Inclusion and Psychological Intervention in Schools

Inclusive Education: Cross Cultural Perspectives

VOLUME 6

Series Editor

Len Barton, *Institute of Education, University of London, United Kingdom*
Marcia Rioux, *School of Health, Policy & Management, Atkinson Faculty of Liberal & Professional Studies, York University, Toronto, Ontario, Canada*

Editorial Board

Mithu Alur, *National Resource Centre for Inclusion, Bandra (West), Mumbai, India*
Susan Peters, *College of Education, Michigan State University, East Lansing, MI, U.S.A.*
Roger Slee, *Faculty of Education, McGill University, Montreal, Canada*
Ronald G. Sultana, *Euro-Mediterranean Centre for Educational Research, University of Malta Msida, Malta*

SCOPE OF THE SERIES

This series is concerned with exploring the meaning and function of inclusive education in a world characterised by rapid social, economic and political change. The question of inclusion and exclusion will be viewed as a human rights issue, in which concerns over issues of equity, social justice and participation will be of central significance. The series will provide an inter-disciplinary approach and draw on research and ideas that will contribute to an awareness and understanding of cross-cultural insights and questions. Dominant assumptions and practices will be critically analysed thereby encouraging debate and dialogue over such fundamentally important values and concerns.

The titles published in this series are listed at the end of this volume

Inclusion and Psychological Intervention in Schools

A Critical Autoethnography

JOHN QUICKE
University of Sheffield, UK

Springer

A C.I.P. Catalogue record for this book is available from the Library of Congress.

ISBN 978-1-4020-6367-1 (HB)
ISBN 978-1-4020-6368-8 (e-book)

Published by Springer,
P.O. Box 17, 3300 AA Dordrecht, The Netherlands.

www.springer.com

Printed on acid-free paper

All Rights Reserved
© 2008 Springer Science + Business Media B.V.
No part of this work may be reproduced, stored in a retrieval system, or transmitted
in any form or by any means, electronic, mechanical, photocopying, microfilming,
recording or otherwise, without written permission from the Publisher, with the exception
of any material supplied specifically for the purpose of being entered and executed
on a computer system, for exclusive use by the purchaser of the work.

Series Editors' Foreword

Within the field of inclusive education, a growing body of literature has contributed to a developing knowledge and understanding of conceptual, empirical, philosophical issues and ideas. However, there is still an urgent need for more detailed accounts of how the struggle for change takes place or 'gets done' in specific contexts involving particular people. This important book seeks to meet some of these needs by providing stories from the working life of an educational psychologist in England, and his interventions in schools in attempting to contribute to meeting the diverse needs of a range of pupils.

In painstaking, sensitive and reflective ways, Quicke offers us some moving insights, detailed observations, challenging questions, which combine to powerfully establish a picture of the complex, social and cultural contexts called schools, in which the struggle for inclusive thinking, values and relations are to be realized.

The author describes himself as a 'reflective practitioner', whose work is not ideologically neutral, but informed by a deep commitment and belief in the well-being of all children. He calls his approach 'autoethnographic' in order to emphasize the self-reflective nature of the activity. Thus, the stories involve insights into the ambiguity, self-doubt, contradictions, dilemmas and real messiness of his position and experiences within his work context. It is a 'critical' activity in which, for example, how barriers to inclusion are defined, the reasons for their existence and the task of removing them are perennial matters of concern. The stories are motivated by a wider set of interests in viewing schools as 'democratic, inclusive learning communities'. This perspective informs the development of such significant questions as: How are particular children's needs spoken about and who deals with them? Does the school also encourage all pupils to actively participate in the development of a community? How far are all pupils encouraged to feel they belong to, and are equally valued within, their school?

Part of the critical framework entails a serious critique of the deficit nature of dominant 'special needs' discourses with their emphasis on 'within-the-child' deficiencies. By using the language of special needs, he argues that an inherently anti-exclusionary distinction between two types of pupils, the 'normal' and the 'special', is legitimated and maintained. Such language and the practices emanating from it are seen as part of the barriers to inclusion and the grounds for the development of an alternative inclusive discourse; hence his vision of schools as 'democratic learning institutions' with their central purpose of 'education for citizenship'. This necessitates changes to the nature of the curriculum, the culture of teachers and teaching, and the expectations and interactions underpinning the learning relationships for all pupils. This is not a narrow vision, but is rather connected to the structures, values, conditions and relations of the wider society of which schools are a part. Issues of power, social reproduction, production, empowerment and social justice are essential ingredients in his inclusive approach.

In self-critical reflections on both his practice and the contents of the stories he has produced, Quicke does not shirk from recognizing and engaging with some of the contentious and complex ethical issues involved. These include the serious and problematic concerns of 'informed consent' and 'anonymity' and the multiple factors involved in particular decision-making within specific episodes. Nor does he refrain from acknowledging the mistakes, compromises and limitations of aspects of his particular engagements. He is not afraid of informed criticisms that have a genuine interest in the possibilities and barriers to inclusive thinking and practice, and hopes that the active reader will raise questions about the work including: Do the readers feel the stories are authentic? Do they believe them? Are they possible? He would welcome criticism, such as: Why did he become involved in a particular process, like statementing about which he had reservations? Why didn't he include the 'voices' of pupils more in this process?

We believe that this is a very important book, which is lucidly presented, accessible and deserves to be widely read and discussed. It is a refreshingly open, honest and self-critical analysis, providing a wealth of rich insights into the complex nature of interactions within particular school settings. It not only raises questions about educational psychologists in the pursuit of inclusive practice, but also reminds the reader that the issues are much wider than those of schools and classrooms. They concern the very nature and purpose of educational provision and practice. We do believe that there is no way more fitting to conclude this foreword than with the words of the author, who hopes that these stories:

Show that there is no quick fix as far as creating inclusive schools is concerned, and that inclusion has to be seen as 'a never-ending search to find better ways of responding to diversity' (Andrew R. Tweedle, 2003, p. 173), and a long term strategy for democratic educational reform.

June 2007

Len Barton
Marcia Rioux

Contents

Series Editors' Foreword	v
1. Introduction	1
Critical Autoethnography	2
Why Write Autoethnographic Stories?	3
How Should These Stories be Judged?	5
Ethical Issues	6
Traditions of Enquiry	8
Inclusion: The Social Model of Disability and Diversity	9
Inclusion and Special Educational Needs: A Professional Dilemma	11
Regressive Practices	13
Professional Knowledge	14
The Stories	16

Section A: Storm, Stress and Standards

2. From Classroom to 'Colditz' via a Learning Support Unit	23
Introduction	23
Developing a Strategy	24
My Brief Interview with Peter	24
The Teachers' Views	26
My Reflections	27
Peer Relationships	27
Further Developments: The Learning Support Unit (LSU)	28
From Classroom to Unit	30
Audrey Under Pressure	30
Audrey is Excluded	32
A Further Review	33
A Further Interview with Peter	35
'Colditz'	35
Coda	36

3. **A Girl Who 'Squeezed in and out of Everywhere'** 39

   Introduction.. 39
   My Interview with Kirsty 40
   My Reflections 41
   Kirsty is Excluded... 42
   The Pastoral Support Plan (PSP) 43
   The Breakthrough 44
   A Further Interview.. 45
   The Drama Project 46
   The Process: 'Hot Seating' and other Techniques 47
   Reactions.. 48
   The Review 49
   The Final Interview: A Box of Tissues........................ 50
   Coda 51

4. **'Giving up on Them': A Tale of Despair** 53

   Introduction... 53
   The Establishment of a 'Nurture Group' 54
   The Inspector Calls Again 55
   'A Failing School'... 55
   Teachers as Scapegoats....................................... 56
   Geoff 'In the Firing Line'................................... 57
   Management Speak... 58
   'Giving up on Them' 59
   Barry.. 60
   Father Gives Me 'The Full Story'............................. 60
   My Interview with Barry 61
   'In his True Light'.. 63
   A Development in My Role 63
   Order in Chaos 64
   'Jolly Good Show, Sir'....................................... 65
   Putting Your Ego on the Line................................. 66
   How Do You 'Love' the 'Unlovable'?........................... 66
   Coda 67

Section B: Against the Trend in Primary Schools

5. **'Off the Differentiation Map': Why Did Inclusion Fail?** 73

   Introduction... 73
   My Interview with David 75
   What had I Learned about David?.............................. 77
   Exploring Support in the Mainstream.......................... 77

	My Reflections on Inclusion in this Context	79
	Strategies	80
	Identifying IEP Targets	80
	'Second Thoughts'	82
	Taking a Step Backwards	84
	Coda	85
6.	**Constructing a 'Disordered' Identity in a Child-Centred School**	**89**
	Introduction	89
	The Approach of John's Class Teacher	90
	My Observations	91
	The Statementing Route	92
	'An Asperger's Child': Retrospective Interpretations	93
	John's 'Voice'	94
	My Interview with John	95
	Health and Safety Issues	96
	A Shoddy Diagnosis Goes Unchallenged	97
	Parental Attitudes	98
	The Statement and Review	99
	The Tribunal	100
	Coda	102
7.	**Action Research, Learning and Football Culture: A Successful Intervention?**	**105**
	Introduction	105
	Identifying the Problem: 'Within Child' Explanations	106
	A Paradox: Playing Down the Importance of 'Research'	106
	An Opportunity for Action Research	108
	Gary and Sam	108
	The Inadequacies of a Cognitive 'Story'	110
	Metacognition	111
	A More Social Approach	112
	The Setting for Paired Work	113
	The Project	113
	My Ambivalence	114
	The Language of Dialogue	115
	The Second Phase: Transfer to the Classroom	116
	Sam Becomes a Teacher	117
	Coda	118

8. On the Social Meaning of 'Throwing a Wobbly' and the Question of Survival in a Primary Classroom 121

Introduction 121
A Class at the 'Tipping Point' 122
Linda's Account 123
Dysfunctional Families? 123
My Reflections on Linda's Account 124
Positive Handling 124
The Science Lesson 126
The Need for Expertise 127
Attempting to 'Manage' Josh's Behaviour and Anger 127
'Circle of Friends' and Pupil Culture 129
Imran 130
The Group 131
Pupils' Reactions 132
Negative Gossip 132
Judith as a 'Crossover' Person 133
Coda 134

Section C: Parents at the Extremities

9. 'We Might be Losing Him' 139

Introduction 139
Betty's Record of Fred's Progress 140
Interviewing and Observing Fred 141
A 'Buddy' for Fred? 142
Fred Gets Agitated 143
Betty's Apology 144
A Revised Statement? 144
The Parents Look to Their Own Future 145
Coda 146

10. 'That's Our Boy Down to a T' 149

Introduction 149
Ben 'Down to a T' 150
An Odd Discrepancy 150
Referral to the Cherry Tree Centre 151
The Full Picture 152
The Question of Abuse 153
Was Ben Faking it? 154
Ben Continues to Make Progress 155
Another Disorder: Pathological Demand Avoidance (PDA) ... 155
Coda 156

11. Conclusion: Promoting Inclusion via the Creation of Democratic Learning Communities ... 159

Inclusion and Reconstruction ... 159
The Role of the Educational Psychologist ... 160
The 'Baggage of History' ... 160
Critically Engaging with the Sen Discourse ... 161
Experiencing the Challenge ... 162
Sustaining the 'Vision' ... 163
Towards a Broader Conversation on Inclusion ... 164
Linking Up With the Curriculum ... 165
The Learning Curriculum ... 165
The Emotional Curriculum: A Way Forward? ... 166
The Curriculum and Democratic 'Communities of Practice' ... 167
Barriers to Learning ... 168
The National Curriculum ... 169
The Secondary Curriculum Review ... 170
Schools as Democratic Learning 'Communities of Practice' ... 171
Final Comment ... 172

Glossary ... 175

References ... 179

Index ... 183

Chapter 1
Introduction

This book consists of a number of 'stories' about interventions in schools to address the educational needs of pupils referred to a local authority Educational Psychology Service (EPS) in the north of England. They are written from the point of view of an educational psychologist (EP) who was employed by the authority. The authority itself had a policy towards inclusion which the EPS was expected to promote and to be involved in as a key player.

As one of the EPs, an important part of my day-to-day work involved identifying the needs of children in schools on my 'patch' (i.e. those schools I served as an EP) who were not benefiting from their educational experiences and then discussing inclusion strategies with teachers and other school personnel. The children and young people were usually those who had been formally referred to the Service. My conversations with teachers did not always relate to specific children but were about general issues to do with inclusion.

The Service itself came under the auspices of the authority's Inclusion Services and was in the process of change. A significant part of its work still related to the Special Educational Needs (SEN) Code of Practice (see Glossary) under the 1996 Education Act, as revised in 2002. I was usually involved at the School Action Plus stage of the Code, but was often called in to give advice at an earlier stage. I also advised the authority in relation to children for whom it might be thought a statutory assessment would be required leading to a statement of special educational needs. But other work was being developed. Intervention for inclusion required contributing to 'prevention' via involvement in 'whole school' and community projects, and the provision of short courses and one-off sessions for teachers and support workers as part of their continuing professional development (CPD). I also participated in multi-agency work and answered requests for psychological advice from schools, the local authority and other agencies.

The aim of these 'stories' is to provide accounts of psychological interventions which do not shirk from describing 'failures' as well as 'successes' and which reflect the general 'messiness' of this kind of work. They are the accounts of an EP who regarded himself as a reflective practitioner and whose professional practice was grounded in a particular moral and political perspective (see later). Professional is a contested concept, but I assume that professional work, far from being ideologically neutral, involves a commitment to a particular set of values and understandings of the 'world'.

Critical Autoethnography

The methodology of the book draws on the qualitative research tradition in social science and education, in particular ethnography and action research. However, it is important to note from the outset that there are two distinct phases of my orientation as a reflective practitioner in the context of this project. In the first phase, my work involved interacting with others and reflecting on processes as a 'natural' part of fulfilling my role as an EP, serving a number of schools on my patch. Although my approach to this work had methodological and epistemological affinities with action research and ethnography, I did not present myself to others as a researcher and the data collected was only that required to enable me to make judgements and take appropriate action in particular situations. Coming from a research background, in the back of my mind was always the thought that at some stage I might write a book or article based on my experiences. At the time, however, I was fully committed to my practitioner role and it was only after I had left the Service that I decided to embark on this project.

The material for the book is derived almost entirely from handwritten notes I made at the time. These were not field notes as such but those I took in the normal course of duty, even if I did regard them as private notes from which I selected material for the official EPS files. It is not uncommon for EPs to record information in notebooks, and perhaps the only difference between my colleagues and me was that I kept all of mine in a safe place rather than shredding or discarding them in some other way when full. The notebooks contained observations and comments but also words and phrases that were spoken to me by others. I noted the language people used because drawing attention to, and often challenging, language was always an important aspect of my intervention. Readers should not therefore be surprised that there are not the usual extensive quotes from field notes or tape-recorded interviews which one finds in most ethnographic accounts. I did not record any interviews because this would not have been an appropriate thing for me to do in my capacity as a support professional.

The second phase might be described as the research proper. It involved constructing in retrospect 'stories' about my interventions over several years. They include what I recall of my reflections at the time. They are intended to be genuine ethnographies, by which I mean accounts which adhere to a particular methodological orientation and view of knowledge, one which involves 'getting inside' a particular social practice and treating individuals as socially constructed, interacting selves within that practice. I have described the stories as autoethnographic because I wanted to emphasize that relative to other kinds of ethnography there is perhaps more self-reflexive comment i.e. where attention is drawn to critical reflection on the self. I also wanted to stress that I was a full participant – a fully reflective participant – in all, or most of, the social action.

However, I appreciate that all ethnography is in a sense autoethnographic or has an autoethnographic dimension. Since in this form of research, the ethnographer himself or herself is the research instrument, it is highly likely that their interpretative work will involve the self-reflexive probing of their own assumptions and conceptual frameworks. The ethnographic school researcher is also always a participant in one way or another. Even if he or she is more observer than participant, they are still allocated a role within an institution-based practice, and will still play a role in ongoing social action, even if this is not always fully understood. Therefore, their self-reflections are as relevant for the account as those of any other role player. However, I saw myself as a participant in a different position from, say, an academic researcher carrying out a research project.

I have also described this book as a *critical* autoethnography. The term 'critical' is used here in both an everyday and a more formal sense; the former to emphasize that what the reader can expect is not just a celebration of success or a self-promoting account of the 'good' work of a professional but one which contains much more ambiguity, self-doubt and even some self-condemnation. But the idea of 'critical' also refers to how actions taken measured up in terms of the moral and political ideals, which I elaborate later in this chapter. In this sense, these accounts might be seen as a form of educational action research for social justice. Following Griffiths (1998), I would see this research (and also the practice on which it is based, which was likewise committed) as predicated upon three aspects: an understanding of social justice as 'what is good for the common interest, where that is taken to include the good of each and the good of all' (ibid. p. 95); an understanding that the purpose of educational research is 'to improve the education of children and students' (ibid. p. 95); and an understanding of the epistemological context where 'there is a requirement to take the interrelations of knowledge and power into account…(and) a requirement to pay attention to individuals and the variety of communities they inhabit'; and where '*all* the principles may always be the subject of critique and revisability' (ibid. p. 95).

My understanding of 'including the good of each and the good of all' involves a notion of inclusion, which sees it as a 'good' for all pupils, not just those identified as having 'special educational needs'. All children have the right to experience relationships with others having different identities, backgrounds, interests and achievements, because otherwise the education of all is impoverished. Research should aim to improve the education of all children, where the appropriate curriculum is one that includes 'education for citizenship' as a top priority. These goals are consonant with a view of practice as inevitably involving issues to do with power in a local and wider context, and with an approach to knowledge which regards it as always subject to critique from different socially and culturally located perspectives.

Why Write Autoethnographic Stories?

This particular genre of writing and research seemed eminently suited to my overall purpose, which was to write about psychological interventions in a way that hopefully generated insights into dilemmas and contradictions, and tried to capture the experience of what it felt like in practice. As Reed-Danahay (1997) has suggested, these personal narratives are a way of connecting the personal to the cultural by reflecting on the role of one's own self as a participant in an ongoing social and cultural practice. This is not to say that the selves of other participants are excluded – far from it – but treating one's own self as a major character ensures that conventional views about 'silent authorship' (see Charmaz and Mitchell, 1997) and the positivist epistemology which informs them are challenged.

I feel these stories need to be written because I am not aware of anyone having done this before in this particular field of practice. To some extent I am challenging the conventional constraints on writing of this kind within my own profession. These constraints take many forms but all of them prevent the development of a more open dialogue about the role and purpose of psychological interventions to promote inclusion. Some are to do with how psychologists and professions, in general, might want to present themselves. This is a particularly difficult time for all professions who work in inclusion services. There are many EPs and teachers who could have written these kinds of stories, but although they would see the point of being self-critical, they might well query the need to make it all public. Like teachers, EPs are going through yet another crisis of professionalism, brought on by the relentless accountability demands of a State intent of micromanaging the implementation of its controversial policies. Would such public displays of 'failure' not merely give more ammunition to those who want to diminish their autonomy still further, and reinforce the 'culture of derision' (see Ball, 1995), which has done so much to undermine EPs' as well as teachers' morale? From a managerialist perspective, would the stories reinforce demands for an audit of their role and performance – how much 'value' do EPs add and do they give 'value for money'?

As someone who acknowledges the importance of the political context, I am only too aware of the dangers that these warts and all accounts may have for professional credibility and status. But I still think more is to be gained than lost by putting them in the public domain. I am not suggesting that professional personnel, whether teachers or EPs, are solely responsible for things going 'right' or 'wrong'. Indeed, in many instances they are on the receiving end of demands from the State which are impossible to reconcile, such as demands emanating from two different agendas – the 'standards' and the inclusion agenda – which, although they may be construed as 'theoretically' compatible, in practice are contradictory.

Yet within professional groups there are competing versions of 'good practice' stemming from different political outlooks (see Annan, 2005). The difficulty is that these are often buried under 'scientific' and technical talk, where issues are discussed in an 'objective' way as if there were no moral or political conflicts at the root of them. In recent years, much of the technical language of managerialism has penetrated the professional discourse of educational psychology in practice e.g. 'performance targets', 'service delivery', 'buyback', 'best value', 'value added', 'evidence based'. Whilst good practice is seen as embracing human rights and anti-discrimination, some commentators have seen EPs as 'well placed to carry out monitoring and evaluation – that is, quality assurance of new initiatives' (see Baxter and Frederickson, 2005, p. 99), and to give advice to the Audit Commission on how to maximize 'value-added' with resources available. They are 'well placed', at least in part, because the dominant definition of research in the profession is still 'positivist', and thus consonant with the prevailing version of evidence-based policy development and evaluation.

In general, I feel that EPs and indeed other professionals involved in inclusion services might have sold themselves short by not writing in an ethnographic way about their practices. They know about the 'messiness' of their work, and they are aware of the contradictions and dilemmas they face when trying to include children with a diverse range of needs in the current school system. They would have some very interesting and insightful stories to tell. Of course, there are various ethical issues to consider (see later), but I feel that a reflective practitioner has not only a right but also a duty to reflect on his or her practice, to act in accordance with those reflections and to make them public, with due regard to the sensitivities and anonymity of others. Rather than undermining professional credibily, this process could only enhance the standing of the profession since it would demonstrate its awareness of the complexity of the social and cultural context in which inclusionary values are to be realized. There is plenty of talk about what psychologists and other support professionals can contribute to inclusionary practices, but very few examples of how these are worked through in relation to specific pupils in a specific school context.

How Should These Stories be Judged?

If personal narratives are a way forward, how can we tell if a story is a 'good' story? I would agree with Holt (2003) that conventional evaluative criteria are inappropriate. He quotes Richardson (1995) who has suggested autoethnographic narratives should be judged according to the following criteria: do the stories make a substantive contribution to understanding life as a practitioner; do they succeed aesthetically e.g. are they satisfyingly complex and not boring; are they sufficiently reflexive; do they generate new questions; do they convey a sense of lived experience? Whether or not a story is 'good' or not also depends on what it evokes in the reader (Ellis, 1995). Do readers feel it is authentic, do they believe it and do they think it is possible? Whose views are sought on these matters and why?

But in addition to these criteria I would also like stories to be judged morally and politically from the point of view of someone who shared the same values and perspective on education, inclusion and democracy as me. For example, I would welcome criticism which asked the following kinds of questions: why did I become involved in a particular process, like statementing, about which I had reservations; what was I hoping to achieve by this; why did I not include the 'voice' of pupils more in the process? I would hope others could point to my insensitivities and suggest alternative strategies that may have been more appropriate in the circumstances. As long as this criticism is derived from a critic's genuine concern about the possibility or, indeed, the impossibility of the realization, through psychological intervention, of democratic and inclusionary values, I would have no problem with it and would willingly engage with it. Criticism which would have no interest for me would be that which suggested this was not 'proper' research or that it was 'ideological' where the critic assumed it was possible to do research in a morally and politically neutral way.

Ethical Issues

Questions could be asked about the interventions described in the 'stories', and therefore about the practice on which the research was based, but clearly questions could also be asked about the ethics of the project itself. There are two issues in particular which I think require further consideration – one relates to the rule of 'informed consent' (derived from the principle of the individual's 'right to know') and the other to 'anonymity' (derived from the individual's right to privacy).

The question of consent, of course, has always been salient for EPs and one which is frequently discussed by services. Most EPs would not see a child without the consent of the parents or parent substitute. The parents' signature on a referral form is usually required, and it is expected that the head teacher, Special Educational Needs Coordinator (SENCO) or some other teacher will have explained to the parent and the child what such a referral entails. Parents and children can and often do refuse to agree to EP involvement. Likewise, it is expected that if one teacher, like the head teacher, makes the referral, this course of action will have been discussed with all relevant staff. But as these stories will show this formal consent is only a part of the story! Parents or parent substitutes can *be* informed but do not really *become* informed because they do not really understand where the process might lead. In general, whether consent is formally obtained or not, some complex questions need to be asked about 'voice', choice and power in relation to all support interventions. I hope these stories will demonstrate the dilemmas and difficulties faced by inclusionary EPs regarding these issues. In this sense, the whole book is about ethical issues in 'special needs' and inclusionary practices.

However, there is also the question of informed consent in relation to the project per se. When I decided to write these stories, should I have returned to the schools and various services, and obtained the consent of parents, pupils, teachers, other professionals and anyone else represented in the stories? There was a dilemma here. I certainly do subscribe to the principle of informed consent, but to obtain it in this instance would have presented enormous difficulties. The stories were written some time after the events took place and many of the 'characters' would have been difficult to track down. Even if I had managed to do this, I am uncertain whether I could have obtained consent that was genuinely informed because at the time of writing the stories I was not sure myself what form they would take, and who or what would or would not be included. It was also possible that seeing various people again would have meant in effect a further period of intervention on my part since I would have felt obliged to take further action if I felt needs had not been met. This may have been an interesting development, but it would have involved a further period of research, perhaps even a different form of research, and would almost certainly have shifted the focus from the action which took place in the schools during the period of my involvement as their EP.

Most educational researchers are faced with dilemmas of one kind or another. A code of conduct, like that produced by the British Educational Research Association (BERA), can be helpful but it is one thing to be au fait with a list of rules derived from principles and quite another to know how to apply these rules and principles in practical contexts. It is not always obvious whether actions taken in accordance with a rule have been successful in realizing a principle, or what rule-based actions relate to what principles, or, when principles conflict, which should be the overriding one. As Pring (2001, p. 414) points out it is a question of making a judgement after a process of careful deliberation 'in which different principles are pondered over within the particular context of the research'.

In this context I judged that the improvement of inclusionary practices (to which hopefully the stories would contribute) overrode the principle of the individual's right to know, provided I took steps to ensure that another principle – the right to privacy – was secured by making strenuous efforts to ensure the anonymity of all participants.

The anonymity of respondents is a rule observed by most educational researchers in both quantitative and qualitative traditions, but it was particularly difficult to apply in the context of the present study. The 'stories' are about particular individuals in particular situations. Any member of the school community or anyone who worked in the school in a support or other capacity, particularly if they had access to official case notes, could probably work out which individuals were which 'characters' in the stories, certainly in the way I wrote them originally. This was not just a question of the right to privacy but also a question of possibly causing hurt to individuals who may have been upset by the way they had been represented.

I felt that changing the names of individuals and institutions would go some way to ensuring anonymity, but would not be sufficient since many of the situations described were unique, even if they had been selected because they raised questions about inclusionary practices which were widely applicable. I was so concerned about this that I took a decision to go though each story line by line, cutting material where necessary but, in order not to emasculate the stories, providing 'equivalents' which would retain the 'truth' of the educational and psychological processes while making minor alterations in the substantive content. These stories therefore might best be described as 'faction'; they are not 'history' but neither are they 'fiction', as these terms would be conventionally understood. It would obviously be counter-productive to give examples of the details that were altered. A fictitious example would be changing the title of a teacher because that particular title was only ever used in one school, or changing the name of a teaching programme which was unique to a particular school and even fudging the details of that programme if I felt this did not detract from the overall 'truth' of the story.

Traditions of Enquiry

I have indicated earlier that I see my position and perspective as deriving from particular moral and political values. I hope the stories I tell will show how these have been interpreted in practice. At this point, in order to provide a context, I shall briefly identify this position in general terms and then more specifically in relation to inclusion issues in schools via reference to some of the relevant literature. My purpose here is not to review all the relevant literature, but merely to locate the stories in certain traditions of enquiry. I have referred to a few key authors but there are many others who would deserve a mention in an exhaustive review.

The moral-political perspective which informs my practice involves an understanding of individualism as conceptually related to political ideas of equality and liberty. As Lukes (1973) has shown in his detailed historical and philosophical analysis of individualism, the four basic ideas of individualism – respect for human dignity, autonomy, privacy and self-development – are linked to each other but are also 'essential elements' (Lukes, 1973, p. 125) in the ideas of liberty and equality. The idea that human beings should be respected because they have an inherent dignity is egalitarian since it asserts that persons are worthy of respect not because of some special talent or characteristic they may possess but purely and simply because they possess human characteristics. Autonomy, privacy and self-development are clearly related to liberty or freedom.

The kind of political system which is both informed by, and facilitative of, the realization of liberty and equality is democracy along the 'classical' lines in the sense used by Carr and Hartnett (1996). In this version of democracy, the emphasis is on democracy as a 'way of life' where individuals realize their potentialities through active participation in the life of their societies, and 'a democratic society is thus an educative society (a learning society) whose citizens enjoy equal opportunities for self-development, self-fulfilment and self-determination' (Carr and Hartnett, 1996, p. 41). An education for a modern version of classical democracy is one which provides equal opportunities for all students to realize their potentialities as individuals and as citizens in a democratic society.

The educational principles deployed are those consonant with and historically related to the formation of the 'good' individual life and the 'good' society, which in democracies gives rise to a view of education as both person-centred and community-oriented. The learner in the democratic learning society is constituted as a person – someone who has actually or potentially the capacity to make moral choices, act autonomously and think rationally– and learning is about the development of persons as unique individuals through being active participants in democratic learning communities. Such participation empowers them to act upon the world around them and transform it, and to act upon themselves in the same way. The more autonomous a person becomes, the more they are able to make use of what they know to create and achieve self-originated goals and the more they will play a part in the development of their own capacities and the development of the learning communities to which they are committed.

Political education will always be a central feature of this form of education because students will need to develop a critical awareness of the ways in which society fosters and, as it is currently constituted, also frustrates democratic aspirations. These social and political processes can be examined on a number of levels – the personal, institutional and societal – and democratic educators would therefore have to deploy a concept of the political which was broader than conventionally understood in contemporary democracy. Ideal relations within communities at all levels must be relations between persons where reciprocity implies concern for the freedom of the other to fully participate as an active agent in the social life of the community. One is reminded here of an earlier account of the morality of persons-in-relation:'My care for you is only moral if it includes the intention to preserve your freedom as an agent, which is your independence of me. Even if you wish to be dependent on me, it is my business, for your sake, to prevent it'(Macmurray, 1961, p. 190).

Inclusion: The Social Model of Disability and Diversity

The identification and critique of social and political barriers which constrain and undermine a genuinely democratic education are central tasks for those writers and researchers on inclusion who adhere to the social model of disability (see Barton, 2003, Oliver, 1996, Tomlinson, 1982). Practices grounded in 'within-child' and medical models of needs also aspire to remove barriers to educational progress, but, as these authors point out, the very act of 'labelling' mystifies the way school and other institutional practices have socially constructed these children's 'difficulties' in the first instance. Paradoxically the 'cure' only makes matters worse by reinforcing the idea that the 'cause' of the problem is within the individual child (see Norwich, 1993). Labels used with good intentions to identify needs only serve to marginalize and devalue such children, separate them from others and reinforce the very barriers which obstruct progress. The faults of schools derive from the underlying exclusionary aims of the system as a whole which creates 'winners' and 'losers', and continues to contribute to the reproduction of hierarchical and oppressive social structures.

The social model is often contrasted with the individual model, but in the light of the significance of individualism in the moral-political perspective outlined earlier this would seem problematical. In fact, the social model is only opposed to individualism when this is defined in asocial terms, as it is when children are described as having an educational difficulty, which is largely determined by a medical disorder or some other form of physical condition (e.g. biological, neurophysiological). When the individual is seen as a person in the sense defined above, there is no contradiction. Indeed, a sense of the individual and the desirability of a school curriculum which celebrates and promotes individual difference and diversity is a central theme of the social model. As Armstrong, Armstrong and

Barton (2000, p. 34) point out: '[D]ifference is not a euphemism for defect, for abnormality, for a problem to be worked out through technical and assimilationist education policies. Diversity is a social fact.' Difference enhances the human experience and enriches life for all. The world we live in is a 'world of difference' (see Minnow, 1997, p. 126), and schools which reflected this would enable children to encounter other children as different individuals.

At another level, the same point can be made about the 'social fact' of cultural diversity. School culture is made up of interactions and conversations between a variety of subcultures and microcultures (i.e. pertaining to one particular group). All these cultures are reflected in individual selves and one would anticipate expressions of diversity to change as cultural interaction proceeded. Diversity in schools is not a fixed phenomenon but one which both reflects and contributes to the production of school cultural practices.

Schools and other institutions which subscribed to what Mouffe (1993, p. 83) describes as the 'articulating principle of democracy' would provide a dynamic framework in which cultures and culturally produced individuals could develop and function in the reflexive, open and self-critical way appropriate to community life in a plural and global society. In effect this would mean developing a multicultural curriculum based on a notion of culture which had certain key characteristics:

(1) a capacity for providing a 'home' and a sense of belonging for its members which was enriching and self-fulfilling for the individuals concerned and which empowered them as agents
(2) a capacity for self-recognition as a social form in the process of 'becoming' rather than as a fixed entity
(3) a capacity for self-evaluation through critical 'conversation' both between elements within its own conceptual framework or, to use Foucault's term, 'regime of truth', and between itself and other cultures.

In my stories there are examples where the celebration of diversity clearly informs practice but there are also issues raised which are common to all debates about democratic school practices. These are expressed in questions like: can we encourage and celebrate all forms of diversity, even those the expression of which inhibits the capacity of others to achieve autonomy; are their forms of diversity which are antidemocratic and have to be challenged rather than celebrated? In identifying barriers to educational progress we should be aware of those that pupils as socially constructed selves 'bring in' with them, so to speak, from home or outside school. The barriers are not just constructed by teachers in school systems, but also by pupils. In the classic ethnographic study of boys in a working-class secondary school, Willis (1977) acknowledged both the positive and the negative aspects of the boys' culture. Thus, he is appreciative of the insights into their social position (described as 'penetrations') reflected in their cultural practices, but he is also critical of the latter's 'limitations' and anti-democratic aspects, like sexism and racism.

Although moral evaluation is central to the process of creating a democratic, inclusive community culture, judgements based on misunderstanding and ignorance should obviously be avoided. A highly relevant example for support professionals would be in relation to pupils referred for 'behavioural difficulties'. A pupil could be a member of a family microculture, where resolving conflicts through physical aggression was encouraged. Such cultures should not be dismissed out of hand but they clearly have to be engaged with. Although 'violence' in any form cannot be tolerated in schools, there is a world of difference between physical assertiveness to protect others or 'stick up for yourself', as it may be understood in certain families, and violence which is used to persecute and oppress the weak and vulnerable, e.g. bullying.

Inclusion and Special Educational Needs: A Professional Dilemma

For the democratically inclusive EP, policies which deploy the notion of 'special educational needs' give rise to a dilemma.

The term 'special education' refers to a wide range of educational provision both inside and outside the mainstream school for pupils with varying degrees of need. Planners have always tried to estimate the numbers likely to require such provision but this is fraught with difficulties. Numbers vary depending on interpretations as to the nature and degree of need, and the particular school context. In some schools a third or more of the school population may be on the special needs register, in other schools it may be only 5% or less. It does not take long for any teacher or support professional new to this field to work out that 'special educational needs' is very much an interactive concept. The numbers identified will be influenced by a variety of factors. It is highly likely they will depend on policy decisions relating to school priorities as a whole rather than just those specifically concerned with special educational needs.

The basic distinction between two identities – the 'normal' and the 'special' – has a long history, and has long been recognized as problematical. It is tenacious even amongst those who recognize the negative consequences of making hard and fast distinctions. This is nowhere better illustrated than in the deliberations of the Warnock Committee, which took place at a time (the 1970s) when the special/normal distinction was coming under fire for being incompatible with the comprehensive principle of non-selection (see Quicke, 1981).

A guiding idea of that report was that the dichotomy between the previous categorization of the handicapped and non-handicapped was no longer necessary or useful. Paragraph 3.24 of the Report reads: '[W]e believe the most important argument against categorisation is the most general one. Categorisation perpetuates the sharp distinction between two groups of children – the handicapped and the non-handicapped, and it is this distinction which we are determined, as far as possible, to eliminate.' But the Report is rife with statements and recommendations which can only be understood in relation to the assumption that operational distinctions can be made between one group – those with special educational needs – and another – those who do not have such needs. There is an assumption in Warnock, as there has been in all special needs policies since that time, that it is possible to separate out a group of children with special educational needs in a way which is relatively uncontroversial. No hedging around the issue by referring to a 'continuum of need' can disguise this.

The distinction is anti-inclusionary because it involves identifying a group of children as having needs so different from the norm that they have to be placed in a separate category and require a special form of provision. It goes against the idea of person-centred education where all children are to be treated as individual persons. Making this distinction also focuses attention on difference in a deficit way, as opposed to regarding difference in the celebratory way alluded to by Armstrong, Armstrong and Barton (2000).

Historically, then, the dilemma for inclusionary EPs has been that although they would like to see themselves as working towards the deconstruction of this special/normal distinction, they are part of a tradition with a long history of providing for the 'special educational needs' of a 'special' group of children. EPs played an important role in the implementation of the 1944 and subsequent Education Acts where pupils labelled as 'handicapped' were brought within the framework of state education provision. One could view this as a first step towards inclusion and at the time a progressive development. Even the terms used then, which today would be correctly seen as discriminatory, were an improvement on previous categories. The term 'educationally subnormal' replaced 'mentally subnormal' or 'mentally retarded' because it was thought that the emphasis should be on a child's educational needs and how these should be addressed rather than on a 'deficit model' of mental capacities. Since that time, EPs have been giving local authorities advice on children's special educational needs and contributing to statutory assessments which ultimately determine resource allocations. And so the issue is: do inclusionary EPs try to avoid reinforcing the system by limiting their involvement in statutory processes, or do they 'play the game' in order to obtain additional resources for the child to support their education in the mainstream?

In the current period this dilemma is still alive and a constant source of tension for inclusionary EPs. The situation now, however, is far more complex. In most authorities, much of the money held centrally for the purpose of mainstream provision for inclusion has been delegated to schools, and inclusion services (for that is what they are now called in many authorities) are bought in by schools. The money is part of the general school budget, but there is a notional special needs budget. The situation differs from one authority to another in its fine detail but generally schools would be expected to cater for the inclusion needs of children at the School Action or School Action Plus stages of the Code of Practice as well as those, particularly in 'high incidence' categories of 'learning' and 'behavioural' difficulties, who might previously have been statemented. Monies retained centrally are for statemented pupils with high levels of needs who require intensive support in mainstream, enhanced provision (i.e. a special unit attached to mainstream) or a special school. Within this provision for statemented pupils, costs are worked out precisely for each type and degree of special educational need. Thus, for example, there might be five levels and four different types of need – learning/cognitive, emotional/behavioural, language/communication, sensory/medical. The highest levels are for special school funding, the lowest for mainstream provision. Overall, it is anticipated that these changes will reduce the amount of statementing, which is often perceived as a costly and bureaucratic business.

In practice what this means for the EP varies from area to area and school to school. Statementing continues, schools know this, and support professionals still contribute to full assessments under the Code, although I suspect that in most authorities this kind of work is on the decline. It certainly was in the authority I worked in. It is easier now for EPs to avoid a preoccupation with assessment and to focus their efforts on developing appropriate 'whole class' teaching and learning strategies to promote a child's education and inclusion. In time, the hope for many inclusionary EPs is that the whole special needs structure will 'wither away'.

Regressive Practices

This is definitely progress but unfortunately it goes hand in hand with other developments, which in my view are so regressive they may well put us back to square one. First, there are developments in psycho-medical and psychiatric 'knowledge' which seem to have had a big impact on how parents, teachers and others explain the behaviours of children who are socially different and often disruptive. The use of terms like 'autistic spectrum disorder' and 'attention deficit hyperactivity disorder' are on the increase and even deployed by EPs in their reports. These out-and-out 'within-child' terms are highly contentious. Even Lorna Selfe (2002), who has a professional commitment to autism, has acknowledged that eccentric children with a quirky view of the world and obsessional interests are now labelled as having Asperger's syndrome, or, as the author recently read, "mild atypical Asperger's syndrome". Children as young as 18 months are being diagnosed in the interests of early intervention' (Selfe, 2002, p. 336).

But this disquiet has not stopped professionals, particularly health professionals, speaking of dramatic increases in the numbers of children with these 'conditions'. Even in my own profession, interest, experience and 'upskilling' in autism and other special 'conditions' are recognized as specialist knowledge, the acquisition of which identifies a specialism for purposes of professional restructuring. The problems that arise for inclusionary EPs are partly to do with their continuing involvement with special provision, but also to how expertise on various 'disorders' is perceived by others as a part of the EP's professional knowledge.

Second, there are policy developments in schools giving rise to various practices (see Booth, 2005) which undermine inclusion. Most schools say they are committed to inclusion but there is often a conflict between this and the 'standards' agenda. Many primary schools have reintroduced streaming and within-class groupings based on erroneous and highly reductive assumptions about 'ability'. Pupils are routinely described in simplistic ways as being at 'levels' of the National

Curriculum and in terms of their performance on Standard Assessment Tests (SATs). SATs themselves generate huge anxieties and encourage schools to waste valuable time and resources preparing for the tests. Leagues tables encourage competition rather than collaboration between schools, reinforce the perception of certain pupils as 'problems' and do nothing to encourage teachers to take risks or experiment with different strategies for including pupils. The values and practices associated with a competitive and meritocratic ideology have become increasingly dominant and it is difficult to see how these can be made compatible with inclusionary ideals, despite all the rhetoric about 'personalised' education. In short, when we talk of children with 'special educational needs' being included we need to ask whether the school environment in which they are to be included is not itself basically exclusionary.

In this context, the lot of children whose needs are catered for under the Code of Practice varies. There now seems little point in putting large numbers of children on the special needs register at the School Action stage, since *all* pupils have targets set and are monitored closely. If the hierarchy of 'ability' is just an accepted fact of life, so the argument goes, there will inevitably be pupils of all levels of ability in schools and less reason therefore to separate out a group of special children with 'learning difficulties'. Paradoxically the deconstruction of the special/non-special distinction in this instance goes hand in hand with the creation of an even more problematical environment from a democratic and inclusionary point of view. The distinction still holds, however, for children with 'higher levels of need' who are perceived as much more of a 'problem' for schools. The growth of 'within-child' special needs explanations are functional here because they evoke a discourse which can 'explain' and account for failure (see Benjamin, 2002).

Professional Knowledge

Another aspect of my position which I feel it is important to briefly sketch relates to how I perceive my own psychological knowledge, since this clearly informs many of the stories. My approach to psychological intervention in schools might loosely be described as 'interactionist' against the background of the moral and political values identified earlier. Some years ago as part of an analysis of the professional knowledge of EPs, I identified the interactionist approach as one of two more sociologically oriented approaches (the other being the 'systems' approach), which could usefully inform practice in educational psychology (see Quicke, 1982). Some colleagues in the past have suggested this is more sociology than psychology, but I have always rejected this. Education in schools involves teaching and learning in social contexts, and understanding context is crucial to understanding the role and purpose of intervention strategies. Educational psychology is inevitably a social psychology, and the most thoroughgoing social psychological model I know is interactionist. More than cognitive psychology or any other form of 'individualistic' psychology, interactionism should have pride of place at the centre of the EP's professional knowledge.

I do not have sufficient space in this introduction to describe the interactionist approach in any great detail. Suffice it to say that it is an approach which assumes that social meanings will depend on the context in which interacting selves are located, and will be derived from perspectives which, according to Woods (1983, p. 7), refer to 'frameworks through which people make sense of the world... construct their realities and define situations'. Interpretative frameworks are nested within discourses which are played out in discursive practices. Discourse identifies a way of thinking, speaking and acting deriving from a particular 'view of the world', essentially a 'language game' associated with a linguistic community in a particular social context (see Peim, 1993).

From my viewpoint, the interactionist approach is totally consonant with inclusionary values. It assumes that learning is social and culturally constructed and that we can examine the learning process from the perspective of an individual self who is at the centre of a web of social interactions. It assumes individuals are discursively positioned (Davies and Harre, 1990) but have a reflexive capacity which enables agency – thus a capacity to think about themselves as learners. Inclusive philosophy also requires us to see the pupil and the teacher as agents, that is, as persons who can become independent, active and powerful through interacting with others in a social context to produce a community where everyone is a participant and everyone is empowered.

One can see the influence of interactionism and several allied theories of culture at work in some current approaches to psychological intervention in schools (see in particular Williams and Daniels (2000), who draw on Miller's (1996) studies of teacher culture). Interactionism also has an affinity with Schon's (1983) notion of reflective practice, which has been acknowledged as pertinent to the issue of the theory/practice gap in the work of the EP (Lunt and Majors, 2000). I have tried to identify my own practice as an expression of self-understanding as a reflective practitioner. My 'knowledge in action', to use Schon's term, includes ideas from formal theory and research but this 'rubs shoulders', so to speak, with a pragmatic, common sense knowledge, some of which is tacit and difficult to make explicit. My 'reflection in action' requires me to examine this knowledge, and in doing so perhaps recognize the inconsistencies and contradictions which at the time the interventions took place were not always apparent. Such inconsistences are often a feature of 'knowing in action' or to use Alfred Shutz's term 'recipe' knowledge. For Schutz (1971, p. 28) 'the knowledge of a man [sic] who acts and thinks within the world of his daily life is not homogenous; it is...incoherent...only partially clear and...not at all free from contradictions'.

Finally, I see this interpretation of professional knowledge as compatible with a more general theory of knowledge alluded to earlier in my comments on educational research for social justice – a theory which defines knowledge as fallible, provisional, uncertain and, as Griffiths (1998, p. 82) acknowledges, 'self-consciously situated in its context, and always subject to revision'. There are two main consequences for educational researchers who hold this view of knowledge. First, since there is no possibility of ever claiming that the knowledge generated by one's research is definitive, one has to present findings to practitioners in ways which allows them to understand that this is still 'work in progress'. Positivist research can also be presented in this way but it is also accompanied by assumptions about the possibility that certain universally applicable 'facts' about 'best methods' will be firmly established at some stage and that many have been already. Second, it is important to clarify one's own position as a researcher, that is to say one's commitment to certain moral and political values in which one's perspectives on research and practice are grounded, even if it is likely that 'absolute clarity is an impossibility, since they (i.e. values) cannot be fully specified' (Griffiths, 1998, p. 83). Griffiths also considers that attention has to paid to the various 'communities' e.g. teacher, Christian, heterosexual to which the individual researcher belongs, 'describable in terms of perspectives and positionings' (Griffiths, 1998, p. 82), although this is only helpful, in my view, in a situation where there are doubts about the meaning and validity of one's political and moral values.

The Stories

In the stories I have attempted to make explicit the thought processes which guided my interventions, even if these are not always expressed in the language of self reflection. The reader should be able to identify my personal 'theories' from how I interpreted my own actions and those of others. With Schutz's comments on everyday knowledge in mind, the reader might also be able to detect contradictions and inconsistencies in some of my accounts. My own impression of the writing process is that I was driven by what seemed to emerge spontaneously as I moved the narrative along. Each of these stories could have been twice as long, or even longer. They are the length they are because of various constraints to do with the later phase of shaping a narrative within a particular space and time frame.

Although my writing clearly draws on theory and research, I have chosen not to incorporate references to literature in the stories themselves. This is partly because I feel that references and quotations would have interrupted the flow of the narrative. The stories are wide ranging and just about every paragraph could be referenced, but this would have made the text unwieldy and far less readable. I am also genuinely not always aware of the sources of the ideas I use. One is conscious of some influences but not others. At the end of each story I have included a coda which is not so much a summing up or a conclusion as just a few final thoughts. References to some of the literature which the reader may find helpful appear here.

There are as many narratives as there are children referred to our Service, and there are thus many stories I could have written. The interventions I have chosen to write about have been selected on several grounds. First, I have tried to maintain a balance between interventions in secondary and primary schools. Work in each sector was substantially different in terms of the extent and nature of my involvement. Thus, I have divided the book into sections. Section A includes three stories, which focus on interventions in secondary schools, and Section B four stories in primary school settings. Section C contains two stories, one from each phase, but placed together in a separate section because both highlight interactions with parents to a degree that the other stories do not. There are more boys involved than girls, which reflects the distribution of referrals to our service where the former far outnumber the latter. (This is a problematical feature of all special needs/inclusion services and raises questions of gender discrimination (see Hill, 1994; Vardill and Calvert, 2000)).

Second, I have tried to select stories which include different techniques and strategies. I have not assumed the reader is familiar with the specific intervention techniques deployed, and where they appear in the stories, I have provided detailed descriptions. Thus, for example, Chapter 8 describes a particular approach – Circle of Friends – which I advised a school to use; and Chapter 7 shows how literacy issues were tackled via a paired learning and 'learning how to learn' strategy.

Third, most of these stories begin with my intervention and end when I ceased to be involved or was less involved for one reason or another. They are atypical in terms of the degree of my involvement. Many of the children referred to the Service may be seen only once or twice a year or not at all, depending on the circumstances. My aim in this book, however, is not to provide an overview of the day-to-day work of an EP, but to tell stories which include psychological intervention as a key aspect.

Finally, I should point out that the stories tend to be more about 'failure' than 'success'. This is partly because I think stories which describe 'failure' tend to be more illuminating. By definition the existing 'recipe knowledge' or, to use Schon's terms, knowing-in-action has been found wanting, and thus more clarification and extended reflection is required than in successful interventions. It is also partly because I feel less than optimistic about the prospects for realizing inclusion via psychological intervention within the current framework. From the stories the reader may get a sense of how practices that derive from good intentions and a pro-inclusion stance are diverted and distorted by day-to-day occurrences which, when examined closely, reflect tensions deriving from conflicting educational values and purposes.

Section A
Storm, Stress and Standards

Adolescence is not inevitably a period of 'storm and stress' but given what young people have to cope today, it is scarcely surprising that this is still an apt description. Many conform to the system and pass exams, and the improving results are heralded as a rise in standards. But even for these 'successful' pupils the testing regime has been experienced as oppressive and the curriculum only engaged with in an instrumentalist way. Those who fail to make headway in the system are individually monitored but often react to this impersonal 'personalized' surveillance by 'kicking over the traces', sometimes for short, sometimes for longer periods. Others whose deviant behaviour is viewed as 'extreme' are likely to be regarded as having 'emotional and behavioural difficulties', and many of these are referred to our Service.

My first port of call in a secondary school is usually the Special Needs Department and my main contact the SENCO, but in two of the schools in the following stories I became more involved on a regular basis with a number of other teachers, particularly those managing Learning Support Units (LSUs); and with Learning Mentors (LMs). LSUs and LMs were created under the auspices of the Government's *Excellence in Cities* programme, which was just swinging into action at the time I took up my post with the Local Education Authority (LEA) and was an important backdrop to my subsequent work in schools.

According to a DfEE (Department for Education and Employment, 1999) document, the purpose of *Excellence in Cities* was to address the issue of poor performance and low standards in inner-city schools. It was hoped that standards could be raised by building on previous initiatives which were still in operation, like Education Action Zones (EAZ). At the systems level there was to be an emphasis on improvements in leadership, teaching and the involvement of parents and governors. The weakest schools, including those which were 'failing', were to be monitored and supported in the development and realization of their educational plans by the LEAs, who were seen as having a key role to play in raising standards.

At the individual level it required removing barriers to achievement, and 'reasserting the principle of an entitlement for every child to reach their potential'. Several innovative programmes were designed to achieve these goals, two of which, the LSU and LM programmes, involved a direct input from the EPS. In the schools on my patch, LSUs quickly became established. In addition to their general contribution to improving exam performance, they were specifically focused on increasing attendance, reducing the number of pupils on permanent and fixed-term exclusions, and reducing the percentage of students not engaged in education, training or employment post-16. The form each Unit took varied from school to school but the two referred to in these stories had similar briefs.

Learning Mentors (LMs) were based in the schools and received training organized by the LEA, which included an input from the EPS. The recruits came from a variety of backgrounds and had usually worked with young people in some capacity, but did not necessarily have a recognized qualification in a relevant curriculum area. Their targets included reducing exclusions and improving attendance, but they also mentored pupils who were underachieving with a view to improving their performance in SATs and GCSEs. They were also, along with pastoral staff, involved in transfer arrangements from primary to secondary, with monitoring progress at Y7 and Y9, and with developing action plans for pupils in need of support.

In each of the stories LMs make cameo appearances, but in two of them teachers described as 'managers' of LSUs are among the main characters. In the first story, 'From classroom to "Colditz" via a Learning Support Unit' (Chapter 2), the Unit manager, Audrey, is almost as much a 'victim' as the other main character, Peter, a boy in his first year at the school. The story demonstrates the morally problematical nature of psycho-medical labelling but also how political tensions around the pastoral structures of a school can result in the exclusion of teachers as well as pupils. I have shown how I attempted to deconstruct the school and clinical identity of Peter by viewing him as a self-reflecting agent as well as a vulnerable person in need of support. It was in the later stages of the intervention that he received support in a LSU. This story has many twists and turns but ultimately it is a story of failure – of how moods changed and how support interventions did not work.

The second story, 'The girl who squeezed in and out of everywhere' (Chapter 3), is more optimistic in that it includes a description of what I felt was a more successful intervention. A number of themes inform the narrative. Kirsty was described by her social worker, Dorothy, as a 'deeply disturbed' adolescent girl who was constantly in trouble both in and out of school. In general, the stories told to me about girls differed from those about boys. In terms of the referrals to the EPS, boys far outnumber girls, but when a girl is referred, so the story goes, she is far more challenging than a boy. Both are described in emotional terms but girls are assumed to be more capable of using emotions to manipulate others. Rather unusually – because the term is more often applied to boys – Kirsty was described by Dorothy as 'a feral child', a term she knew and used about herself.

Kirsty received support in LSU. Some of the possibilities for promoting inclusion via the LSU are described. I was particularly impressed by a strategy involving drama techniques used by the Unit Manager, Pat. Her approach, with its emphasis on the curriculum and collaboration, seemed to be a better way forward than the previous approach with Kirsty with its managerialist emphasis on targets and Pastoral Support Plans. In the Coda I speculate on issues to do with Kirsty's mental health, on gender issues, on the question of therapeutic intervention and the role of teachers like Pat.

The title of the final story in this section, 'Giving up on them: a tale of despair' (Chapter 4), speaks for itself. It is about a SENCO, Geoff, who had worked in the same secondary school for nearly 30 years – a school which, as he said himself, had seen better days (it had been identified by OFSTED as having 'serious weaknesses'). His current frustrations were very real but an unfortunate consequence was the change in his attitude towards pupils in trouble. I was involved in his attempts to 'prove a point'. The story includes a detailed account of Barry, who was one of those pupils whom Geoff said he had 'given up on' and who were responsible for his retiring earlier than planned.

Geoff was opposed to a major innovation in the school, the establishment of a 'nurture group', which he felt had been imposed on him and the Special Needs Department by Senior Management. In the Coda I identify the rationale behind such groups and the doubts I have about their role in secondary or for that matter in primary schools. Although as critical as Geoff of this innovation, I try to explain why I did not share his feelings of despair, and why I could not support his attitude towards certain pupils in the last few months of his teaching career.

Chapter 2
From Classroom to 'Colditz' via a Learning Support Unit

Introduction

Peter was referred to the EPS because of concerns about his behaviour and educational progress. His secondary school, Westbourne Park, reported that he had 'concentration problems' and was constantly disrupting other pupils' learning. He could also be confrontational with staff and very abusive. In general conversation and in class discussion it was evident that Peter was able to understand ideas and reason logically at a good level relative to peers of his own age, but his literacy skills were said to be weak for a boy of his obvious ability. He had not received a statement from the LEA but was being supported at the School Action Plus stage of the Code of Practice, which involved an Individual Education Plan (IEP) and some individual input from a TA (teaching assistant) and from a LM.

The school informed me that the parents had recently become much more cooperative. Apparently their attitude had changed after they had, as they said, 'at last found out what was wrong with him'. After several sessions at the Child and Family Psychiatric Service (CFPS), Attention Deficit Hyperactivity Disorder (ADHD) had finally been diagnosed and medication prescribed.

Although I was pleased that the family was now working in partnership with the school, I am never happy when I learn that a pupil has received this diagnosis. Was it going to be another occasion, and I had experienced many, when a medical category was going to be deployed as a substitute for actually addressing a pupil's needs? Was it merely going to be a way of suppressing further self-reflection on the part of the parents and Peter himself? Would reliance on medication merely reinforce this suppression? And what about the possible side effects, which no one, not even psychiatrists, seemed to know much about?

In the local area in which I worked, the psychiatric services were stretched to the limit, with the number of referrals increasing rapidly. Treatment for ADHD could involve in-depth family counselling and therapy but whether the CFPS had sufficient resources to do this was often unclear. Although everyone knew that medication was not a cure, in effect drug 'treatment' was all that was provided, even when family relationships were acknowledged as contributory 'causes', as in all probability was the case here. Peter was described by his mother, Diane, as having a love–hate relationship with his stepfather, Richard, who was, according to school reports, generally passive and gave the impression of not being very interested in Peter. Diane told the school that she had been very ill and with five children to look after (three of her own and two of Richard's) this was a very difficult time for her. Peter had maintained contact with his birth father but it had always been stressful for him.

Peter had another appointment with the psychiatrist but this was some way off. The school felt the family now saw Peter's illness as the main cause of his 'difficulties' and the problems he caused in the family. The parents had said none of their other children had been troublesome despite at least two of them experiencing a similar family environment historically as Peter. None of them locked themselves in their bedrooms and refused to come out or threatened to put a brick through the television set.

Developing a Strategy

I discussed Peter with the assistant head, Norman, who reported that Peter had done well in his first term at secondary school but things had gone 'a bit pear shaped' and the school needed advice from me about some possible strategies. Norman knew about the ADHD diagnosis. He felt that whatever the problems at home, it was important for the school to give Peter 'a goal and purpose' and an opportunity for him to mature morally and emotionally. Maybe this would help the family too at some point, as Peter became more reflexive and able to see things differently.

When responding to a referral, my initial contact in this school is usually one of the assistant heads, in this case Norman, who was also the SENCO. From this point on, my enquiries can take several directions, not all of which involve interviewing the pupil concerned. I may, for example, choose to work with teachers, TAs or mentors rather than the pupil if this seems the most appropriate course of action. But usually I like to see the pupil just to obtain an impression of them – of how they react to an unfamiliar adult, how they see the situation in school and what issues are important for them – which however superficial gives me a starting point for developing an understanding of their 'voice'.

My Brief Interview with Peter

A familiar stereotype of the adolescent is of one who gives minimalist responses to adult questioning – a clear 'yes' or 'no' or 'I dunno' if you are lucky, and mumbled responses or shoulder shrugs if you are not. For me, there is no such typicality. The young people I see vary enormously. Some are extremely chatty, others are almost totally silent, and the rest are at various points between. Peter was at the extreme end of chattiness. He seemed to relish his conversation with me, and wanted to talk and talk.

He told me all about his ADHD. I was not sure whether he had really internalized the label or was using it strategically or both. He said he recognized the symptoms in himself. He got bored very easily and was very easily distracted. He had no patience and did things on impulse. He was easily 'wound up' by others, particularly when they called him names. On the whole he liked coming to school and was particularly keen on computers, but he felt that 'no child was over the moon about coming to school' and that applied to him. His main problem was his handwriting, which had gone from bad to worse over the years and was now like that of a 'three year old'.

Writing was certainly a problem for Peter. He recognized that there was a huge gap between his ability to express himself orally and his ability to get things down on paper. Other literacy skills were fine. He could read well and in fact loved reading books about the Second World War. In the small amount of reading he did for me, he read fluently with understanding and demonstrated that he could reflect critically on what he read. But in general, although writing was not his main problem, it was certainly holding him back and contributed to his difficulties overall. Unfortunately, he did not want any special support for this; that is, support other than that provided by the subject teacher. This was clearly because of the stigma of being seen to need help of the kind provided for pupils whom he described as 'thick'.

A paradox here was that although Peter did not want to be seen as different from his peers in that way, he did not mind being seen as having ADHD. Attitudes to labelling are not always what one might anticipate. Some pupils like labels, others do not. Some, like Peter, like some labels but not others. ADHD could have attracted pejorative name-calling like 'nutter' or 'loopy', but it did not seem to in Peter's case. He was, however, on the receiving end of other forms of name-calling which he detested, like being called 'thick'or 'fatso'.

As far as the teachers were concerned he felt some of them 'had it in for me'; with them, it was personal. He was bored in lessons and felt he had to do too much writing. Other pupils created the disturbance and he got the blame, or others were involved in the disturbance but he was the one singled out or other pupils picked on him and the teacher only saw his retaliation. He was only doing what everyone else was doing. He often could not help what he was doing because of his ADHD.

I had heard such complaints many times before, in fact, apart from the reference to ADHD, they were almost word for word the standard responses of adolescents trying, usually unsuccessfully, to defend themselves against teachers' accusations by shifting the blame on to others. Sometimes they had an element of 'truth' in them, sometimes they did not. I was never sure, but it was of no consequence in this instance because all I was trying to do was get a sense of Peter's attitude towards his situation and some understanding of his potential. What struck me about Peter in these conversations was his capacity for argument. He was articulate and understood how to present a point of view in a way that took account of arguments against it. Yet at the same he was clearly upset by how he felt he had been treated in school by teachers and some other pupils.

At the end of the interview, I told Peter that I was now going to discuss his situation with the assistant head and asked whether he felt anything he had said to me should not be passed on. I had already given assurances that the interview with him was confidential within certain limits. Far from not wishing me to do this, he insisted that the assistant head should know about his views and 'do something' about staff who failed to recognize the difficulties he experienced as a result of his ADHD!

The Teachers' Views

From the outset, in order to accentuate the positive, I told Norman that I had been very impressed with Peter's ability to articulate his views and argue his case. The gap between his oral and writing ability must have been frustrating for him. Norman agreed but confirmed that Peter kept refusing specific help. He suggested that perhaps this help could be delivered in ways other than via the Special Needs Department. As for his capacity for argument, he said these 'skills' appealed to some teachers but not others. One of the teachers had called him a 'barrack-room lawyer' who often claimed to represent the views of his classmates. This was fine in principle, the teacher had said, but was usually irritating at best and extremely disruptive at worst because he tried to 'defend the indefensible'. Thus, he would argue that teachers were unfairly picking on pupils in the class because they personally disliked them, or that the teachers had misinterpreted evidence about a bullying incident – what looked like a case of bullying was in fact just 'normal joshing'.

Some of the teachers also thought Peter used his skills in argument to plead for special treatment on grounds of his 'illness'. He obtained brochures on ADHD and would hand them to teachers before the start of lessons. They felt he did this in a very strange, patronizing way as if he were the expert and they were ignorant! The handout was accompanied by a verbal declaration of how they should expect him to behave. He could not concentrate for long and therefore it was unfair for them to keep punishing him for talking to others or being out of his seat. And queuing up was a problem for ADHD pupils. As he said to me during the interview: 'A person with ADHD should not have to queue up.' Would it be possible therefore for him to be allowed to always go to the front of the dinner queue? The teachers I spoke to about this could see the funny side, but they believed that Peter could sit still for longer periods than he claimed to be able to. One of them told me that Peter often 'forgot himself', became absorbed in his work and would work for half an hour or so without leaving his seat and without talking to anyone. This was particularly true when he was working on a computer. It was less true on those occasions when the task involved writing.

My Reflections

From these interviews, I obtained a sense of Peter as an individual active agent who had interests which he attempted to realize in his relations with others. Not all emotionally oppressed pupils exude this sense of agency but in my experience one can always get an idea of their potential in this regard in the right conversational context.

To describe Peter's behaviour as derived from some form of 'disorder' is to go along with a deterministic view stressing vulnerability but not agency. But one could err in the other direction and see him as nothing but a manipulative active agent. In many of my discussions with teachers I have found myself emphasizing agency or vulnerability depending on the situation. Thus, Peter, as demonstrated earlier, could be 'manipulative', and many teachers described him as such. In some ways this was no bad thing because at least his capacity for agency was recognized. Unfortunately, this was often used as evidence of his 'swinging it' and of his not being as psychologically 'ill' as the ADHD diagnosis would suggest. In a sense, this was understandable, but it could have resulted in a hardening of attitude, which dismissed the whole idea of Peter as vulnerable.

The important point was that Peter was an agent but at the same time he was also vulnerable. One always had to keep in mind both ideas. I felt that Peter's vulnerability was expressed as an inability to make friends and this probably stemmed from uncertainties about his self worth. The teachers felt he had very few friends and those he called his friends did not reciprocate.

Peer Relationships

In order to explore this aspect further, I asked Norman if he could arrange for a sociometric questionnaire to be administered in Peter's tutor group i.e. the group with whom he had most contact. This is a simple device for identifying the friendship structure of a class. Pupils are asked which other pupils in the class they would like to work or play with. They are usually, as in this instance, asked to name three. From their responses a diagram is drawn up with choice lines identifying pairs, triangles, stars, isolates, and other features such as cross-gender and cross-race choices.

An analysis of the questionnaire responses confirmed that Peter had no mutual friends in his class. Nobody chose him, and his choices were not reciprocated. Yet Peter himself felt he had a large number of friends, more than the three he was allowed to name on the questionnaire. I was not surprised by this. Peter's claim to represent the class on certain matters, as if he had been somehow chosen to be their leader, was merely a reflection of wishful thinking on his part. He may have been trying to ingratiate himself with others by demonstrating that he was not only on their side but even willing to get himself into trouble in order to help them out, a fairly typical strategy of a friendless pupil.

Unfortunately not only was this strategy unsuccessful in that it did not enable him to obtain more friends, but it led him into further trouble by causing him to adopt attitudes which led to more confrontations with teachers. For example, he was heard to express racist views apparently in order to curry favour with a group of disaffected white pupils. He felt there was an injustice, which he explained to me as follows: White kids in the class were always 'getting done' for making racist comments and yet when 'the Asians were racist to us', they did not 'get done' or at least not in a way that involved severe punishments like exclusion. He felt there was 'one law for them and one for us', and he articulated this view in front of the class, which contained a minority of British Asian pupils.

I could see incipient racism here but I did not think that Peter himself, who was 12 years old at the time, was motivated by racism. There was a certain logic to what he was saying. It was indeed the case that racist language directed at British Asians was outlawed under the school's anti-racist policy and the penalties were severe. There were never any exclusions resulting from racist comments directed at white pupils. Since many of the latter regarded racist comments as just another way of insulting someone, it seemed unjust that they should be picked on in this way. This claim to victimhood by whites is typical of racist discourse, but many of the whites from poor backgrounds in this school did themselves feel like victims and indeed were victims.

I tried to explore these matters with Peter in a later interview but did not get very far. He had an answer for everything. His saving grace, if it can be called that, was that he was so desperate for friends he would have welcomed overtures from anyone. Thus, a few months later he teamed up with a British Asian, Ehsan, who himself was short of friends.

Peter's attitudes towards girls and women were also problematical. He was developing an unhealthy interest in pornography and used his computer skills to access obscene pictures on the Internet, which he printed out and circulated clearly in the hope of 'getting in' with certain boys in the class. These strategies worked for a time but after he had been used for a while by his new 'friends' he would be dumped again.

Further Developments: The Learning Support Unit (LSU)

I discussed the results of the sociometric questionnaire with Norman and it was decided to focus attention on the issue of friendship, and perhaps ways this could be addressed via the Personal, Social and Health Education (PSHE) curriculum and by using techniques like Circle of Friends (see Chapter 8). But before any strategies could be put in place, things started to go from bad to worse. The staff were becoming more frustrated with Peter's lack of progress on the behavioural front and his poor achievement. He was being thrown out of lessons on a regular basis, and was continually playing truant. The school had introduced an attendance card which pupils had to 'swipe' before entering a class. Peter was one of the first

Further Developments: The Learning Support Unit (LSU)

to find out that the card could be swiped outside any classroom and his attendance would be recorded. This caused mayhem for several weeks.

I had had several conversations with the LM who was counselling Peter on a weekly basis. What line was she taking? She had mostly been using a package of support materials designed to improve his social skills, but although he responded quite well in the one-to-one, there was no transfer to the classroom context.

At this point there was a development in the school's pastoral facilities, which everyone felt potentially would be of great help to pupils like Peter. The school was in the process of establishing a LSU, which was to be run by a LSU manager who was an existing member of the teaching staff. There was provision for the employment of one other person, hopefully a teacher but more likely an experienced TA. The proposed Unit was supposed to cater for pupils with a variety of needs and problems, as defined in the official DfES Guidance (2005): lack of self worth or confidence; poor anger-management skills; difficulty with accepting sanctions; aggression, insolence and belligerence; lack of respect for authority; poor social and communication skills; shy, withdrawn, anxious; difficulty with adjusting to new situations e.g. asylum seekers and refugees; difficult family or social circumstances or Looked After Children; long-term absentees; bullied and bullies; victims of crime, domestic violence ; pregnant school girls.

The LSU would consist of two rooms situated near the Special Needs room and the base for LMs. There was to be a structured system of referral to the Unit, which involved an admissions group consisting of a member of the senior management team, heads of year and the Unit manager. Some pupils would spend whole days in the Unit but placement for shorter periods would be more typical. Sometimes pupils would be taught individually but usually they would be taught in groups, this being the only practical way to organize teaching for the 20 or so pupils who were to be 'on the books' of the Unit at any one time. The curriculum would be flexible, but generally involve either 'packages' of pastoral materials aimed at developing various attitudinal and learning competences, or materials provided by teachers in particular subject areas, especially English, maths and science.

The overall purpose of the Unit was to address the needs of pupils who had become disengaged from classroom learning by teaching them 'skills' which would help them to become 'better' learners and 'better' behaved in school. Concomitant aims were to reduce the number of exclusions and use the Unit as a base for the reintegration of pupils returning from a fixed-term exclusion.

The guidelines for the Unit had been drawn up by the teacher, Audrey, who had been appointed as manager. I had previously had several discussions with her about its role and function. She was adamant that it should not become a 'dumping ground' or 'sin bin' or a place of punishment. What were called Isolation Rooms, basically punishment rooms, were to be established later but Audrey thought it was generally accepted by staff that the LSU was not for that purpose.

As she pointed out, the main aim was to address the pupils' needs and 'get them back of track'. It was important that the Unit was not isolated as a 'bolt-on' provision but was part of an overall pastoral framework, which reflected an inclusive philosophy. She thought part of her role was to work with teachers as well as pupils.

She would need to have enough time out of the Unit to liaise with teachers, particularly subject teachers, and share with them her experience of teaching approaches with Unit pupils. Subject teachers themselves might be timetabled to work in the Unit for a few lessons a week. This would be beneficial for all concerned, including the pupils who would have a chance to relate to a teacher in a more relaxed atmosphere outside the normal classroom context.

From Classroom to Unit

My own view was that some of the basic ideas behind the Unit were sound, but there were a number of issues which were likely to crop up. Pupils referred to the Unit were likely to have different needs. It would not necessarily be the case that a pupil whom teachers expected to be placed in the Unit would be able to fit into any of the teaching groups as currently constructed. As the staff of the Unit were the only ones in a position to make judgements about this, Audrey would have to have the final say on who and who was not admitted. If the Unit was to be effective, it was absolutely crucial to create viable groups. If this did not happen the whole project would be jeopardized.

However, the first step was to ask teaching staff to name those pupils who they thought might benefit from placement in the Unit. Each department drew up a list. The names varied from one department to another but there were some names on every list, and Peter's was one of them. Even though it was understood that no pupil could be admitted to the Unit without the Unit staff agreeing, there was pressure on Audrey to take Peter, which she duly did. Because he and a few others could not realistically be refused admission, the groups had to be built round these pupils. This was not an easy task because they were pupils who had clashed with each other in the past and were currently not on good terms.

Audrey Under Pressure

In the next few weeks there was enormous pressure on Audrey coming from a number of directions. A TA was appointed who had a good relationship with her but who, though experienced, required some further CPD, which Audrey had to supply without any time allocation or extra resources for the purpose. Although a structured referral system was set up, some teachers did not fully understand the purpose of the Unit and those who did often had their recommendations turned down on grounds they wanted to contest. The Unit had teething problems and its actual role and function still had to be negotiated. The guidelines were one thing but the 'reality' was always likely to be different. Audrey to her credit was aware that she was part of a process. She felt 'things never work out quite how you expect them to' and 'that's just the way things are in schools; you have to make compromises.'

Audrey and Jane, the TA, managed to set up two viable groups, and decided to work individually or in pairs with pupils who for one reason or another could not be fitted into the groups. However, the months went by and Audrey was still not able to fulfil all aspects of her role. The main problem, she said, seemed to be that teachers generally saw the Unit as 'about changing the kids but not about changing themselves'.

I shared Audrey's view. The Unit took pupils out of the mainstream classroom and tried to give them the 'skills' and attitudes to enable them to reintegrate, but without changes in the classroom environment itself the 'triggers' to dysfunctional behaviour remained. Under these circumstances, a high 'recidivism' rate was likely. Of course, other aspects of the school's behaviour policy, like the revamped pastoral system, might eventually make an impact on the classroom environment, but it was important to work on all levels at the same time. Changes needed to occur that would facilitate the reintegration of pupils like Peter in the here and now not at some point in the future when general behaviour policies began to bite.

There was a politics at work here grounded in different views of the Unit stemming from different interests. LSUs are often a contested innovation because staff from different departments have their own subject-based interpretations of pupils' needs. It is highly likely that there will be different expectations of the Unit based on these different interpretations. As an EP, I was aware of this but my knowledge of the situation was inevitably limited. I visited the school only once a fortnight and was not party to all discussions about the Unit and its operation. My 'theory', backed up by experience of such developments in other schools and my recollection of similar policies in the past, gave me some preconceptions of what was likely to occur but I was not able to act on these. I was already involved with several pupils in the Unit and currently had a particular interest in one pupil, Peter. Although I tried to think in broad terms about the role and function of the Unit, I also had to think what might happen next in matters specifically relating to him.

One of the anticipated scenarios was that despite all the talk about not wanting the LSU to become a 'dumping ground' that was what in effect it was in danger of becoming. It had not been established very long before Audrey was complaining that she did not have enough say on admissions and was just being asked to take pupils whom teachers, in her words, 'had almost given up on'. Everyone was aware that this should not have happened and several meetings were called over a period of time to review the Unit, but the recidivism rate in fact increased, which was a sure sign that the Unit was not working as everyone had hoped. There were several reasons for this negative development, which I cannot for lack of space go into detail about here. Suffice it to say that ultimately it was about priorities. A section of the staff were genuinely not convinced about the value of the LSU, and thought the resources could be better deployed elsewhere.

In the event Peter was unable to cope with group work in the Unit and had to be worked with on his own. In the coming months various attempts were made to reintegrate him, all unsuccessful. Whenever he did join a subject group in the mainstream, the same behaviours recurred as he responded in the same way to what he perceived as the same provocations.

Audrey is Excluded

At this point I felt that Audrey's position was becoming untenable. She was in the crossfire of conflicting forces in the school, which had reduced her to an almost permanent state of anxiety. She felt she had taken the job on a false prospectus. She told me that she was becoming 'stressed out'. Not everyone in her position would have reacted in this way. These kinds of jobs in schools are not inherently any more stressful than, say, subject teaching. The manager of a Unit only interacts with pupils in small groups or pairs, and often sees pupils on their own. Their timetable is more flexible and can change from week to week. All teachers have to work under pressure and not all do so in conditions which are to their liking. Individuals differ in their response to pressure, but I have known many teachers in her position who have reacted in the same way to similar kinds of frustration – feeling that they cannot do a good job because of the way an educational facility has been interpreted by other staff or because of underfunding.

Audrey's own development as a Unit manager entered the equation. An EP has to take account of the individual teacher's situation and their relationship with the pupil. In fact, contrary to the conventional view, it is often this relationship they are supporting rather than one or other individual. Since Peter had been re-referred to the Unit and was now almost permanently in the Unit, his key relationship was with Audrey. This was not a good thing for him or for her. I had experienced many situations like this in other schools where usually a TA but sometimes a teacher was forced into a situation where they had a continuous interaction with a pupil over a long period of time. Although this usually kept the pupil out of trouble for a while, it also created more difficulties. Peter was a complex boy who needed care and attention but did not need to spend his school life relating to one adult in a LSU.

I felt the situation was becoming impossible for Peter as well as Audrey, whose own vulnerability was becoming a factor. Since it was now evident that even an approximation to her ideal role was never going to be realized, she gradually began to exclude herself from the mainstream. She began to stress the differences between Peter and other pupils, and focus more on his ADHD diagnosis, seeking advice from the CFPS about how to 'treat' him. When this did not materialize, she sought guidance from a clinical psychologist working for another health-based service. She began to stress the need for a form of therapy, which would involve Peter coming to terms with his psychological difficulties. Like all of us, her understanding of his problems was a projection of her own situated theories and concerns, but I felt she was herself becoming too vulnerable to achieve the reflexive distance needed to evaluate her practice.

It was acceptable to develop a close relationship with a pupil but the nature of her closeness with Peter was such that they seemed, as it were, to be colluding in the exclusion of each other. Her interventions on his behalf were fraught with dangers. Better perhaps not to intervene at all than to project on to him what looked to me like half-baked psychological theories about 'lack of love' and 'poor early nurturing', and his need for 'a therapeutic environment'. Not that her theories were necessarily inappropriate, but I felt her outlook was becoming too constrained by her own anxieties for her to 'let go' of Peter and achieve his inclusion.

Of course, I cannot pretend that at the time I was fully cognizant of these 'dangers'. In any case, as a genuinely reflective practitioner, I had to acknowledge my own uncertainties. Audrey may have been right. Maybe intensive therapy was the answer, provided it did not involve further exclusion.

However, I still felt that it was practicable to include a boy like Peter in the mainstream provided an appropriate, well-resourced 'cocktail' of support was arranged. This may include some co-counselling in the Unit, but every effort should be made to wean him from his relationship with Audrey. The latter would be difficult. It was in everyone's perceived interests that he should remain in the Unit. Some of the subject teachers felt he would always be too disruptive to be in the mainstream. And Peter himself wanted to remain in this therapeutic environment, which he regarded as a right for a child with ADHD.

A Further Review

Was I right in calling for yet another review? Norman, who was in general very supportive of my role in the school, had a different perception of the 'problem'. He thought Audrey's relationship with Peter was the only positive aspect of the whole situation. 'She is about the only one who can keep him in school and out of trouble', he had told me. He was aware that Peter was taking up a great deal of her time but felt this 'would not be forever', and it was worth it in the here and now just to 'keep things on an even keel'.

Maybe he was right. Maybe we needed to accept Audrey's relationship with Peter de facto and build on it. After all, in other contexts, as Norman reminded me, I had recommended that a pupil be assigned a key worker, that is, someone who would coordinate support, be available to see the pupil at short notice, be proactive in developing support structures for the pupil in different areas of the curriculum, and work with the parents on a regular basis. But I felt Audrey was not able to perform this role because of the way she now perceived her relationship with Peter, as a quasi-therapist rather than a teacher and coordinator of support.

In the end, Norman agreed that a further review could do no harm. I was hoping for an outcome that would involve Peter having less to do with Audrey. It was important to have another look at how Peter related to different teachers in different subjects, and to see if it was possible to identify a subject teacher as an alternative key worker. Was there any evidence that in some lessons with some teachers Peter had got on relatively well? This was all slipping into the past now since Peter had not attended many classes for several weeks. But up until now we had not really had a close look at it. Although all departments had referred Peter for placement in the Unit, it was not clear how individual teachers perceived Peter. I hoped that there would be at least one teacher who appreciated some of his strengths, like his capacity for argument, for example, and who thought they could channel this constructively.

I asked Norman to obtain a 'round robin' on Peter, which involved all his teachers, 12 in all, writing a sentence or two about him. From this, four things were apparent. First, although all the teachers had recommended Peter for the Unit, it was clear he had been better behaved in some lessons than others. Second, those lessons in which he behaved well were not necessarily those in which he was relatively better academically, and vice versa. I suspected that his poor spelling and writing skills were a factor, but only if the teacher was too demanding in this area, forced the issue too frequently and made few allowances for pupils with poor skills. Third, some teachers did have a good word to say about him. One noted that he always made positive and interesting contributions to class discussion. Fourth, the comments about his behaviour outside lessons were all negative. He had lots of run-ins with other pupils, and had, as one teacher put it, occasionally 'flipped his lid', like when he picked up a girl's dinner in the hall and threw it at her. He could still be abusive to staff, particularly female staff.

After this review, another support 'package' was constructed, which identified two or three subjects where Peter might be able to cope, because the teachers seemed more sympathetic. It also involved further sessions with a LM, but only a couple of sessions a week in the Unit where I hoped Audrey could involve Jane more, particularly as a support of his writing difficulties. Audrey reluctantly accepted this. I talked to her about the need for 'weaning' and she eventually agreed that perhaps she had become too involved with him, but I felt that at an emotional level she did not really accept this. I may now have lost her trust but I was not sure what I could do about it.

What of the key worker? I suggested a young history teacher, Joe, might be approached. From his comments, it was clear he had a lot of time for Peter whom he regarded as a 'bright' youngster, but he said that even in his lessons he was frequently involved in low-level disruption, which sometimes 'boiled over' into something more serious. In any case, he did not see how he would have the time to be his key worker. He only saw Peter for two sessions a week, and was unsure how such an arrangement would work. It was not his job to coordinate support.

I knew this would be the response to my suggestion, but I still thought Joe was the best person, and that even a little of his time would have been greatly appreciated by Peter who enjoyed history and obviously respected this particular teacher. As with other subject teachers, all that could be negotiated was a slightly more proactive approach in relating to him, perhaps by making sure he was spoken to in a friendly way at the start of each lesson and when he was passed in the corridor. As in many secondary schools, the academic were split from the pastoral structures, and there were various pressures on staff to maintain this. One subject teacher told me that he would have liked to deal with 'personal issues and problems' but he just did not have the time, and in any case it was the job of the pastoral staff.

It was also agreed at the review that the parents, Diane and Richard, should be seen again to check up on how things were going at the CFPS. On interview, both parents said they were at the end of their tether with Peter. Whenever they sent him to his room, he escaped through the window and wandered the streets. He 'stole' the television from the living room and refused to give it back. He had put a lock on the inside of his bedroom door so none of the family could get in. They were not sure if he was still taking his tablets. The CFPS had given them another appointment in six weeks. Although things were bad at the moment, they did not want any involvement with Social Services or anyone visiting the home, apart from the Education Welfare Officer (EWO) because he was the only one who could get Peter out of bed!

A Further Interview with Peter

Norman suggested that it would be a good idea if he and I had a further discussion with Peter to outline the new support arrangements and inform him that we considered this to be a fresh start. I made the mistake of agreeing to this against my better judgement (why does this happen?). I did not like conducting joint interviews with assistant heads. There was a danger the pupil would perceive me as too closely aligned to the authority structure in the school. When pupils like Peter saw what the set up was, they understandably often went into defensive mode. And this was what Peter did. When confronted with two adults in authority, he knew what line to take and how to manipulate the rhetoric. Thus, he gave out the usual spiel of having been unfairly treated and picked on for minor infringements of rules, which were inconsistently applied.

The general thrust of this interview was predictable. Norman explained the new support procedures and then proceeded to act in the way Peter himself probably anticipated, challenging Peter's own account of his behaviour but also accepting that he had a right to make these points. He told Peter he would follow up his complaints and criticisms but we both knew he would not spend much time doing so. Norman was at the top end of a hierarchical-line management, which already had built into its thinking the idea that Peter was the problem.

Norman understood this and gave Peter a 'talking to' which was in part Dutch uncle and part hanging judge. It was not something I strongly objected to because the 'discourse of punishment' was clearly subsumed under a caring approach, but I knew that for Peter it was like water off a duck's back. Although very sensitively handled by Norman, it could not possibly have had much effect, because we all, including Peter, knew that no one was in a position to deliver on promises. Peter would only have to be abusive to one teacher on one occasion for him to be back in the dock, so to speak, again.

'Colditz'

In the event the new support arrangements soon broke down. Peter, by now a much larger boy, had started throwing his weight around and attacked a girl in his class with a rucksack. There was now a serious Health and Safety issue. The teachers felt that he 'blew up' at the slightest provocation. Audrey felt that his behaviour had become worse because he resented not being able to spend more time in the Unit. Some of teaching staff felt that Peter was 'getting away with it', so they asked Norman if he could be sent to the Isolation Room. As indicated earlier, unlike the LSU, this was more about punishment than rehabilitation. Pupils were sent there for a given length of time ranging from one lesson to a whole day. In the room, they had to get on with their work in silence without speaking to other pupils and with only the minimum contact with staff. Norman, with his disciplinary hat on, agreed that it was appropriate for Peter to do a spell in here.

I disagreed with this move and felt the matter should have been discussed with me and support staff. I was beginning to feel pessimistic, and now that I had been left out of the 'loop' (and in a sense been excluded myself) was wondering if I should be spending any more time on the 'case'. I was not really sure. I decided to see Peter again for an update. During my interview with him, he bitterly complained about having to go to the Isolation Room, which he described as 'Colditz', after the castle used by the Germans in the Second World War as a POW camp. I asked him how he was coping in school but on this occasion he was not in the mood to say much. I asked him about his ADHD and whether or not he was still receiving medication. 'Yes', he said, 'still getting my little pills, but I don't take them. Sell them to girls as slimming tablets.'

This was the last time I saw him. The school had other 'cases' they wanted me to see urgently. Eventually I received a copy of the notification to the LEA that the Governors had agreed to Peter's permanent exclusion. Audrey had by this time retired on grounds of ill health. The Unit was to be revamped. I was at least invited to discuss the new referrals to the Unit, most of whom were on my books. What would my advice be?

Coda

In her critical analysis of the concept, Lloyd (2003) refers to the 'unproblematic view of ADHD as a clear, measurable, clinical disorder, significantly under-diagnosed in Britain, and manageable through medication' (Lloyd, 2003, p. 106). I have certainly found in the course of my work as an EP that this unproblematic view is becoming increasingly dominant, particularly amongst health professionals. It is worrying that large numbers of children and young people have been diagnosed as suffering from a 'disorder' for which, as Baldwin and Cooper (2000, p. 598) have pointed out, 'there are no reliable scientific criteria for making a diagnosis.' Even my own professional association, the British Psychological Society, has produced Guidelines which, though acknowledging disagreements over the concept, implicitly accepts a highly uncritical view, making frequent reference to the 'nature of ADHD'. The reasons the concept flourishes in the current period are complex and relate to the interaction of a variety of social and historical factors comprehensively analysed by Neufeld and Foy (2006).

In Peter's case, the diagnosis of ADHD was welcomed by the family probably because it seemed to explain his problems in a way which fitted with their own needs and concerns. Peter's own perspective was more ambiguous. From his cavalier approach to his medication I wondered whether deep down he really accepted that he had a 'disorder'. He certainly embraced the label on certain occasions, but there was a suggestion he only did so when it suited him. The teachers were more circumspect and several felt that he was manipulative and on occasion showed more self-control than someone with ADHD would have been capable.

Audrey's stress was certainly in large part a function of lack of job satisfaction. The link between job satisfaction and occupational stress has been well documented in the literature (for an overview see de Nobile and McCormick, 2005). Teachers' confidence has taken something of a battering in recent years due mainly to the Government's managerialist, 'top down' approach towards professionals in public services as mentioned in the Introduction. According to some commentators, this is particularly evident in relation to 'difficult pupils' (see Mittler, 2000) where many teachers feel that they do not have the knowledge and skills to teach these pupils inclusively. Lack of job satisfaction and lack of confidence can be tackled through CPD work, but this would not improve matters unless the underlying issues were addressed. Teacher's stress needs to be looked at not just as a function of psychological factors but of processes endemic to schooling in our society.

What exactly are these processes? The National Curriculum together with its associated assessment system plus the network of controls from league tables to performance assessment have alienated many teachers, stoking up stress whilst undermining the collaborative and collegial relations that can best deal with it. It is not just an English problem. In her study of teachers in Australia, Munt (2004) found that one-half of the participants complained of 'stress related health problems' but she felt that 'these problems were not able to "become" political issues related to teachers' work because they were framed as "individual" illnesses to be "managed" by the appropriate psychological, medical or management experts'(Munt, 2004, p. 588).

Many of the teachers I speak to in schools appear cynical about my role, but they are often just being realists. The only way the LSU could have acted as a force for inclusion was if it had been linked organically to a programme of radical curriculum change and innovation. It was not so linked because there was no such programme, and most teachers knew this. Audrey was isolated because what she initially tried to do was counter to a powerful hidden agenda; one that involved regarding the Unit as a facility for excluding rather than including pupils. In the end she opted for what in my view was the 'wrong' solution to the difficulties she experienced, but that is how it often is with people who are suffering from stress. The problems are compounded.

Chapter 3
A Girl Who 'Squeezed in and out of Everywhere'

Introduction

Kirsty Myers was a recent re-referral to our service. Dorothy, her social worker, said she was a young person who was 'never at home'. She was what the newspapers described as a 'feral child'. It was not clear if her father, with whom she supposedly lived, ever knew where she was. Kirsty was quite open about her movements in the neighbourhood, and it amused her to think she might be called 'feral'. 'That's me', she told me on one occasion, 'I'm a right little animal…squeeze in an out of everywhere.'

She had been on our books in the primary school, but the 'case' had been closed because, as my predecessor had noted, the 'situation had improved'. Now it had all blown up again. Kirsty was said to be running wild in the neighbourhood. In school her behaviour was appalling. She was abusive to teachers, calling female teachers 'shag-bags' and 'perv lessies'. She skipped lessons and wandered round the school peering into classrooms. On one occasion she assaulted a student teacher in the corridor, or at least it was alleged that she had, her version being that she was only responding to verbal abuse from the student.

Those teachers who said they knew her well told me they felt she was on the fringes of more serious delinquent activities. She was in danger of becoming a 'bit of a gangster's moll', and had been seen smoking in the back seat of a stolen car with her boyfriend joyrider at the wheel. She had a recent history of drug abuse and although she was now clean, in view of the company she kept outside school, was obviously still at risk. The pastoral staff knew her social history – how her mother had been very ill when Kirsty was a toddler, how her father had originally deserted the family but had returned and how the housing conditions had always been very poor. Kirsty herself thought she had been failed by the various welfare services who had never taken appropriate action in relation to her family's problems.

Some of the staff felt that when Kirsty was on her own or in a small group she could be a cooperative and amenable young person and in many ways was very mature for her years. Her form tutor, Jenny Woodward, felt that she was one of those youngsters who had had to fend for themselves from a very early age, and had had to 'grow up quickly'. Despite her disruptive behaviour and verbal abuse towards staff, she had a nice side to her. She had a certain way of talking about herself and her relationships, which seemed quite insightful, and on the whole, staff did not dislike her and felt that sometimes she could be a 'delight' to talk to.

However, although Kirsty might have been 'worldly wise' and in a sense 'mature' for her age, it was generally felt she was an emotionally vulnerable child who was very much at risk. She herself had said on several occasions that she thought she was 'going mad' and was finding it very difficult to 'control herself' either inside or outside school, and this got her into a 'lot of trouble'. She had been referred to a psychiatrist who reported a number of symptoms commensurate with depression and described here as having 'an internal sense of rage and symptoms of emotional stress'.

My Interview with Kirsty

The school was not sure what line to take with Kirsty and wanted my input. She was in Y 10 and would be leaving school next year. I interviewed her with Dorothy in attendance. She gave the impression of someone who liked to talk about herself and who had strong views about what was going wrong for her in school. Like many pupils in trouble she blamed the teachers, or at least some of them, the ones who had 'no sense of humour' and 'couldn't take a joke', but she also blamed herself. She was not easily led and in fact felt she was more of a leader in the peer group, but nevertheless she had developed a reputation for messing about and there was pressure on her to fulfil a particular role as someone who 'took no shit' from teachers and gave as good as she got.

Despite a somewhat anti-school view, she made interesting observations about the process of teaching and learning, which went beyond the usual criticisms of lessons as 'boring'. She had views about how teachers should teach and what they should teach – that pupils should not be asked 'to write all the time' but encouraged to discuss things and express themselves verbally, and how lessons could be improved by 'starting off with stuff that interested us'. She felt that some teachers 'didn't have much life in them', were 'not exactly exciting in themselves' and had not done much apart from go to school then to college then back to school. 'What sort of life was that?' She liked a few teachers, those who were 'good with kids', like the ones who dealt with special needs or who were tutors.

There were a number of issues Kirsty did not want to discuss with me, because, as she pointed out, it would 'take too much time'. She was clearly ambivalent about her mother, who at one point she claimed to 'detest' but later spoke about with more affection. She lived with her birth father and her brother, but usually she was either at her mate's house or at that of one of her two grandmothers. I did not delve into her motives, but clearly there was a possibility that keeping in with the grandmothers provided a safe bed for the night away from home, not that home was ever more than a few streets away.

I asked her what were the 'positives', if any, about school. She said that the work experience the school had arranged for her 'had gone off well' and she wanted more of this, although perhaps of a different kind. She had had experience in a nursery and a hairdresser's and would now like to do something more interesting. Reports written by her supervisors were mixed. When she was at work she could be cooperative and hardworking but she often turned up late and sometimes not at all. She was said to be very good with children. Wanting to accentuate the positive, I said this seemed to be one of her strengths. At this, she gave me a sideways glance and shrugged her shoulders. She told me I was beginning to sound like a teacher! Intrigued, I asked her what she meant. Teachers apparently were always telling her that she was good with children, but she felt they were just trying to push her 'into a corner'. I asked what she thought she was good at. 'Having a good time and then getting depressed!' She was not particularly interested in working with children, although she did not mind doing it for the experience. Why would she want to spend the rest of her life as a 'drudge, looking after kids for a pittance?'

The bell rang and I had to terminate the interview. It had been brief and I felt we had not got very far. Did she want to continue next week? Yes, she would not mind. 'It will mean I won't have to go to lessons!' She gave me a quick grin and then left.

I asked Dorothy how she thought the interview had gone, and she said that Kirsty seemed to like me although was not 'telling me half'. In fact the people who had written reports on her work experience were letting her off the hook. Neither placement had been successful. She had been far too 'bolshie' in each context. Dorothy felt that Kirsty was a deeply disturbed adolescent who had 'gone off the rails'. There were a lot of ambivalent feelings towards her mother and father. She said she loved them both but in the next breath called her mother an 'old cow' whom she did not want to see again, and her father an 'idle sod' who could not even make his own bed. She had better relationships with her grandparents, but the situation was getting out of hand and Social Services were thinking of taking her into care and placing her with foster carers.

My Reflections

I had many questions in mind at that point. Her 'wild' lifestyle and the company she kept after school seemed to be committing her more and more to a 'delinquent' identity. She regarded herself as a 'rebel' but what was she in rebellion against exactly? Kirsty had told Dorothy that she often felt like 'a caged lioness' and was so bored at school that it was 'unbearable'. She often said being in school was like being in prison.

This was really a version of the 'bored teenager' explanation writ large in Kirsty's case. But what was different about her? How were home and school linked? As indicated above, Dorothy felt her behaviour was a function of a deep-seated emotional disturbance stemming from the way she had been treated at home in the past. She became caught up with a 'dodgy bunch of kids after school' because it gave her a 'home of a kind' rather than because she was bored and just seeking thrills. She did not intend to be bad but had just drifted into activities, which involved lawbreaking.

Some teachers saw Kirsty as more emotionally manipulative than male pupils who had similar track records. Girls who misbehaved were often perceived in this way (Peter in the previous story was an exception), as if they possessed a greater capacity for expressing and using emotion simply because they were girls. This was clearly part of a picture of female 'deviance', which reflected a gendered understanding of girls' 'nature' and Kirsty may have been 'living out' stereotypes available to her in the school context.

Another salient aspect of gender oppression was to do with her relationships with older boys, usually ones who had left school. Like many girls of her age, she felt boys in her year at school were too immature for her. For some girls the age-based year-group system of school organization was just another reflection of the oppressive nature of schooling. As Kirsty put it in her interview with me 'The boys in my class are like little kids. All they do is fight and mess about.' An older boyfriend outside school was a status symbol and made girls feel more adult, but this was often not a solution that was in their best interests. In the company she kept, particularly outside school, there were three options available in these allegedly more adult relationships – 'wife' or 'missus', 'slim and sexy dolly bird' or 'gangster's moll'. She told me that girls were often forced by boys to take drugs in order to keep slim. She said she thought she was too fat, even though she was in fact underweight for her age and height.

Kirsty is Excluded

Dorothy thought whatever strategies were used in school, they were unlikely to work unless there was some security in the home context, even if this meant a foster home. The situation where she was sleeping here, there and everywhere could not continue. There had to be some stability. I agreed with this but was unsure what the school could do, which they had not done already. The flexible curriculum with more options, which had been put in place for Y10 pupils, had not really worked in Kirsty's case. Sending her out of school on work experience would have been fine if the supervisors in the work place had had more time for her. The whole 'support package' was too fragmented, but I was not sure it would have worked even had it been more coherent. She had received some counselling from a LM but the various strategies around the idea of 'anger management' had been too superficial.

I decided to have a further interview with Kirsty because I wanted to obtain a clearer picture of how she felt about school and what subjects or activities might be of interest to her. However, a few days later Dorothy rang me to say that Kirsty had been given a fixed-term exclusion for verbally abusing a teacher. Moreover, things had taken a turn for the worse outside school. Kirsty had found out that her mother had been taken to court on a drugs charge and was likely to end up in custody. Also, it had transpired during the course of a police investigation that her mother, whom Kirsty said she hardly ever saw, had been supplying her with drugs, certainly cannabis and ecstasy tablets, and possibly even some cocaine. And worse still, Kirsty had been caught shoplifting in a local store and the police were considering charging her for the offence. It was not clear whether she was stealing to fuel a drug habit or whether it was something she had just done on the spur of the moment. It seems the latter was more likely because she had only stolen one relatively inexpensive item – a baseball cap! – which she alleged was not for herself but her boyfriend. This was not a serious offence but she had been cautioned for a previous one and the police had decided to charge her. Dorothy thought the outcome of this would be a period of probation and that the Youth Offending Team would probably been involved.

The Pastoral Support Plan (PSP)

I decided that it would be inappropriate for me to see Kirsty again at this point – she would have had numerous interviews recently – and that I could best help the situation by contributing to the planning of a reintegration programme. The school felt it was imperative that such a plan be part of a revised Pastoral Support Plan (PSP) and should be in place before she returned to school. Such plans were seen by the LEA as a crucial element of the inclusion process and as an example of 'good practice' in pursuit of goals in accordance with the Government's wider 'social inclusion' agenda. Under the plan, the school was to ensure that all relevant parties were invited to a planning meeting, including school staff, birth parents/ foster carers and representatives from outside agencies. The pupil was to be properly prepared for the meeting, and, if they did not attend, their views were to be represented and the outcome fed back to them. An action plan would be decided upon, which included targets to be achieved, and a key member of the teaching staff would be identified who would implement and coordinate the plan and liaise with parents/carers and outside agencies. Information would be disseminated to all relevant parties. Methods of monitoring the effectiveness of the plan would be identified, and a date for review set.

In previous meetings of this kind, the whole business of target setting had been a turn-off for Kirsty, who later told me she felt she had to agree to certain things because that seemed to be what was expected of her, and although she was asked her views, she felt unable to express what she really felt, because there were just 'too many things going on inside my head'.

As a support professional, one attends many such meetings. They are useful when they foster greater collaboration and reflective conversation between professionals, parents and pupils, and between professionals themselves. But too often they do this in only a limited way. They are 'packed' with professionals all of whom have to have their say. Genuinely creative and critical thinking are at a premium. Predictable 'solutions' are identified from a limited range of options, and there is always an overemphasis on the identification of appropriate targets usually defined in behaviouristic terms.

At this particular meeting there were four members of the school staff (Head of Year, SENCO, Manager of the LSU, LM), two representatives from Social Services, the foster carers, the EWO, a representative from the CFPS, a member of the Youth Offending Team (YOT), and me. Neither of the parents was able to attend. Nor did Kirsty herself attend although the SENCO had obtained her views by asking her to fill in a questionnaire. Yes, she would like to come back to school. What lessons did she think she could do well in? Drama and English. What lessons did she think she would have a problem with? Science and maths.

The social worker and foster carers provided an update on behaviour at home. The member of the YOT explained that Kirsty had eventually just been given a caution and outlined what he thought the contribution of the Team could be. They would probably do some drugs education with her. The representative of CFPS said they would be able to see Kirsty again in about a month.

The Breakthrough

I did not expect much from the meeting, but in this instance I was wrong! Certain suggestions were made, which seemed to open up some interesting possibilities. The representative of the YOT asked if it would be useful for Kirsty to work towards an ASDAN (Awards Scheme Development and Accreditation Network) in drugs education. If so, the YOT could make an input to this. It so happened that the new Manager of the LSU, Pat Downey, who was a drama teacher seconded to the Unit from the English Department, had the night before been reading on TeacherNet about a case study where drama was used in drugs education in an LSU. She would be keen to have a go at this with the support of the YOT.

From my point of view, this seemed a golden opportunity to reinforce 'organic' links between the LSU and the English Department and between the school and an outside agency, which would help Kirsty but also develop the role of the LSU. Kirsty could begin her re-engagement in the LSU and drama work would help her access the English curriculum in the mainstream. The YOT could advise and support Pat. It meant that Kirsty would not be isolated in the Unit but would still receive the support she needed. It would enable her to obtain an ASDAN award, which was a recognized award and one that would be useful for her. I asked if the LM could attend some of the drama sessions on the grounds that it was important for her to understand what Pat was trying to do.

The Head of Year was not convinced at first. He felt we needed to 'flesh out' a fuller timetable for the whole week. Kirsty was entitled to further work experience and access to the National Curriculum, including a basic skills input. The drama-drugs project was a good idea but what else would she be doing?

And what targets should be identified? But there was a general feeling that the whole of the reintegration 'package' should be built around this project. There was no need at this stage to identify targets. Her other point of contact with the school would be sessions with a LM of her own choosing, but the key worker would be Pat. The focus at this stage should be on getting Kirsty back into school and addressing her immediate social and emotional needs. The rest could wait. It was this view that prevailed.

The problem would be devising a drama input in time for Kirsty's re-admission next week. Pat saw no problem with this. She had plenty of material on drugs education and a whole repertoire of drama approaches at her finger tips. A member of the YOT would attend the first session and become as involved as she or he had time to be. Pat said she would appreciate an input from them on drugs in the community. When Kirsty was informed of the outcome of the review, she agreed that it 'sounded OK'.

A Further Interview

I interviewed Kirsty again (with Dorothy present) at the school's request just before she started back. She told me she had not been shocked to find out that her mother had been 'banged up'. Her mother's latest boyfriend was in prison and she had been caught trying to get drugs to him. I did not want to talk to her about drugs because this ground would be explored by others, but she did volunteer that she intended to turn over a new leaf and that a new Kirsty would shortly emerge. Rather than a 'caged lioness', she now thought she was a chrysalis that would shortly come out as a butterfly! Her main problem was the people she associated with both in but mainly out of school. She had had to 'ditch' her last boyfriend because he was a 'druggie' and this meant she did not go out as often. She had settled down quite well with her foster carers, whom she liked, and was looking forward to living a normal life.

I must admit I had my doubts. I could not see how she could easily put the past behind her when it was still on her doorstep, so to speak. The foster home was only a stone's throw from her old stamping ground, and her emotions in relation to both parents were still in turmoil. I asked her about her visit to the CFPS. She kept the appointment and had an interview with 'a doctor bloke and someone else'. They discussed her depression with her but she felt they were hinting at 'causes' which she did not recognize – 'that wasn't where I was coming from'. She would have liked further interviews to explain herself more fully, but was told this was not possible (This was her version; in fact, the CFPS told me they had offered further appointments).

Kirsty had changed a little since I last saw her. She seemed calmer and less volatile, but I was still not optimistic. Why? It was partly to do with my attitude towards drug abuse. I have great difficulty in thinking positively whenever I learn that drugs are involved. I do not accept there is such a thing as a drugs culture; drug abuse seems to me to be inherently anti-culture. But this was related to another factor. I knew from past experience that outcomes for girls in Kirsty's position in this area were often negative, and I just could not imagine someone like Kirsty resisting the pressure to take drugs. Although in some ways she appeared tough and assertive, she was still vulnerable and I could see her becoming emotionally distraught about issues relating to her mother and taking the easy way out.

The Drama Project

I did not having anything to do with Kirsty for several weeks. I knew she had returned to school and that the plan agreed upon had been put into operation. A review meeting was due and I thought I ought to have a talk with Pat Downey prior to this. The set-up in this school was superficially no different from the one I described in the school referred to in Chapter 2. There were still the same issues about staff viewing the Unit in different ways, about some wanting to use it as a 'dumping ground', about which pupils should attend etc. But whereas in that school things had not turned out well, in this one the LSU manager, Pat, had managed to accomplish her role in ways which were helpful to the pupils and drew other teachers in. She was an established member of staff who already had good relations with her colleagues, and she saw the importance of negotiating and collaborating with staff from all departments. I was particularly impressed with her belief in drama as a teaching method in all subjects. She had a very interesting approach to 'bringing science alive' via a dramatic reconstruction of famous discoveries which, even though it was described by one teacher as 'off curriculum', nevertheless so intrigued members of the Science Department they invited her to give a demonstration.

Thus, much of her conversation with staff was about teaching and learning processes as well as about individual pupils. I felt this was exactly the right balance for a teacher in charge of a LSU. Fortunately, she had managed to negotiate enough time for this broader role. Overall, she felt the project had been a valuable learning experience for her and had helped her deepen her understanding of how drama could be used to support youngsters like Kirsty.

Pat said that she and Kirsty had had their ups and downs but basically she was a 'treasure' whose street knowledge was 'impressive'! She had proved to be 'a good little actress' and had made a useful contribution to all aspects of the process of putting a play together. The basic idea was similar to the one that had been outlined at the review meeting. Kirsty worked with two other female pupils in creating and producing a play. They knew their work was to be accredited and this certainly helped to motivate them initially. They took great pride in producing a play that looked 'professional' and Pat felt the exercise had boosted their confidence and self-belief.

The Process: 'Hot Seating' and other Techniques

I was intrigued by Pat's teaching approach and wanted to know more about it. It is not often acknowledged that EPs adopt what I call a benign 'thieving magpie' role as they move from school to school. They see a good idea at work in one school and pinch it! Another school then gets the benefit of this bright idea. It is what teachers do when they interact in person or on the Internet, but in this instance it involves the EP as a go-between. The EP can hone the idea to fit a particular situation and include it as part of a 'whole child' approach to addressing needs.

Kirsty and the others had started off by trying to think of characters and a story line. They had each chosen a character and then put them in the hot seat! Hot seating is a technique which is supposed to help actors to 'fill out' and shape a character. Each of them took it in turns to sit in front of the other two and Pat. Sometimes the LM, a member of the YOT or an interested teacher from a subject department was also involved. They remained in character while the others fired questions at them. Some of these questions were about family background and childhood experiences, which Pat at first thought might touch on areas that were too sensitive, but it did not seem to worry any of the pupils. Kirsty in particular painted a very imaginative and colourful portrait of the character she was playing who was not unlike herself – a female adolescent who had been encouraged by her mother to slim, and was addicted to slimming tablets. She was asked why looking slim mattered, and the responses she came up with triggered more questions. Why did she want to please boys so much? What drugs were involved ? etc.

Pat said there had been a very interesting question-and-answer session about drugs between Kirsty's character and a member of the YOT, which she herself found enlightening. The YOT member had asked the character why she had taken drugs. She replied that everyone took drugs of one kind or another and it was a question of whether they used them properly or misused them. But were not some drugs more addictive than others? Kirsty's character replied that crack cocaine was not necessarily more addictive than cigarettes or alcohol.

At this point Pat felt like intervening but as the YOT member pointed out Kirsty's character was only voicing the views of some health experts. He was impressed with the way she or at least the character handled herself. She went on to point out that drugs were a part of many young people's lives and to 'get in a panic' about it did not help to solve the problem. People managed to get by even with a heroin habit. This only led to stealing if they were poor. If they were a member of a pop group like the Rolling Stones they might end up in court but not for 'thieving'. Drug use did not make any one less of a human being. Pat said she thought Kirsty's character had put up a stout defence of drug taking, but Kirsty herself seemed to recognize that she had been playing devil's advocate.

Interestingly, Pat's skills were such that she allowed the question and answer session to drift away from drug-related issues. Kirsty's character talked about her rapping skills – how she could make up rhymes very quickly – and then gave a demonstration.

Pat felt the other two pupils were 'not in the same league' as Kirsty who was clearly the dominant character and the most streetwise. They looked up to her but this was not a problem because the whole process seemed to bring out Kirsty's 'good side'. Pat was grateful that she had been able to choose two other pupils whom she felt would gel in a group with Kirsty, and that there was some value in keeping this an all female group. In fact, there had only been two other female pupils referred to the Unit. The other 12 were boys.

Pat then asked them to write a play based on these characters. They put it all on a computer and printed out drafts, which they altered in rehearsals. In its final form the play addressed many issues relating to drugs but its storyline revolved around several other themes. It was about a girl who wanted to become a rapper but was continually being put down by male rappers. The girl eventually got together with other girls and formed a band. The story that unfolded was about the rise and decline of the band. Parents cropped up at various points. Some of the characters were stereotypes but Pat had made an effort to encourage less stereotypical approaches mainly via hot seating techniques and this seemed to have worked. Kirsty's character was complex and nuanced.

Reactions

The most controversial part of the process was playing in front of an audience consisting of pupils from the girls' classes. In Kirsty's case this was the class in which she was taught English – a mixed ability group, which included some of her friends but also, she felt, a 'lot of enemies'. The play was clearly going to be controversial and the Head of Year and the Head of English were beginning to have cold feet about it. The Head of Year said he had strong religious beliefs, which he did not foist upon the pupils, and he was certainly against any form of indoctrination, but he was against drug taking in principle and thought the play, which he had seen in the Unit, was a 'bit near the bone' in that it may have been construed as celebrating drug use. The Head of English also felt that the morals of the play were questionable.

However, from Pat's point of view, and I agreed with her, this was not intended as a didactic tale about the evils of drugs but a creative piece of self-expression about life as an adolescent today. The girls had put a lot of effort into it. In artistic terms it was good. The plot had a well thought-out structure, not all the characters were stereotypes, the acting was convincing, the language colourful and pertinent, and far from being morally questionable Pat felt it raised and dealt with issues in a way that other pupils could readily relate to.

In the end the play went ahead and was a great success. Kirsty was the star although both she and Pat insisted that there were no stars! There was no doubt that all three would obtain their ASDAN award. In Kirsty's English class, it led to further developments. Other pupils wanted to write and perform plays and go through the same process. Pat suggested that Kirsty could act as an adviser, a role which she performed with great enthusiasm.

I saw part of the play myself in the Unit and was very impressed. As mentioned above the whole idea of a 'drugs culture' was anathema to me, but I felt my own attitude was beginning to change. I had long believed in drama as the best medium for teaching about controversial issues and totally agreed with Pat about avoiding didacticism. In fact, I had done some CPD work with LMs in another school on how to use drama in their work with small groups. The secret was to know about what made a good play and the process you needed to go through to achieve this. Role play, a typical pastoral strategy, had its uses but it was not equivalent to the process described above. In general, I argued against using drama merely as a vehicle to get a message across. A good play is judged in relation to aesthetic criteria and you need to be a bit of a specialist like Pat to appreciate whether these criteria have been realized in the final production. A good play can help to develop insights into moral and political issues but these have to be teased out through dialogical engagement with interpretations of the play's meaning.

Pat understood this. She wanted people to discuss the play as a play in a wide ranging way, and not get hung up on particular moral issues. I personally could not think of a better way to re-engage a disaffected youngster like Kirsty. Moreover, the model developed by Pat, which involved a variety of staff and other adults, was a way of making the work of the LSU much more inclusionary.

The Review

At the next review meeting, it was generally agreed that Kirsty had made excellent progress and should be on a full timetable as soon as possible. The school hoped she might be able to obtain a few GCSEs if she buckled down to work there and then. The situation out of school was more stable and she had clearly made an effort not to run with the usual crowd. She had visited her mother in prison and felt sorry for her. Her father had taken her out shopping on a couple of occasions, although he still managed to upset her. The YOT praised the school for its flexibility and in particular for what Pat had done.

Kirsty herself was not present at the meeting but she expressed her views via Pat. She thought she might be able to cope with a full timetable but would like to avoid certain teachers and certain classes. It was generally felt that Kirsty had turned a corner and was making a good effort to 'turn her life round', although she still had a long way to go. She was still occasionally very volatile in class but in general much more controlled and there were no reported incidents of her hurling abuse at staff.

Dorothy told me after the review that she thought two developments had really helped Kirsty – first, the drama activity with Pat, and second the fact she had been placed with excellent foster carers, Mandy and Fred. Mandy had left school without any qualifications. She had had 'reading difficulties' as a child and as an adult continued to finding reading 'hard work' although she could read well enough to fill forms in and read newspapers. There were hardly any books in the home and

Mandy spent most of her time knitting for her grandchildren and watching soaps on television. But she was a woman who had a lot of time for children, was an extremely good listener and quite astute in her own way. Kirsty struck up a very good relationship with her. Mandy was the carer, but on occasion it was as if the roles were reversed! Kirsty insisted that Mandy got out of the house more! She was also helping her to improve her reading skills. Dorothy thought this may have been an example of Mandy's 'canniness'. Allowing herself to be 'taught' by Kirsty helped to bring out the latter's 'best side' and encouraged her to develop a sense of responsibility.

The Final Interview: A Box of Tissues

I was rather surprised to learn that Kirsty had requested another interview with me. Dorothy was not sure why she wanted this but could it be arranged? I was currently visiting this school virtually every week and so it was not difficult to fit her in. By this time Kirsty was well into her final year at the school, and was looking forward to going on to college.

I saw her for about 20 minutes in a new rather comfortable interview room located at the front of the school, adjacent to the school secretary's office. Although wearing a school uniform that had seen better days, she looked much smarter and tidier than on the previous occasion. I began by congratulating her on the progress she had made and then asked why she had wanted to see me? She said that she had just wanted to 'put the record straight'. She was aware that a file had been kept on her since the infant school stage and she now wanted to make sure that her recent progress was recorded. This was certainly a young woman in the know!

But I felt there was more to it than this. My general impression was that she wanted to prove something to me but I was not quite sure what. She began by going over her life, all the bad times, the broken home, a violent dad, a druggie mum – and then, when in full flow, she suddenly stopped and said 'I bet I've surprised yer haven't I?' Well, that was true she had. 'You thought I was going to be a druggie didn't yer?' Yes, that was possibly true. 'I still get fed up yer know.' I said I hoped she would get help for this. 'No thanks,' she replied, 'I've come this far on me own.'

That also was largely true. I certainly had not done much, although I felt Pat deserved some thanks. 'Oh, yeah, Pat. A great lady. There aren't many like her'. She then went on to tell me that a week after the performance of her play she had smoked some cannabis in a crack house with some old mates and was thinking about returning to a 'life of crime'. But why did not she? 'I dunno. Just decided to change me ways.' What, just like that. 'Yes, just like that.' She imitated the comedian Tommy Cooper. You are too young to remember him are not you? 'Yes', she replied, 'but he's my mum's favourite.'

I have no idea why Kirsty had wanted to have this conversation with me. Her life had changed for the better, but she seemed to want to stress she could have made this happen at any time. She seemed to be saying that despite all the interventions, particular the drama (which she knew I thought was the best thing since sliced bread), she herself had made the decision to change and that was the top and bottom of it. Was she thanking me or just making sure this part of the record was straight?

Towards the end of the interview, I had an attack of hay fever. My eyes started to water. I reached inside my pocket for a handkerchief. 'Here', said Kirsty, 'use one of these'. She plucked a tissue from the box on the coffee table, which lay between us, and handed it to me with a wry smile.

Coda

Dorothy had always felt that Kirsty was a 'deeply disturbed child' and on several occasions had pushed for further appointments at the CFPS. A psychiatrist had identified symptoms of a possible depression, but this was never followed up mainly because of Kirsty's failure to keep appointments and alleged failure to cooperate even when Dorothy or Mandy made sure she turned up. I was not surprised by this. Although her behaviour could be extreme and she seemed to recognize herself as someone with emotional problems, I felt she had not really internalized the psychiatric interpretation of her difficulties. Dorothy thought that some form of psychotherapy or intensive counselling would have been the best option, but unfortunately from her point of view it was an option that was not available. I had doubts in any case about whether this would have been an appropriate way forward. What did it mean to say Kirsty was 'disturbed'? As far as I could see most of her actions and reactions made perfect sense once you understood her situation. She was able to talk quite openly about her feelings and attitudes, and in her final interview with me seemed to want to portray herself as someone who made her own decisions. The drama intervention had been more educational than therapeutic in the psycho-medical sense, and seemed to prove that 'good education' was what pupils like her needed.

One can speculate about what it is feasible to ask schools to do with respect to mental health issues. Surely there will always be some problems which schools neither have the facilities not the expertise to deal with, even with support from outside agencies? There will always be, it might be argued, some pupils who require help in addition to or even, in certain circumstances, as an alternative to that which the school can realistically be expected to provide.

But we do not know what might be possible in schools where inclusive policies and practices were fully developed. In such schools, teachers like Pat, who are able to make positive, educationally productive relationships with the most troubled and troublesome youngsters, would be a powerful force. At present, they are respected by other staff, but their potential for facilitating inclusion across the curriculum is not always fully appreciated.

I often wonder how many teachers there are like Pat. I have met several of these exceptional individuals over the years, but are they a dying breed? Perhaps if we had a different approach to teacher recruitment there would be plenty of Pats in schools? Even someone like Mandy, despite her weak literacy skills, had something which many subject teachers lacked. At present, recruitment is hidebound by selection criteria derived from the need to teach the current National Curriculum subjects to a particular standard. This gives rise to an excessively restricted field of recruitment in secondary schools since one of the main criteria for selection is a degree in one or more of these subjects or an equivalent qualification.

Finally, it is worth noting that the main pedagogical strategy described in this story was derived from arts education in the form of drama. For many authors (see e.g. Nussbaum, 1997; Minnow, 1997; Greene, 1995) arts education is particularly relevant in teaching for difference and diversity. A study by Griffith et al. (2006, p. 363) showed how children who 'apparently felt they had no place in a public space' were enabled via arts-based work to find 'new possibilities for agency.' Drama, like literature, provides opportunities to teach about human relationships in ways which encourage analysis of personal feelings and the development of empathy for others in a dynamic context where issues highly salient for pupils can be addressed. It provides a way of enhancing pupils' abilities 'to be for others as well as for themselves' and enables 'the imaginative identification with others unlike oneself' (Minnow, 1997, p. 103). It achieves this by working with forms which conform to certain moral and aesthetic criteria as to what constitutes a 'good' play, thus focusing on the development of character, the interaction between characters and the resolution of issues.

Chapter 4
'Giving up on Them': A Tale of Despair

Introduction

Geoff had been working at Thornbridge Comprehensive School for nearly 30 years. He had been a PE teacher for most of that time but a few years ago had decided to apply for the position of SENCO and was duly appointed the same year. He felt that this was necessary career move, not an untypical one for a PE teacher who was beginning to find the job too physically demanding with age. He thought he was 'good with all kinds of kids', particularly those who were 'a bloody nuisance' in most other lessons and who were 'at the wrong end of the school'. At the time of his appointment he knew the school had just received an unfavourable report from the inspectorate, OFSTED, and was judged to have 'serious weaknesses'. He had thought of taking up an appointment in another school but in the end had decided he did not want to leave Thornbridge. Having been a pupil in the school himself many years ago, he felt he had an affinity with the pupils' social cultural background and could make a useful contribution to raising their self-esteem and improving their motivation.

The Special Needs area at this school was well off the beaten track. It existed at the far end of a long corridor, away from the reception area and the head teacher's office but also from the staffroom and the tutor rooms. Even the nearest classroom was 40 or so yards away on the other side of a storage and library area. This had suited the previous SENCO who had taught in a special school and had in fact remarked that it was so cut off it was almost like being in a special school.

Geoff, however, was keen on inclusion and thought the geographical isolation of what he called the Special Needs 'suite' was a problem.

He wanted the rooms moved to an area near the newly established LSU and mentor rooms, which were both adjacent to the Heads of Year and Student Support Tutors' rooms. Geoff liked 'the general hubbub' of this area, which was noisy, but he felt it helped pupils on his list to feel more included. As he pointed out, all pupils were sent in this direction for 'something at some time', and he would have been happy for other pupils who were not on his special needs list to use any of his rooms. Or should I say room, for the move here would have entailed shrinking the Special Needs Department from two and half rooms to one fairly large, comfortable and pleasantly decorated single room. Space was as much a bone of contention in this school as it was in any other. Geoff would have been unhappy with the shrinkage but felt there was more to be gained than lost by the move.

The Establishment of a 'Nurture Group'

He was, however, to be disappointed. Not only did the Special Needs Department remain where it was but it was also to house a 'nurture group'. I had come across such groups before in a primary but never in a secondary context. Sarah Parkes, an Assistant Head at Thornbridge, quoting from the relevant internal document, explained it to me as follows: a nurture group was for those 'vulnerable children usually of very low ability and poor attainment, who were very immature for their age and would normally be placed in special schools.'

I asked how children would be selected for this group. They would be chosen from those who had been statemented in the primary school. What would be its purpose? Basically to give such pupils a 'staging post' on their way to full inclusion in the mainstream. They would be 'shielded' for a time from the hurly-burly and the rough and tumble of secondary school life. They would have a modified curriculum, be taught by a small team of teachers and use the Special Needs area as a base.

Many of their lessons would take place in the base, which meant teachers would go to the pupils rather than the other way round. But they would join other classes for some lessons, usually when this involved going to a specialist room like the gym, the drama studio or CDT (craft, design and technology) room. The group would be kept small with a high pupil–teacher and pupil–TA ratio. The staff would include a special needs teacher redeployed from the English Department plus several TAs. There would be minimal contributions from Geoff and from teachers seconded from the various academic departments.

Sarah seemed to be excited by this new arrangement. She felt it was a 'breakthrough on the inclusion front' and obviously thought of it as a development of which I and other personnel from Inclusion Services would unreservedly approve. There would even be a small room attached to the special needs/ nurture group area where support professionals like me could see children individually. But I was uneasy about it. There was certainly much to said for children in the first year of the secondary school being taught by a small team of teachers; and also for the creation of a 'home base' for pupils where most of the teaching would take place. In the 1980s, I was involved in several initiatives of this kind, like the creation of mini-schools or schools within schools, which usually went hand-in-hand with attempts to develop an integrated thematic curriculum. But the nurture group was only for a small number of pupils not for the whole of the year group. For the rest of the pupils it would be business as usual, with no home base to speak of in the school and only the ill thought-out National Curriculum to look forward to.

And would not this school within a school in fact be a special school within a school? The idea was to move children out of the nurture group when they were 'ready', but when would that be? It was envisaged they would attend the group for a year, but it could be longer. In any case, why a 'nurture' group? This seemed to hark back to days when 'handicapped' pupils were regarded as needing 'care' rather than education.

However, the nurture group had not been discussed with me and was a fait accompli by the time I heard about it. The only questions were: which children were to be admitted and how could such children be 'nurtured' in the most inclusive way possible? Its history and development is really a story on its own. I mention it here because its establishment contributed to the development of a context which was increasingly alienating for Geoff.

The Inspector Calls Again

Troubles come not in single spies and the nurture group had only just got going when the inspectors called again. This was the second visit in two years. As mentioned above, the school had been identified as having 'serious weaknesses'. The special needs policy and practice in particular had come in for criticism. The inspectors felt that Geoff was a very good teacher but his administrative and coordinating skills were poor. Geoff disliked the paper work involved in being a SENCO, a great deal of which he thought was unnecessary, but he appreciated that from the inspectors' point of view this was one of his weaknesses. However, he strongly objected to being described as a poor coordinator. He felt because of his geographical isolation, plus his marginalization and relative lack of power/status as a special needs teacher, he had not been given the opportunity to show what he could do as a coordinator. He was 'working on it', however, and had not given up, because he was committed to inclusion, and coordinating provision was a vital part of creating the school as an inclusive community.

It was during the period of the second inspection that Geoff asked me to come to the school and help with 'getting the books in order', and it was in the process of supporting him with this that I got to know him better. The story he told about the school was germane to what happened subsequently. Geoff thought the school 'had seen better days'. His account of this drew on a familiar but still potent narrative of the school and its catchment area.

'A Failing School'

Geoff really objected to Thornbridge being called 'a failing school' mainly for two reasons. First, the school had a number of weaknesses but it did have a number of strengths, like, for example, 'some very dedicated teachers who had taught at the school for a long time.' These were not 'stick-in-the-muds or time servers', but staff who really cared about the school and were prepared to consider any change that would improve the education of its pupils. Geoff was a member of the NASUWT (National Association of Schoolmasters and Union of Women Teachers), had held office in this union in the past and was very loyal to his colleagues or 'comrades' as he sometimes, with a touch of irony, called them.

Second, it was quite obvious that whatever its internal problems, the school had had to cope with the effects of massive changes in the surrounding economic and cultural environment. The demise of the coal and steel industry was now many years in the past, but it was apparent that the area had still not recovered from this seismic shift in the economy. Many of the jobs that had been created in recent years were part-time and/or poorly paid, and were perceived in this traditional working class area as women's jobs. There were almost as many women working as men, and in many cases the woman was the only breadwinner.

Although the official unemployment rate was low, Geoff felt the amount of unemployment was concealed by the large numbers claiming invalidity benefit. Community ties were weakened as a result of growing differences in people's circumstances. Those families lucky enough to have both parents in reasonably well-paid employment were in a totally different situation from those where only one parent was working on a low wage or both were out of work. Whether you were in work three months or three years depended on whether you were in the right place at the right time and what choices you made about employment and training opportunities.

As Geoff and most other teachers were aware, alongside the formal economy, there was a growing black economy and its worst feature a growing drugs economy. There was an increasing amount of family breakdown, of stress in families and of parents not being able to cope; and increasing levels of so-called anti-social behaviour and truancy. Geoff thought, however, that the extent of social breakdown in areas like this could be exaggerated. In the catchment area, which was a large, low rise, post-war estate of predominantly municipal housing, 'problem families' only constituted a minority of the total number of residents. But in certain neighbourhoods it was a much larger percentage. As far as the school was concerned this minority took up a disproportionate amount of staff time and energy.

Teachers as Scapegoats

Geoff felt that the school could not cope alone in these circumstances. It seemed obvious to him, as indeed it did to me, that all local services needed to make a contribution, but that above all a huge investment in jobs and training was required. He was suspicious of schools in these sorts of areas who claimed to have made huge improvements in standards (as measured by exam results), and to have been, in management jargon, 'turned round' by dynamic and innovative head teachers and senior management teams. Undoubtedly, one could improve the ethos of a school, the way things were organized, the teaching and learning, the curriculum etc. but teachers should be allowed 'to get on with the job' and not be constantly 'chivvied up by the Government' who assumed if they did not constantly monitor them 'teachers would come in late and leave work early'. Most teachers were 'pissed off' with this lack of trust. In schools like Thornbridge, every teacher put in a 'huge effort', usually over and above the call of duty, to address the changing needs of communities in difficult circumstances, but instead of being respected for this and supported accordingly, all they got from the Government was 'a kick in the teeth'.

Geoff felt that Thornbridge had been compared unfavourably with another school in the area which was said to be in similar circumstances but when you looked into it there were crucial differences. Although each school had roughly the same number of pupils on free school meals, the housing stock was different in each area and Geoff felt there had been a subtle process of selection going on, so that 'problem families' tended to end up in Thornbridge's catchment area. He suspected from his conversations with parents, the numbers of persons in full-time employment also differed. The drugs culture was probably more dominant in one area than the other. These were impressions which were difficult to substantiate, but they might all add up to making the two catchment areas significantly different despite their both being 'disadvantaged'. And there were also school factors. Thornbridge had 'a longer way to go' because it had had a number of set backs, like, for example, the trauma caused by the sudden death of two well-respected teachers and an arson attack, which only affected two rooms but had destroyed pupils' art course work.

I have gone in to some detail about Geoff's views because I wanted to stress that as far as I was concerned he was a loyal supporter of the school and a dedicated teacher. I sympathized with most of his views, which I felt were derived from an understanding of the social and political context which I shared. He was a supporter of inclusion and understood what needed to be done to make Thornbridge a more inclusive school.

Geoff 'In the Firing Line'

What happened next bordered on the tragic. Geoff's loyalty and professional commitment would count for nothing. In the upshot of the OFSTED report a number of departments and individual teachers were pinpointed as in need of 'support' for 'further professional development'. Geoff was one of the teachers who was 'in the firing line', as he put it, but the nurture group was not. This was praised by OFSTED inspectors as an imaginative and innovative approach to inclusion.

Geoff thought he had been pinpointed for reasons other than his inefficiency on the administrative front which, as indicated earlier, he was willing to acknowledge. He felt it was to do with his views about the nurture group and possibly also with his trade union activism in the past. He did not see eye to eye with the present head teacher on a number of matters, and had had a few run-ins with him over policies like performance assessment, which Geoff felt was a divisive, morally questionable policy.

He thought the whole business of rewarding individual teachers for achieving targets, even if these were negotiated, set teacher against teacher, failed to acknowledge that teaching in a school was inherently a team effort and went against the whole idea of creating the school as an inclusive community. As he put it, teacher X may have done well because 'teachers like me had removed the most difficult kids from their lessons.'

I do not like to discuss teachers with senior managers but in Geoff's case I felt I had to put in a good word for him with Sarah, who seemed to have a down on him. Geoff was not described as a 'failing' teacher but the word was getting round and others were beginning to look at him in this way. A certain psychological language was being used to identify and explain his failings. Sarah told me 'in confidence' that Geoff was in poor health and had had a lot of time off (which was true), and that he tended to 'bottle things up' (which was not true). She felt he used to 'worry himself to death about certain things'. Just before the school inspection he had driven himself into 'a frenzy', and had been 'chasing his own tail for weeks, trying to get paper work in order and worrying about which lessons the inspectors would want to observe'. Poor old Geoff! He was just not a good manager of special educational needs, and in fact was not 'management material' even at this level. He was 'good with the kids but these days you needed to be more than that'.

Management Speak

There was something patronizing about the way Sarah spoke about staff and this was an example of it. She was au fait with all the clichés of management speak. Geoff was a fine teacher with a fine record but would find it difficult to get a job as a SENCO anywhere else because of his 'lack of leadership qualities'. He had not 'delivered' on his targets and in 'turning the school round' there was definitely an 'issue here that needed to be sorted'. He was committed but he was not 'adapting to change' and was not one of those teachers who would go 'the extra mile'. All management speak irritates me, that last phrase more than any other. Teachers who went 'the extra mile' were typically those who were willing to give up free time after school and even at the weekend to help the school 'raise standards' and 'achieve a world class education'. Such teachers were also usually those who had curried favour with senior management.

I have noticed that in recent years there has been a growing divide between management and staff amongst teachers in secondary schools. There is much talk about 'shared leadership', 'shared responsibility' and 'collaboration' but this is being emphasized precisely at a time when structures are dictating the very opposite in relations between teachers. Head teachers and senior managers often talk about their staff in a patronizing way. At conferences, these managers all talk to each other about management issues, which include how to handle, motivate, consult, employ etc. 'them' i.e. the staff in their school, in the same way a manager in industry may talk about his or her workers.

Geoff was described as being 'one of the old school' which indeed he was but I felt he was more in tune with the 'whole school' and 'whole curriculum' implications of an inclusion policy than Sarah or for that matter any other member of the Senior Management Team. However, the situation was to get worse for Geoff who was beginning to feel isolated. Some of his long-standing friends on the staff had taken early retirement. In his hour of need, the loyalty he showed to others was not reciprocated. He was feeling under more and more pressure, and more and more alienated from the school.

'Giving up on Them'

Geoff was increasingly unable to cope with the pressures put upon him and I was not surprised when he told me he was thinking about taking early retirement. To me the reasons were obvious. There was only so much pressure a person could take, and Geoff had decided enough was enough. I thought I understood him quite well. I could see how someone with his educational ideals would feel deeply frustrated in the current situation.

But I obviously did not understand him well enough. During our lengthy conversation, he acknowledged that although he disliked 'the way things were going in the school', the main reason he decided to retire was to do with 'certain kids in the school' whom he felt he could no longer relate to. He never used the word 'evil' to talk about anyone, especially a pupil, but in recent years he said he found it unavoidable. He appreciated that people like me always wanted to give the pupil the benefit of the doubt but he had reached a point where he could no longer be so 'charitable'. These kids were 'thugs, plain and simple'. He did not like 'giving up on them' but he felt he was wasting his time.

Why had he never expressed this view before? As indicated earlier, Geoff was a good teacher who had good relationships with pupils, particularly those who 'kicked over the traces'. I had always admired him for this. Why was he now making statements about certain pupils which I felt were unprofessional? He seemed to have developed a view that there was a 'new breed' of youngster who rejected the 'old values' of solidarity in working class communities, and who had become 'anti-social thugs and hooligans', and 'really evil bastards'.

Had I been wrong about Geoff all along? Or had he changed? Perhaps these views reflected his feelings of alienation, and should not have been taken at face value? I just did not know. This was not the first time I had been wrong about a person and it would not be the last. A psychologist's view was as fallible as anyone else's! In retrospect, perhaps I should not have been surprised. I had experienced the attitude before particular in my dealings with teachers in the NAS/UWT who had always argued that violent, aggressive and disruptive pupils were part of their 'job conditions', and used this to argue for the setting up of special units. But I was still disappointed that Geoff had spoken in this way. When I challenged him, his riposte was not unexpected – how did I know? I did not have to teach these kids day in and day out. There was one pupil in particular, he said, who almost single-handedly was responsible for his retirement. I knew the pupil he meant and why he had named him. And he knew that I knew. The pupil's name was Barry. My involvement with Barry began several months before and what transpired is germane to how Geoff and I came to part company.

Barry

Barry Brown was a large 12 year old who, in the jargon of special educational needs, had 'learning and behavioural difficulties'. He was referred to me mainly for alleged violent behaviour towards other pupils and for 'going up close in a threatening way to a female member of staff' but when I looked into it, matters, as usual, were more complex. Despite his size, it appeared he may have been as much a victim of bullying as a bully. He complained bitterly about other pupils' verbal and physical aggression towards him. They used to call him 'hippo', because of his size and the fact his blazer was often covered in mud. He was not obviously poorly coordinated but always seemed to be slipping over – particularly when crossing a muddy patch of ground on his way from one classroom to another. This did not used to be so muddy. In fact, it was once a green lawn with an herbaceous border, but an annex had been built nearby and pupils now used it as a short cut. Everyone brought mud into the school. Barry, according to his peers, used to 'wallow' here before moving on.

When Barry was 'wound up' by other pupils, he retaliated by hitting them with his rucksack, on one occasion a rucksack which contained a couple of large stones. A fellow pupil was bruised on the upper arm and Barry was immediately excluded from school. Dan Brown, Barry's father, requested an interview with the EP, and Geoff and I saw him on the day Barry, by this time full of remorse, was due to be re-admitted.

Father Gives Me 'The Full Story'

Geoff knew about Barry's background but he said it would be 'good for me to hear it'. I did not realize at the time the full significance of this remark. On interview, Dan Brown said he wanted me to know what he described as the 'full story' and went on to volunteer information about the family situation. He said he had been on the point of 'smacking Barry in the face' but had held back 'because he was only twelve'. He felt that Barry was a 'Jekyll and Hyde character' who could be very loving and caring towards others in the family and the neighbourhood but when he 'blew up' he could be very 'cruel'. 'You never knew how he is going to react.' He was always being given money to go to the shops. For Christmas, Dan had bought him the 'best fishing tackle money could buy' and also a new mountain bike. He had smashed up three new bikes but they bought him a fourth to 'keep him quiet'. He had also bought him a new computer 'which did everything'. But still, and this was the nub of it, when asked to take the dogs for a walk, he had told his mum and dad to 'fuck off' and claimed that it was not his 'fucking job'.

He felt Barry had had a tough life, but no tougher than any other family member. His wife, Barry's mother, was in bed 95% of the time, and the 'only thing normal about her was her blood pressure.' She was diabetic, arthritic, asthmatic and had other illnesses, which required his administering ten injections a day between 3.30 a.m. and 11.30 p.m., which he regarded as his work and resented anyone saying that he did not have a job. In addition he had to look after his daughter who was physically disabled and attended an integrated resource in a mainstream school. He felt she was less of a problem than Barry. She was 'a tough nut', a brilliant wheelchair athlete who could 'give as good as she got'.

He felt that although Barry could be aggressive, on his 'other side' he was a 'gentle giant', who 'walked in fear of bullies at school' and who often 'came home black and blue as a result of his nipples having been twisted', a form of violence which the perpetrators knew they could get away with because the victim would usually be too embarrassed to show his bruises to a teacher. However, Barry himself was 'no angel'.

Dan was willing to explore with us what Geoff put to him was 'the root of the problem', which seemed to be to do with his need for 'attention'. I went along with this because it seemed a reasonable assumption, but also because I knew from past experience in this school what the consequences of this construction of Barry's motivation would be. It would mean he would be given another chance, an effort would be made to give him more individual help and an opportunity would be provided for him to talk about his problems with a LM. When you have worked in a school for some time, you get to know what forms of action certain words imply.

These strategies would require further discussion but I felt quite hopeful now that father was on board. I suggested that we needed to think about the details of how Barry's attention seeking would be addressed in school. Geoff agreed to observe him in a few lessons, identify what he thought was attention-seeking behaviour, and then discuss this behaviour with Barry to find out what his own perceptions were. He might agree or disagree about this description of his own motivation, but the important thing was to foster a more reflective approach towards his behaviour. The next phase would be to help him to develop a 'script' he could use with a particular teacher who would be briefed to respond in a positive way. The 'script' would take the form of sensible, curriculum-related questions he would ask the teacher and for which he would get the attention he craved in a way that would be educationally productive.

My Interview with Barry

In the event, these strategies had to be rethought because Geoff was absent the next week and by the time he returned Barry had got himself into further trouble and had been excluded again. I decided to interview him in the hope that I might obtain some clues as to what to do next. In the one-to-one he was chatty and spontaneously acknowledged his role in the running conflict with an ex-friend, which had precipitated the recent exclusion. He continued to insist that his responses were retaliatory and that he had not started the feud. His main grievance was the way the other boy 'took the piss out of him' about having to care for his disabled sister, whom Barry had been observed pushing around in a wheelchair on the estate. The way he 'got at' Barry about this was quite subtle. All the other boy had to do was to move his hands and arms in a way which suggested pushing a wheelchair and Barry knew precisely what he meant. Barry knew the other boy knew he was extremely sensitive about this, so much so that the latter eventually only had to make minimal movements with his fingers to get an angry response.

My initial impression of Barry was of a boy who was not coping with tensions experienced in the home. There were a number of positives. He had managed to obtain a St. John's Ambulance qualification for First Aid. In view of his mother's illnesses and his sister's disability, his dad thought it would be a good idea for him to have these skills. But although he seemed quite happy to do things for his mother, he seemed to resent always being called upon to help out with his sister, who he said was 'always getting away with things'.

When I asked him about his alleged attention seeking, he immediately said that this was not 'true'. As if to prove the point, he went on to list all the things his parents had bought him in the last year or so, which matched what father had told me previously. His dad took him fishing when he had the time. When the whole family made a trip to a local shopping mall, he always got 'a surprise present'. I did not press the point but it seemed obvious that Barry had his own idea of 'attention'. There were clearly some deep-seated tensions in the family. Perhaps I needed to contact the agencies already involved with them.

Barry then went off on a different tack and started to ask me personal questions about my job, my family situation and other matters. I was not surprised by this. Pupils are often curious about me. If they know I am a psychologist, they often want to know who else I am seeing in the school and why. They often want to know if I have any children of my own. Sometimes such questioning makes me feel uncomfortable. I have had several experiences of pupils commenting on my dress – 'that's a nice tie, sir' or 'do you always wear that brown jacket?' – or asking me where I lived and what car I drove. Probably all this was harmless, but I was never sure about it. Barry was one of those whose questions seemed to reflect something other than mere curiosity. No sooner had I given my usual anodyne answers, than he went on to talk about his dad having gone to prison for beating someone up. 'He broke this bloke's leg and liked the sound of it so broke the other one!' Then he spoke about his uncle who had killed someone in self-defence and who had also gone to prison. He had an odd expression on his face when he was telling me about these matters, as if he expected me to get the point, which I did not!

'In his True Light'

When Geoff returned, I told him in confidence about my conversation with Barry. He said he thought that it was probably better if I did not see Barry on my own again. Female staff in particular were wary of him. He tended to be 'overfamiliar' with them, and on one occasion, as noted in the exclusion report, his behaviour appeared to be threatening. Usually, when interviewing in the one-to-one, I insist on someone, a teacher or more typically a member of the clerical staff, being in adjoining room with the door open, but it is not always possible in the hurl-burly of school life to arrange this. In any case, secretaries often get called away. I would never in any circumstances see an adolescent girl on my own, but I often take a chance with boys.

Geoff apologized and said that it would not happen again but thought it might have been useful for me to have seen Barry 'in his true light'. This seemed to hark back to a previous comment he had made about it being 'good for me' to hear about Barry's background. Geoff seemed to have made up his mind about Barry but I was not sure what he was trying to tell me. I still had more questions than answers and I had some reservations about the strategies we were using.

The focus was now on 'thinking creatively', as Sarah put it, about a re-integration plan for Barry. But, as usual, there was nothing particularly creative about her proposals. It was the same old off-the-shelf package consisting of the usual elements – a modified subject timetable avoiding 'flashpoints' with certain staff, timetabled periods of mentor support, short spells in the LSU, plus some support for literacy and numeracy in a small group. As mentioned earlier Barry was described as having learning as well as behavioural difficulties. Literacy and numeracy skills were well below par for his age, probably due to prolonged absences and poor motivation rather than specific difficulties in these areas. In the chicken and egg of what 'causes' what in the world of special educational needs, it was felt that in this case behavioural difficulties and factors associated with them were the prime 'cause' of learning problems.

A Development in My Role

The reintegration plan was being put into operation at a point when I was having further discussions with Geoff about my overall role in the school. He had always agreed with the broader role I had advocated, and there was now an opportunity to develop this. There had been requests from teaching staff for LM in the school to do some small group work with selected groups of pupils, and the mentors had asked for advice as to how they should go about this. Could I make some suggestions, perhaps even do some CPD work? Since it was a new venture, it might be useful for me to postpone other activities and to take a group myself for a few weeks to gain some insights into what went well with what pupils etc. I was delighted with this development, and agreed that a useful first step would be for me to do some work with a small group in a room adjacent to the nurture group room.

The group was set up and it included Barry plus three other boys who had been referred to me in the past. For some reason, perhaps because it was a group situation, Geoff thought this would be 'safer' for me. I went along with this, but on reflection it was really no 'safer' than a one-to-one. He said a TA would be in a nearby room, but in fact she never materialized.

I was not certain what to do with them but I thought it would be useful to begin with a 20 minutes chat about their preferences for this slot for the next few weeks. My hope was that we could work through issues which cropped up on a daily basis in their school lives e.g. bullying, boredom, teachers picking on them etc., but I wanted to start with a session where they could voice their own concerns and priorities.

Thornbridge is a badly designed school with leaky flat roofs and a number of damp classrooms. In some rooms the ceilings are crumbling. The corridors are too narrow so that there are always 'traffic congestion' problems at lesson changeover times and breaks. The special needs area, as indicated earlier, was at the far end of the school. The room I was allocated was like an oasis. It had been refurbished and was part of the suite of rooms for special needs purposes. The furniture was upholstered in bright green in contrast to the dominant classroom colour of mucky brown. Comfy chairs had replaced plastic seats and an elegant coffee table with a glass top had been placed in the middle. There were bookshelves full of resources, filing cabinets, a computer, a telephone, a mini-fridge and a water dispenser with a tower of plastic cups by its side.

Order in Chaos

I arrived early and set the scene, arranging chairs around the coffee table, making sure there was enough space between them to avoid 'he kicked me' opportunities. I located my own spot near the mini-fridge. Five minutes later, the group arrived. They charged into the room, shouting and swearing, completely ignored my overtures of welcome, immediately shifted the chairs away from the table and slung their rucksacks on the floor.

What I thought might be perceived by them as a welcome opportunity for an informal chat with a sympathetic adult who was not a teacher at the school was clearly interpreted by the group as an opportunity of a different kind. Here was a person who was more like a supply teacher than a proper teacher, and therefore was not in a position to 'do them' and see it through. Nor was this a proper lesson. Disorder ruled from the start, or you might say an order was imposed which was different from the official order! They egged each other on. The mini-fridge was looted and some of its contents seized. I had to physically stop them tipping over the water dispenser. Cups were taken and crushed under foot. One of them said he was hot and started to take his tie off and the rest followed suit.

What were they up to? Each had recently been excluded for bad behaviour. Were they conveying a message to me, along some such lines as: 'We know why we've been sent to you. It's because we're the naughty ones. And this is what you are going to have to deal with'? Were they 'testing the boundaries'?

In any event I did not have much time to reflect on these matters! The EP is in a difficult position in this situation. He or she is not there to discipline the pupils, at least not in accordance with the school's official disciplinary code. But I had to do something. I could not allow them to trash the room.

After issuing a few threats about terminating the session and sending them back to class, I managed to get them all seated and facing in the same direction. None of them, probably for good reasons, wanted to acknowledge having seen me before, apart from Barry, who made boorish comments about my being a 'psycho-man'. They were seated but were still talking to each other rather than to me. I decided to try and go with the flow. I said something along the lines 'What Barry said then was funny but we all didn't hear it. If we all quieten down, we could hear each other's funny stories.... I could hear them too. Who else has got a funny story?...' I was trying to get them to speak in turn and listen to each other, and this seemed to work for a while, although I had to tolerate stories full of bad language and questionable morals involving some dubious activities like 'happy slapping'.

'Jolly Good Show, Sir'

I then tried to move things on a bit. Could we each talk about something we were good at? Or an interest we had? Or something interesting that had happened to us? This went well for a short while. All but one said they thought they were good at fishing and that fishing was what interested them. Barry spoke first and most of the others seemed to be taking their lead from him. After a while, I said that as they all seemed to want to talk about fishing, and as I did not know anything about it, perhaps it would be a good idea if they 'taught' me about it. They then proceeded to blind me with science, telling me about different kinds of bait and the intricacies of the tackle. I tried to ask questions but they talked through me, and I could not get a word in edgeways. Eventually, things started to get out of hand again. The fishing talk became a fishing demonstration, and the demonstration went beyond methods of casting lines to methods of killing fish and this involved hitting each other.

At that point I decided to end the session, but not before making a final error. I felt I had to bring them to order, sum things up and ask if they wanted to come back next week and if they did what they would want to do. I praised each of their contributions, mentioning each of them by name. By this time they were standing up and ready to go, and clearly not interested in what I had to say. I felt a little put out by this, and made the mistake of asking them if they had enjoyed the session. This, I think, was interpreted as a sign of weakness. A 'proper' teacher would have tried to end on a positive note but not before warning them about the consequences of bad behaviour. Barry was the first to seize on it and the others followed. 'Yes', he said, 'we did enjoy it.' Then he started to mimic my accent, using a voice which would have been interpreted by the others as 'snobby'. 'Yes, sir, that was a jolly good show, sir, yes, sir, jolly good, old boy.' And they all took left the room shouting 'Jolly good show, sir!'

Putting Your Ego on the Line

I was left on my own in the room to pick up the pieces, both literally and metaphorically. I have always thought that one of my professional strengths was my interviewing technique. I could put even the most inhibited pupils at their ease and usually engage the more extroverted and chatty ones in conversations, which they seemed to enjoy. Pupils told me things which they did not always tell teachers. And so this episode left me a little put out, to say the least. Teachers talk of 'putting their egos on the line' when dealing with difficult classes, and I know exactly what they mean. My ego was intact, but one could imagine a whole term of this would probably take its toll.

The original purpose of my involvement was to help the school to draw up a scheme of support work with groups of pupils. I had something to say about this after my experience – be careful how you choose the groups, start of with an 'easy' group just to get the hang of it, perhaps work in twos, have a clear idea of what you want to do. But this did not address issues which were all too common in relation to handling 'difficult' pupils. The pupils had really been 'dumped' on me. It was always a relief for the teacher if they were sent out of the classroom. Whatever the rhetoric on inclusion, there was an institutional bias towards 'offloading' such pupils at every opportunity.

How Do You 'Love' the 'Unlovable'?

But the experience had given me a further insight into Barry. He had a track record as a carer and could be honest about his problems and difficulties, but I began to see what Geoff said he disliked about him. And it was after my next conversation with Geoff that I realized what he had been driving at when he spoke of seeing Barry 'in his true light'. I think he wanted me to experience what he had experienced with Barry, which was not at all pleasant. When I told him what had happened in the group session, he said it confirmed his view that Barry was now turning into a 'ringleader of bullies'. The narrative was the familiar one of son imitating a violent father and seeing violence as a solution to problems.

Teachers in this school refer to some 'difficult' pupils as 'rescuable' and others as 'out of reach'. They often describe the latter as having become 'thugs' – a term which implies they are no longer 'lovable rogues' or 'just lads kicking over the traces'. In sociological terms, their deviant identities have become fixed and cannot easily be deconstructed. In moral terms, they have been demonized – dismissed as human beings who have 'gone bad', who have malicious intent towards others, of whom nothing good can be said.

And I think this is why Geoff was now ambivalent about boys like Barry. He had seen this happen too many times. He wanted to show me why a pupil like Barry now caused him so much stress. Of course, I could not go along with this. Professionals working with young people should never give up on them. What happened when they left school happened, but whilst they were in the school's care, efforts to 'include' them had to continue. Yet teachers and psychologists for that matter cannot always control their negative emotions. For Geoff, the question – how do you 'love' the 'unlovable'?– no longer nagged so much; the answer seemed to be 'you don't have to'.

The final straw for Geoff was when Sarah told him that she thought a possible answer to the Barry-problem was placement in the nurture group. He was opposed to this because he felt that to put someone like Barry in there would be asking for trouble. It was not supposed to be a place for pupils with 'emotional and behavioural difficulties' but immature pupils with 'learning difficulties' who had been statemented. It was symptomatic of his increasing lack of status that his views were not listened to. But underneath I suspected that Geoff felt a 'nurturing' approach was now inappropriate, and would be perceived by Barry as the school "going soft". Shortly after this, Geoff took early retirement.

Coda

It is depressing that school life turns sour for some teachers. I was particularly disappointed with Geoff who was someone with whom, at an earlier stage, I felt I had much in common. I shared his concerns about the school's inclusion policy, particularly his concern with the establishment of a 'nurture group'. Such groups have received positive evaluations as an inclusion strategy in primary schools (see Iszatt and Wasilewska, 1997; Colwell and O'Connor, 2003), but I have doubts about their role in either primary or secondary school. They are underpinned by a conceptual rationale, which leads to a 'deficit' view of pupils as a starting point for intervention. Advocates like Bennathan and Boxall (1996), drawing on Bowlby's attachment theory, refer to impaired early learning and distorted social, emotional and cognitive development, but many of the pupils I see are perfectly capable of rational thought and their emotions are often 'normal' reactions to difficult circumstances. Barry's view of himself and his situation is certainly an interpretation to be critically engaged with, but it is not a view that derives from a 'cognitive distortion'. Such theories can easily lead to the identification of a special 'deviant' group and their permanent separation in the name of inclusion.

I was thus as critical of the school as I was of Geoff. The head teacher and the Senior Management Team had pushed through 'reforms', which I thought had taken the school backwards not forwards as far as inclusion was concerned. I did not think the school had really come to terms with the changing nature of its clientele or was appreciative of the full impact of changes that had taken place in the local economic and cultural environment. Many of the 'problems' referred to me could readily be related to tensions produced by the breakdown of traditional occupation-based working class communities and the development of a 'new economic order'. The socio-cultural effects of these changes have been well documented in the national and international sociological literature (see e.g. Weis, 1990; Dolby and Dimitriadis, 2004). It was not surprising that most 'behaviour problems' were disaffected male pupils from poor homes, with one or both parents unemployed or in insecure, poorly paid jobs. In Barry's case his oppressive economic circumstance were compounded by other factors, but this is nearly always the case if one takes a close look at the individual circumstances of any vulnerable youngster.

Geoff's general attitude in his last days as a teacher may have been out of character, and a function of his being under a great deal of pressure. I had every sympathy for him but I could not go along with his cynicism and despair prior to early retirement. Studs Terkel (2003), the renowned oral historian, used a quote from Jessie de la Cruz, a retired farm worker, for the title of his book – Hope Dies Last, 'La esperanza muere ultima.' The book contains stories of committed people whose hope, in Terkel's view, was 'born of activism and a stubborn determination to change the world'. But it is also grounded in an appreciation of human life as it exists warts and all in the here and now, because if we cannot see any value or meaning in life *as it is* we cannot possibly have hope.

My own hope is kept alive by the thought of a better future but also by glimpses of possibilities in the present. School per se is not the problem. Modern state secondary schools have many faults but they are dynamic places, which have to constantly adapt to the needs and aspirations of a new and 'unknown' generation. They have to harness the huge energies of young people in a diverse, fast changing, multicultural society in a political context where they (i.e. schools) are pulled in different directions by policies reflecting different often contradictory versions of schooling.

Section B
Against the Trend in Primary Schools

In all the schools on my patch I was locked into the special educational needs (SEN) discourse right from the start. Much of the work I inherited was already described as a 'caseload' and the pupils concerned as 'cases'. But in the primary school involvement with official SEN procedures was particularly taxing. I was already committed to contributing in some way to the annual reviews of statemented pupils and to attending other reviews of children supported at various stages of the Code of Practice. I picked up referrals which continued to flow into the EPS at a steady rate. On each referral form was a description of the type of 'difficulty' it was thought the child might be experiencing. I often felt obliged to assess a child and write a report for the school, a copy of which often went to the LEA's Special Needs and Inclusion Panel for their consideration.

Nevertheless, I was hopeful I could work in a way that was not too compromising of my own moral and educational values. My actions often involved the strategic use of ambiguity, redescription and redefinition as I engaged with the SEN discourse, accentuating some of the potentially more progressive aspects and downplaying the more questionable. Fortunately, the whole approach to special needs was changing in the Authority. The inclusion agenda was becoming well entrenched and the number of pupils for whom a statement was thought necessary was decreasing.

However, as the stories in this section show, it was for others and me an uphill and not always successful struggle. The problem was that although inclusion policies were often out of kilter with and represented a critique of the powerful standards agenda, the SEN discourse with its emphasis on individualistic explanations was perfectly compatible with it. Indeed, aspects of the discourse were becoming increasingly influential in mainstream schooling. Diagnostic assessment, planning, target setting, individual monitoring, rigorous testing, 'labelling', grouping by ability were features of traditional special needs policies, which schools were now applying to all children in the regular classroom.

Some of these tensions are evident in the first story, 'Off the differentiation map: why did inclusion fail?' (Chapter 5), which involves a description of the process leading up to a child being placed in a special school. Simon, the head teacher of a primary school, called me in because he was concerned about David a boy who was said to have 'moderate learning difficulties' and whom he described as 'so weak he was off the differentiation map'. David had already been statemented and was being supported in the mainstream with the help of a TA, paid for with monies generated by the statement. Part of my role was to help the school identify further targets for inclusion and to evaluate how the extra resource was being used by the school. I reflect on the role of a TA in this context. Despite my opposition to the move, wheels were set in motion for David's eventual placement in a special school.

In the second story, 'Constructing a "disordered" identity in a child-centred school' (Chapter 6), I describe the events, which reinforced the social construction of a boy, John, in the infant section of a primary school as a child with a 'disorder'. The Head teacher of the school, Deborah, was someone for whom I had the utmost respect. She described herself as committed to a 'child centred ethos' and was opposed to many Government policies, which she felt flew in the face of her educational principles. She was particularly concerned about initiatives, which she thought were not in the best interests of children who were the most challenging with respect to inclusion. She disliked labels and thought that all children should be regarded as individuals. However, despite her good intentions, she ended up colluding in a questionable process. Resources had to be secured even if this meant exaggerating the difficulties the staff were experiencing with John, who had been diagnosed with Asperger's syndrome. The label identifying a psycho-medical disorder proved to be just too powerful, and the views of medical personnel were never properly challenged. The psychological intervention involved addressing a number of controversial issues relating to the statementing process and engaging with the parents who thought John was not receiving sufficient support.

The third story, 'Action research, learning and football culture: a successful intervention?' (Chapter 7) provides a blow-by-blow account of how a strategy was developed to support one pupil, Sam, whose reading was well below what one would have expected of a boy of his age, level of language development and all-round knowledge. It identifies ideas derived from the psychological assessment and dyslexia research informing previous interventions, and describes how, in order to make a 'fresh start', Janet, the SENCO, and I decided to tackle reading indirectly via an action research project focusing on 'learning how to learn'. Somewhat controversially an approach was developed in a context which relied heavily on these male pupils' identification with football culture. The issues arising from this are reflected upon. Was this a successful intervention?

The final story in this section, 'The social meaning of throwing a "wobbly" and the question of survival in a primary classroom' (Chapter 8) raises a number of questions about the interaction between the cultural context and psychological interventions. Sometimes a head teacher will want to see me about a whole class rather than just an individual pupil. David Grant was the Head teacher of one of the most disadvantaged primary schools on my patch – a multicultural school with a large British Asian minority and several other groups, including the children of asylum seekers. He wanted to discuss a class where there were numerous 'problems' and where the class teacher, Linda, was at her 'wits end'. The most challenging pupils had already been referred to our service. I outline Linda's account of the 'problems' as she saw them, and reflect on this. I then go on to describe the school's approach, which included 'positive handling' and 'anger management', and how it was possible a policy-induced 'culture of anger' had developed. A behavioural approach was then used with one pupil, Josh, and a 'circle of friends' strategy with another pupil, Imran, both of whom had thrown temper tantrums or 'wobblies' as Linda described them. I describe how an attempt was made to relate 'circle of friends' to the ongoing cultural practices of the pupils, particularly those aspects which might be construed as 'negative' like derogatory gossip. Finally I reflect on the question of racism and issues to do with making interventions of this kind against the backdrop of certain political and cultural realities.

Chapter 5
'Off the Differentiation Map': Why did Inclusion Fail?

Introduction

Simon Barnes, Head teacher of Fotheringham Primary School, asked me to have a word with him about David Connell. David was now 11 years old and due to transfer to a secondary school next year. Simon felt his progress in recent years had been minimal. He had been referred four years previously and had been assessed by my predecessor who felt that in all areas of development he was considerably 'delayed' and that he should go forward for a full assessment by the LEA. There were many children with similar profiles to David's who managed to cope in mainstream, and under its inclusion policy the LEA agreed to issue a statement with resources to support him in the primary school. A sum of money was duly allocated, which enabled the school to purchase two hours of TA time per week.

Simon described himself as an 'inclusionist' but he felt David was so far behind his peers that he was 'off the differentiation map'. He felt they had reached the stage when David needed more support than the school was currently able to provide, and at the very least he needed a revised statement with more resources if he was to be retained in the mainstream. Simon said he would like the case to be reviewed urgently.

His argument, with which I was only too familiar, was as follows. We all believed in inclusion but not if it was done on the cheap. There was an unholy alliance between inclusionists and those who wanted to cut budgets. Some pupils who used to go to special school could be accommodated in the mainstream but pupils like David who were of very low ability could not be without a massive extra resource. This was what Simon meant when he said David was 'off the differentiation map'. He referred to my predecessor's report, which quoted an IQ figure of 62 and a reading age of 6.3 at the age of 8. This IQ, as Simon pointed out, was probably the lowest IQ he had ever had in his school. Under the inclusion policy he accepted that a child with such an IQ would not automatically go to a special school. They had tried to include him in the mainstream but the situation now needed to be looked at again.

Within the rationality of the special needs discourse, Brian's account had a certain plausibility. There was no doubt that in terms of measurable progress in literacy and numeracy, David was well behind his peers, and after making some progress initially seemed to have had gone backwards recently despite all the support. His reading age on a standard reading test was 6.6 when he was nine, then it went up to 7 when he was 9 years 6 months then back to 6.3 when he was 10. The class teacher could identify few strengths. He was weak in all areas. As the SENCO put it he was 'slow cognitively, poor orally and not in very good shape physically'. His drawings were immature and apart from computer games he showed no aptitude for any form of technology. He had moreover just started to truant, which the class teacher put down to 'lack of control at home' and 'having switched off at school'.

There were several children on my patch who were in a similar situation to David. They had been monitored by the school and the support services from the early years; and had received support at various stages of the Code of Practice, but because of poor progress and low functioning they were eventually put forward to the LEA with a request for a statutory assessment of special educational needs with a view to a statement being issued. With the extra support attendant upon the statement, they might respond for a time, but each year it was a struggle to maintain progress, and they often slipped back.

David's progress had been reviewed by the Learning Support Service and the SENCO once a term and by me once a year at the annual review. I had discussed his progress or rather his lack of progress on several occasions. The school felt they had tried everything and Simon said they were now 'at the end of the road'. David's needs were not being met in the school. Secondary school was looming, and he clearly would not be able to cope in this larger and more complex environment.

David came from a large family. Several of his brothers and sisters attended Fotheringham, and all had been on the Special Needs register. Both parents were out of work, and the children were on free school meals. Two children already attended special school and the parents wanted David to go as well. They had been in two minds about special school but his lack of progress, in their view, was proof that inclusion did not work, and so now he should be placed in a special school as a matter of urgency.

However, times had changed and although a special school was a possibility, the main purpose of my role, as I interpreted it, was to explore further strategies for including David in mainstream. Although the school felt they were 'at the end of the road' – and indeed the reason Simon had called me in was to reinforce this – my own expectation was that the inclusion strategies deployed so far needed to be looked at again. This set me slightly at odds with the school from the start. Although Simon acknowledged that the role of the EP had changed and that I was there to give advice on inclusion, he knew special schools were still recruiting children with 'moderate learning difficulties' and that if anyone was an appropriate candidate for such a school it was David. It was not therefore, from his point of view, a question of more advice so much as urgent action to review the situation with a special school placement the likely outcome.

My Interview with David

I had a thick file on David but had never actually seen him. I normally did not see pupils in connection with their annual reviews but in view of David's poor progress and the fact he was due to transfer to a secondary school, I decided to do a full review, which meant seeing David individually, observing him in class and discussing him with the class teacher.

I waited for David in the staffroom. It was just after break and staff had clearly left in a hurry. There were half-drunk cups of tea and coffee on the central table, and a biscuit tin had been left open. This was unusual in this school. The staff were quite scrupulous in making sure the staffroom was left clean and tidy. It was often used by visitors like me. I usually had priority but sometimes had to have 'space negotiations' with another professional, like a speech therapist, who could also, like me, claim to be a rare visitor who had fixed up an appointment weeks sometimes months beforehand.

From the window, I watched David leave his classroom and walk across the playground. He was a small child for his age and not very well coordinated. Some children are hesitant and fearful about seeing a strange adult in school, for others it is just routine, while others regard it as a special treat, perhaps because it involves being given the undivided attention of one adult for up to an hour. David was in the last category. He knocked on the open door of the 'inner sanctum', as the staff called it (the 'outer sanctum' was the secretary's office next door) and on entering greeted me as if I was an old friend from way back! I apologized about the state of the table and he offered to help me clean it up. He asked if he could do the washing up and I said we did not really have time for that. Then he asked if he could have a biscuit, a chocolate one. Not mine to give, but I agreed.

I explained that I just wanted to see him for a short while to find out how he was getting on in school and what he thought about going up to the big school next year. He immediately spoke enthusiastically about the transfer to Bretton Park – he used the name – which was the community comprehensive school he was likely to go to, assuming he did not go to a special school. He knew all about special schools because, as he said, two of his brothers went to Priory Grange, and he felt he might go there too. Clearly, there had been some discussion in the family about this, but my first reaction was to note that despite his obvious naivety and immaturity, he did have a view, which, regardless of his alleged expressive difficulties (he did not say much in class), he clearly expressed to me. Moreover, this view seemed to have been formed in the light of some awareness of the alternatives.

I asked him what he liked doing in school, and he immediately replied 'playing at running after'. In the playground? 'Yes'. That is your favourite thing in the playground, what is your favourite in class? 'Computer'. What about reading? 'Yeah, I'm good at reading.' Number? 'Yeah, I'm good at number.' Is there anything you do not like very much? 'Writing, sometimes'.

I think it is important to obtain a pupil's views but the way to do it is not to quiz them in this way! I often make this mistake when I am in a hurry. With pupils like David, it just ends up with me asking questions and them giving brief, often just one word answers, usually answers they think I want to hear. They will claim to like everything and be good at everything. My initial approach was better, just a statement about why I had come to see him rather than a direct question. His response about going up to Bretton Park comprehensive school was spontaneous and on that account I had a hunch it was probably valid, a point which is difficult to get across in a formal report.

I felt the best way to proceed was to engage David in activities where he could show me rather than talk to me about what he could do. I asked him to read to me from his reading book, which he duly did, and we then had a conversation about the story and the various characters. He said he liked drawing and so I asked him to draw something for me, and then talk about it. I also carry around items from the Wechsler Intelligence Scale for Children (WISC) test, which most children love to do, like the Block Design and Picture Arrangement test. The WISC or the British Ability Scales (BAS) were still the stock in trade of EPs in this LEA, although used less frequently now a consultancy model had been adopted. David had been assessed some years before, but I knew that in view of this possibly being a contentious case, I would be expected to reassess and say something about his 'cognitive skills'. A few items from the WISC would be sufficient for this purpose.

The Block Design test is a timed test, which involves making patterns of increasing difficulty with a number of two coloured blocks. David immediately cottoned on to what he had to do. He completed the first four quickly and correctly and the next three correctly but more slowly. All the way through, he voiced his opinions. 'I can do this, this is easy; it's good this.' Even when the task became too difficult for him, he persevered. At the end, I asked him if he had enjoyed the test, and he said he had and asked if he could do some more. I showed him the Picture Arrangement test and he did this with the same enthusiasm as he had the Block Design. It consists of a number of picture cards which tell a story. They are laid out before the child in the 'wrong' order, and the child has to put them in the 'right' order to make a sensible story. David's response was similar to that on the Block Design. He expressed his enthusiasm and managed to complete several items successfully. After this 'cognitive warm up' exercise, I asked him if he did tasks like this in the classroom and went on from there to discuss in more detail what activities he did and did not enjoy.

I then decided to see how David would respond to teaching. I showed him how to do a more complex design on the Block Design test, one that he had failed previously, and then asked him to do it on his own. He failed again but had a better stab at it and then was successful on the third attempt after I had demonstrated the strategy of giving the blocks more than one turn. I did the same with Picture Arrangement but this time used a more scaffolded approach, asking him to complete a sequence that I had started. David clearly enjoyed these activities and seemed disappointed when they came to an end.

What had I Learned about David?

Although his reading age was at the 6-year-old level as measured on norm referenced tests, he was able to read his book to me and talk to me about its content. On the WISC subtests, I could not of course score the teaching session. His scores on the first run were similar to those he obtained previously, corrected for age, and put him in the bottom 1% of his age group. These are norm referenced tests and unsurprisingly David came out at the bottom end. The 'bottom 1% of his age group' is a phrase which could be used as evidence supporting the case for placing David in a special school. The test results would not be the sole determinant but they would be an important part of the evidence.

But this is typical of an exclusionist way of thinking. It is the kind of information used to demonstrate that child X is 'off the differentiation map' i.e. so poor relative to peers that it is impossible to differentiate teaching sufficiently to cater for their needs. Yet even from this limited sample of behaviour it was clear that David was teachable in a way that involved nothing out of the ordinary in terms of teaching and learning strategies. He could apply himself to and show enthusiasm for a cognitive task that interested him. There were many pupils in the class who could have achieved at a higher level than him on these tasks, but that was not the point. He appeared to me to be quite a sociable boy who enjoyed company and had up until recently enjoyed coming to school. If ability and teachability did not explain why David had gone backwards in the last year, what had gone wrong? Was it something to do with the way the teaching and learning context had changed?

Exploring Support in the Mainstream

To explore this further, I decided to have a closer look at the support arrangements in the classroom. David's class teacher, June Withers, was aware of the need for differentiation. She told me she had experimented with different forms of differentiation but was finding it increasingly difficult to 'personalize' learning for David. I observed her carrying out some typical strategies for including all children. In the literacy hour, using modelling and scaffolding techniques, she made every effort to help David access a shared text, which he would not have been able to read independently. In plenary sessions, she also made a point of asking David questions which she knew, with a small amount of help from her, he could answer. She had purchased books that were suitable for David and other children in her class with similar levels of achievement, and although David was on his own with the TA, Sandra Shaw, for guided reading and some other reading activities, she included him as a member of a group in other activities like small group discussion about a text.

She seemed to use Sandra in a flexible and educationally appropriate way, and was aware of the need to ensure he did not become overdependent on her. She adopted similar procedures in the numeracy hour. She told me that she went out of her way to encourage interaction between David and other children in a whole range of contexts.

I told June I thought the inclusion strategies she was using seemed to be appropriate, even though he was not making much measurable progress in basic skills. But June was less certain. My period of observation just happened to take place on a good day! In fact, she was finding it increasingly difficult to sustain these strategies. Why? There were a number of pressures which limited her freedom to teach in the way she wanted. These took various forms, but they all tended to revolve around preparation for Standard Assessment Tests (SATs), which were a year away but still in the 'forefront of all our minds'. She found that because of these pressures it was easier to 'get through the work' and prepare for SATs if pupils were in homogeneous ability groups for literacy and numeracy. If she wanted to move a child from one level to the next then the easiest thing to do was sit them with children who were at a similar level and others near to that level. It made it easier to raise scores if she targeted certain groups who were at level 3 and had a good chance of moving on to level 4.

Because of the increasing emphasis on SATs, pupils at similar levels were in each other's company for longer and longer periods, and pupils aiming for higher SATs levels had less and less to do with the likes of David. Could this explain why David was not making the progress we hoped he would? Was he in fact becoming demoralized and developing low self-esteem?

Another source of pressure were some of her more conservative colleagues, who in the topsy-turvy world of present day educational politics thought she was the conservative one (!) for sticking to what they regarded as a 'romantic' view of the nature of ability. There was no school policy on grouping. Simon, the Head teacher, always said he was 'laissez-faire' on this. It was up to the individual teachers to decide what worked best for them. Staff had carte blanche to organize their teaching groups in a way that accorded with their beliefs about 'ability'. For some of them, as June pointed out, children like David who had 'moderate learning difficulties' were 'the proof of the pudding'. Such children were 'dull' in all areas and this reflected their low ability. These teachers organized their classes into groups, which they called red, green, orange and purple but everyone knew they were ability groups and everyone knew their place. In one class there was even an SEN table where two 'SEN pupils' sat together for a large part of the day. Some teachers were starting to call this 'personalized learning'.

All this acted as a pressure on June who was opposed to organizing her teaching in this way but the problem was her results were no better than anyone else's. At least, that is what was said. In fact, I was not so sure. It depended in what sort of 'results' one was interested. I felt that June's was a more inclusionary class, and that was a result that mattered more than any other. But the counter-argument was that in these other classes even 'SEN pupils' got as good if not better test results than in June's class. I did not know the children well enough to argue convincingly against this, but I could see why June often said to me

'Why do I bother?' Since teaching homogenous groups was both easier and allegedly made no difference in terms of results, why indeed bother to waste all that energy differentiating in an inclusive way?

My Reflections on Inclusion in this Context

Having seen David and discussed matters with June, I left the school wondering about what to do next. I had my own ideas about inclusion, which did not accord with what I was seeing in some primary schools. For me the main aim of a school was to realize itself as a democratic community of learners and for all of its pupils to participate in this community. The school was a microcosm of society and good schooling should reflect one's vision of the good society. Including pupils like David was a test for the school, a marker as to how far the school had moved towards the creation of a democratic community. For a school to support structures and foster attitudes, which resulted in David's exclusion meant the school had 'failed', whatever its SATs results. However, Simon was clearly proud of the school's achievement in raising SATs scores (although he was critical of SATs) and saw the school's 'failure' with David as problematical but as almost inevitable in the current context, as if somehow therefore it did not detract a great deal from the overall success of the school.

Inclusion as the development of a democratic community of learners contrasts with another view of inclusion underpinned by the ideology of meritocracy. Within that framework, more progressive inclusionist policies are criticized for not stretching the brightest pupils, for being unrealistic when it comes to ability grouping, and for often resulting in more children in fact being excluded due to the lack of a systematic and rigorous identification and remediation of literacy and numeracy difficulties. For me, inclusion implies that all children should be stretched; that grouping should be fluid and flexible; and that more rigour is certainly required but across the whole curriculum not just in relation to literacy and numeracy skills. For example, how pupils understand, value and behave towards each other is a crucial aspect of the curriculum, requiring the rigorous application of quite specific strategies which take full account of the complexity of the school environment.

I have rehearsed these arguments here, albeit in a truncated form, because they are an intrinsic part of the story. As a reflective practitioner, I am always willing to examine what I perceive as my most deeply held beliefs, and revise them if necessary. This is not something I do everyday, but in a situation like this when several years of intervention appear to have failed, it is necessary to go back to fundamentals. Simon is considered to be good head teacher, and he himself would say he subscribes to the values which underpin inclusion. If pushed, he would probably agree these values were to do with freedom and equality. But I profoundly disagreed with him about David, and I wanted to make sure I was clear about why. In addition I knew from past experience that going over this ground again in my own mind might help me to come up with practical suggestions about ways forward.

Strategies

What could I suggest at the annual review that would shift things on, address David's educational needs and improve his chances of being included? I decided to begin by thinking in broad terms about the curriculum, and in particular about the English Curriculum. Up until now the focus had been on developing David's literacy 'skills'. This had meant that Individual Education Plans (IEPs) had identified targets relating to various aspects of literacy but mostly his 'word attack' skills. June felt he had a poor memory and would only retain basic skills if he 'overlearned' them. Everyone was aware that constant repetition might 'switch him off', but with the focus always on basic skills it was difficult to avoid this. I had discussed this issue at previous annual reviews but although other targets were identified, these were always too narrowly conceived, and made no impact on David's educational experience overall.

In the English curriculum at Key Stage 2 (7–11 years), the programmes of study include giving pupils opportunities to talk and think in a range of contexts for many purposes: for exploring, extending and explaining ideas; for planning, prediction and investigation; for sharing ideas, insights and opinions, and so on. They should be taught to listen to others and to question them. In relation to David none of this had ever been seen as a priority. The school knew that in recent months there had been a growing emphasis on 'speaking and listening', which relative to other elements of the English curriculum like reading and writing, had been a neglected area. In a DfES Guidance document various curriculum strands were identified, which included speaking and listening but also specifically group discussion and interaction. I pointed out that these aspects were rarely emphasized in reviews of progress of pupils like David, and, if they were, usually came under the heading of 'social' rather than 'curriculum' goals.

Identifying IEP Targets

I suggested that it would be helpful if we selected targets in speaking and listening, and also defined a target more broadly and less behaviouristically than we had in the past. Teaching this aspect of the English curriculum would involve a collaborative and interactive approach, and this would have several advantages. First, although it was obviously important to be mindful of his literacy needs, to de-emphasize literacy might take the pressure off David and help with his motivation.

Second, it would give him an understanding of how he could learn from his peers. Third, it would include David in an activity from which he had a tendency to be excluded. When others were doing group work, he was usually receiving individual attention.

Fourth, in this class, as June herself acknowledged, the group work itself was not usually of a very high standard. In fact, as I explained to her, I had never seen any genuinely collaborative work. Emphasizing targets in this area for David might act as a spur for 'whole class' development in group work, which would assist in the creation of the class as a learning community, thus helping all pupils.

Fifth, I felt it was important for other pupils to be given the experience of relating in a learning context to pupils with profiles of skills similar to those of David. In a democratic society, it is important for citizens to try to see things from the point of view of the 'other', and to develop an understanding of difference and diversity. The mixed ability group gives pupils an opportunity to learn to do this. In this sense, David himself would provide a learning opportunity for others as much as they would for him.

I put these points to Sandra and June at a pre-annual review meeting. Neither of them was happy about excluding literacy skill targets, but they thought a useful compromise might be to identify two literacy and one what they described as 'social' target.

Targets have the advantage of making the evaluation of a support strategy more transparent by pinning down more precisely what it is hoped the child will achieve. But the disadvantage is that in order to be measurable, observable and unambiguous they are too behaviouristic and their scope therefore inevitably limited. Broader targets like participation in group work, even if broken down into a hierarchical sequence of small steps, are still often considered a bit too 'woolly' and subjective from a behaviouristic viewpoint.

When suggesting targets, I feel it is always important to bear in mind their possible broader impact on teaching and learning in that particular classroom context. 'Good' psychological practice ideally involves 'whole school' or 'whole class' intervention. But this is difficult to realize. If you start with a discussion of strategies to address the needs of individual pupils, you often do not get beyond this, even though it seems obvious that there are implications for all other pupils and that the strategies will not work without a reorganization of teaching and learning in the class as a whole.

In this instance, though, the signs were more hopeful. June had agreed that David needed broader targets and also acknowledged that her existing approach to group work left much to be desired. She agreed it would be important to think about the role of group work generally in class. It was not just David who would have to be tutored on how to work in a group. The rest of the class might need some input as well, because it could not be assumed they had acquired collaborative learning 'skills'.

At the review meeting, however, we focused initially on how June and Sandra could work with David to facilitate the attainment of group work targets. We agreed it would be useful to 'work up' to small group work via paired work, and the first pair could be child/adult i.e. David and Sandra. To begin with it might be useful to play games involving turn taking just to get him used to the idea of reciprocal exchange before moving on to more sophisticated interactions involving 'listening', 'asking questions' and 'allowing everyone to speak'. The target related to what we hoped David could achieve by the end of the year – which might be something like 'expressing an interest in what someone else had said and commenting on it'. It would be important, though, to integrate this activity into the 'whole class' setting. The target, therefore, would include David demonstrating he could use these newly acquired skills in the context of a regular lesson. This implied, of course, that he would be given an opportunity to do this, which in turn implied June would have to think about how she would facilitate group work as a routine teaching/learning process in her class. Sandra's role would be to work with David in a pair and then a small group and then assist in the transfer to the classroom situation.

'Second Thoughts'

But as the day of the annual review drew nearer, June and Sandra told me they had begun to have 'second thoughts' about this approach. Later, I managed to discuss the issues with each of them separately. From Sandra's perspective, her training, such as it was, had mainly been for literacy and numeracy support and as a TA she did not feel confident about teaching pupils how to work in groups. I said that I would be quite happy to do some CPD sessions at the school on group interaction. But she also felt that my suggestions would be a problem because they required her having more detailed discussions with June about the connection between her work with David in a small group and what June was doing in the classroom, and there just was not time for this. What she seemed to imply was that although June liked to think of herself and Sandra as 'working together as a team', when it came down to it there was little opportunity for genuine collaboration.

I had had many discussions with both Simon and June about the role of the TA. June appreciated that a TA paid to support a pupil for a specified number of hours did not have to devote all that time to one-to-one contact. This 'velcro' model often led to pupils becoming overdependent and passive as opposed to autonomous and active learners. Her preferred model was of a TA with a 'roving brief' in the classroom, involving possible contact with all pupils, but giving support when necessary to the statemented pupil. This support might also involve paired work or group work. And the intensive contact need not always involve the TA. There should be many occasions when June herself would interact with the pupil individually or in a small group.

Nevertheless, although they did not say much about it, I knew there were differences in outlook between June and Sandra, which seemed to reflect the difference in their status and position in the school. June liked the 'roving brief' model because it took account of all aspects of the classroom context, which impinged on the teaching of an individual. She felt that even if support was provided inside rather than outside the classroom, this could impact negatively on the pupil concerned. 'Other pupils might still see them as different in a negative way'. But she felt that if Sandra could, from time to time, give support to all pupils, the possible stigmatizing effect could be minimized. However, she was not optimistic that derogatory 'labelling' by peers could ever be completely eradicated in this way. I agreed with her on that point. Such 'labelling' was a function of wider aspects of social and education policy reflected in pupil culture in such a way that 'status hierarchies' would have emerged whatever support strategies were deployed. Nevertheless, in engaging with this culture, thinking about how pupils interacted in learning groups and what could be done to enhance learning in such groups was a good place to start.

Sandra, however, felt that the 'roving brief' model was fine but the demands placed on her by June were often inconsistent. Just when she would have expected June to teach David herself, Sandra was asked to support David in an aspect of curriculum for which she felt she had not been trained.

I discussed this with June who accepted there were a number of ambiguities. Sandra made judgements about pupils' understanding and interacted with pupils in small groups and this was a central aspect of teaching, and yet the word 'teaching' was not used to describe what she did; she 'assisted' the teacher. A second ambiguity related to the nature of the relationship between Sandra and herself. All descriptions of the TA role in helping to make classrooms more inclusive referred to the importance of collaborative partnerships with teachers. This meant involving the TA in curriculum planning and review as well as teacher and TA working together cooperatively in the classroom. She certainly felt her relationship with Sandra was collaborative and hoped the feeling of trust was mutual but it could never be an equal relationship. I felt the issue here was not whether Sandra and June could be 'equal', in the sense that their roles became interchangeable, but to do with the kind of 'inequality' they both envisaged. It was clear that June was expected to manage learning support effectively but it was not clear if she would have to play a major role in training Sandra.

There was also a confusion from the pupils' viewpoint. Sometimes June asked them to take their work to Sandra, at other times they were asked not to do this. Sandra felt that the pupils knew she was not a 'proper teacher' even though a lot of her activities would come under the heading of teaching rather than supervision. In some ways some of the teaching she did was more like 'proper teaching' than what June was doing. She would interact with the child in ways which June never seemed to have time to – listening to David when he wandered of the point, using his current interests as a starting point and interacting rather than just giving 'single shot' feedback.

I felt that these kinds of issues were at the root of the problem and made a direct impact on the school's ability to include David. June said she wanted to collaborate with Sandra but in effect collaboration could only go so far. The professional difference was reinforced by a material difference because the job conditions of each were also markedly unequal. Why should Sandra do June's job when, to put it bluntly, she was receiving much less money? Why should June expect Sandra to collaborate as an equal when she was not professionally at the same level? The potential for dysfunction becomes particularly acute when it is obvious that the TA is in fact a better teacher than the teacher! This was not the case here but I felt Sandra had skills in relating to pupils like David which June, good teacher though she was, did not have. I was not sure if June saw it in this way, or whether Sandra was conscious of it, but it was probably an important contributing factor to Sandra's and June's 'second thoughts'.

Taking a Step Backwards

On the day of the annual review, June asked to see me before the review took place. She said that she had been thinking about my proposals and had thought that it was not possible in the time available to implement them. She was not opposed to identifying group work targets but thought these could only be addressed in Sandra's work with David. She herself did not have the time to think more creatively or reorganize her teaching because of the SATs. It would have entailed a great deal more planning than she had time for, to say nothing of the training she would have had to give Sandra. Sandra could certainly benefit from some sessions with me, but how would it be funded? She doubted if Simon would agree to providing a resource for this. June was already having to argue against Simon's insistence that for a few weeks prior to SATs, Sandra might need to do 'extra duties'. I knew what she meant by this – money could be found to employ Sandra to help boost SATs scores but not to include David.

The inclusion policy needed a shot in the arm. I could not see it succeeding without a radical change, but such a change now seemed unlikely. Had June been able to enthuse about the approach we had discussed, this may have made a difference. But at the meeting, although she agreed that 'social targets' were important, she still thought the focus should be on literacy. Simon said that he supported this, but the main thing was to consider whether the statement should be revised.

It was also evident that the parents still wanted David to go to a special school. They said this right from the start and clearly wanted the matter discussed. Both June and I explained it was not the function of an annual review to make a recommendation about placement in a special school. Its purpose was to review David's progress and suggest what needed to be done to meet his current needs. But Simon chipped in at this point and said that we could identify David's needs in a way which would 'imply placement in a special school' even if this was not stated explicitly.

From my own interview with David I could confirm that he thought he was going to the local comprehensive and that he seemed quite happy with this. I saw no reason why he should not go there. The parents, however, argued that since David had gone backwards in his reading and his number this year that was proof enough inclusion had not worked. Their other children were quite happy at Priory Grange, and they felt David would accept a placement there eventually. I said that it was important to recognize two things. First, David had already expressed his wishes regarding a school next year. How were we going to take account of this? Second, although his academic progress had been limited, he had benefited from his attendance at Fotheringham Primary in other ways. But the parents could not be persuaded to give the matter further thought. Unusually for an annual review, where matters are normally talked through to a consensus, we agreed to differ and these differences of opinion were noted on the official form.

By the end of the meeting I felt quite dispirited. There was a mountain to climb. I realized I had made a mistake in not engaging with the parents at a much earlier stage in the proceedings. Even seeing them for a one-off interview before the annual review would probably not have been enough. The AR had been diverted from what I regarded as its main purpose and had been hijacked by an exclusionary agenda. I knew it was the system that was at fault but I could not help blaming Simon. The AR had taken place in the summer term just over a year before the transfer to secondary was due and I suspected Simon was hoping that a special school placement could be arranged over the summer, which would mean David would not be returning to Fotheringham.

I have always argued against the 'blame culture' but in practice when faced with a situation like this, I sometimes tend to react in this way. It is a mistake though. In a sense I was as much to blame as he was. I have to maintain a relationship with a school if I am to do my job. They are not obliged to refer children to me or invite me in. I would like to have told Simon that he was giving in to externally imposed demands, which a few years ago he would either have ignored or got round in some way or other. He had changed under pressure. But I did not challenge him sufficiently. I also knew he had a heart condition and had had a lot of time off work. My relations with him remained friendly. The next time I saw him we discussed his golf handicap and shared a few jokes.

Meanwhile, the LEA had looked at the evidence and it was only my report, which seemed to suggest that David should transfer to a comprehensive rather than a special school, although I had not named a school (it was policy for professionals to advise the LEA about needs and strategies but not placement in specific schools). To its credit, the LEA did not go along with the head teacher's and parents' views, but I knew the parents would appeal and it was likely that David would end up at Priory Grange. My reservations would be taken into account, but it would be argued by the parents or their representatives that the weight of 'evidence' was against inclusion in a mainstream school. This evidence, which had been built up over several years and included 'objective' measures of progress or in this case the lack of progress, would not be easy to challenge.

Coda

The pressures on teachers at Key Stage 2 stemming from the standards agenda and the 'performativity discourse of assessment'(see Broadfoot, 2001) have been extensively documented (see Webb and Vulliamy, 2006). In their research study on the impact of New Labour's educational policies Webb and Vulliamy found that the 'unremitting pressure' of the government's standards agenda 'had created a culture whereby however hard teachers worked they never considered it adequate to meet expectations'. (Webb and Vulliamy, 2006, p. 147). One teacher spoke of pressure 'coming from above' so that the head, who was constantly under pressure to perform, 'puts the pressure on us, we put the pressure on the children and then everyone is just under immense pressure and stress' (p. 148).

If this pressure were a function of the relentless and successful pursuit of raising standards for all pupils, then some may feel it was justified. But the source of pressure for many teachers in primary schools is the contradiction they experience between their moral and professional commitment to a child-centred approach to teaching and learning, and how they are expected to teach in order to achieve good SATs results. The former is about teaching the 'whole child', involves a broad curriculum and exploratory, collaborative and creative approaches to pedagogy, the latter involves an overemphasis on testing, a narrow curriculum and a rigid and overly structured approach to teaching. The worry is that all the extra effort they are being asked to put in is misdirected. Levels of test performance are being raised but 'real' standards are not.

As indicated above, June was inclined to a more progressive stance but felt inhibited by the performativity culture, which was becoming increasingly dominant in the school. To develop an educational environment in which David would have been included would have required a sea-change in teaching approaches and the curriculum. But what actually occurred, I felt, was demotivating for David and damaged his relationship with June and Sandra. It was a symptom of what was going wrong in the system as a whole – too little time allowed for responding to children's 'voices', for creative and critical reflection, and for professional collaboration.

Another issue highlighted in this story relates to the role of the TA. The use of TAs to facilitate the inclusion of pupils deemed to have special educational needs is now common practice. Indeed many educationalists think that they are a key factor in bringing about greater inclusion for this particular group of pupils (see Rose, 2000).

The debate about their role has revolved around issues to do with how and by whom they are managed; how support should be provided e.g. within the classroom or in withdrawal groups; and whether support was primarily for the teacher rather than the child. Richard Rose (2000) in his study of the use of support in a primary school concluded that the effective management of TAs could provide benefits for all pupils and that collaboration between teachers and TAs at all stages was essential.

The importance of collaboration cannot be overemphasized. It includes joint curriculum planning and review as well as working together cooperatively in relation to specific pupils in the classroom. The good TA will be trusted by the teacher to make crucial judgements about interventions to address pupils' learning needs but as indicated above the relationship cannot be equal and, if not, we might then ask what kind of relationship is it and what would we like it to be? Is it like that between 'manager' and 'managed' or more like that between 'tutor' and 'trainee'? Rose refers to the need for teachers to develop skills to manage learning support effectively but it also seems that teachers have to play a major role in the training their assistants.

As I have pointed out elsewhere (Quicke, 2003b), a possible way forward would be to accept that since, for all practical purposes, assistants will be teachers, they should be trained as teachers and on taking up employment in a school should be required to register on a school-based modular teacher education programme.

What are the implications of this proposal? One negative possibility is that this requirement would create a recruitment problem since only a percentage of people who apply for jobs as TAs would want to go on to become teachers. The recruitment base typically consists of people, often local women with children, who want part-time work at the local school, and, whilst they might welcome an induction course and some further training, do not envisage themselves becoming teachers. Selection criteria would inevitably have to be more stringent and they would be put off applying.

However, I would argue that there should always be a rigorous selection process, since working in classrooms at any level requires being able to relate appropriately to children in learning contexts. But rigour does not imply all recruits have to have formal academic qualifications. For those with few if any such qualifications, a more practice-based course involving accreditation of prior learning/experience and 'banking' of modules could be devised, one that did not involve the lengthy process that school-based teacher training does now, when for this group it can take up to ten years. Some, of course, may subsequently want deferments or want to drop out (with the option of returning later) but the principle that all assistants should be trainees would be retained.

Another objection might come from teachers themselves. They might want adults in their classes who were just plain non-teaching assistants. But it seems to me this implies a division of labour in the classroom, which is unhelpful and undesirable. NTAs inevitably do some teaching, particularly if their brief or part of it is to support pupils described as having special educational needs. Interacting with all adults is a learning experience for pupils. Pupils should not learn that there are some adults in the classroom who are not really teaching, particularly when these adults spend more of their time with pupils with 'difficulties' than with other pupils.

There is a qualitative difference between the teacher/assistant and the teacher/trainee relationship, with the latter being more functional for educational purposes. The former is essentially 'master/servant' and the latter 'expert/novice'. Both imply a hierarchical relationship but there is one crucial difference – the former involves power over the other solely to secure the attainment of predetermined targets, the latter involves power over the 'other' to construct a relationship where the development of 'self' and 'other' is an intrinsic part of goal-directed action. In practice, the former involves a division of labour where the teacher defines the roles in a way that will secure outcomes irrespective of the development of the assistant's autonomy; the latter involves a changing relationship of collaboration, which secures outcomes through the developing autonomy of the novice or trainee. The latter is a more inclusive idea if we define inclusion as action which empowers all members of school communities.

The key to this reform would be the development of an apprenticeship model of teacher education (TE) where all practising teachers regarded being a teacher educator as intrinsic to their professional identity. This reconstruction of their role would involve seeing TE not as an 'add-on' but as a central feature of their work and indispensable for the creation of genuine learning and inclusive communities. As such, it would have to be properly resourced.

Chapter 6
Constructing a 'Disordered' Identity in a Child-Centred School

Introduction

Deborah Marshall was a primary school head teacher for whom I had the utmost respect. Despite the increasing formalization of the curriculum and the assessment system, the school had continued to retain what Deborah described as a 'child centred ethos' with plenty of opportunities for creative play. The school usually met its targets for literacy, numeracy and science, but all the teachers felt there was more to education than this. As Deborah put it, they had to conform to Government guidelines 'to keep OFSTED off our backs' and create space for the development of the school's own priorities. She thought that SATs and the National Literacy and Numeracy Strategies were at present something they could live with, and that her school was 'successful' despite these Government-imposed policies rather than because of them.

She was one of those head teachers to whom I liked to talk about educational matters generally because she could reflect critically on broader issues but was also keen to give detailed examples of how she attempted to put her principles into practice. She knew all the children and most of the parents, and she spoke about children in a way which was affectionate and optimistic. She disliked labels and was all for inclusion, though like many teachers she felt more resources were required to make it work.

So when she said she wanted to discuss John Gregory an 'unusual' boy in the infant section (Y1) whose current behaviour was a worry to staff, I knew she and the staff would have discussed John at length and have tried several strategies before approaching me. If they were worried, there was usually something to worry about.

What exactly was the situation with John? There had been medical involvement at the nursery stage and his current teacher had been asked to complete an autism checklist. I asked Deborah what she felt about this and she said although she disliked labels, a diagnosis might help secure more resources to support John. She showed me the checklist and I was not too happy with it. It seemed to emphasize a deficit view of the child stressing what John could not do rather than what he could. Deborah agreed with this but thought 'what you put on a piece of paper for administrative and financial reasons is one thing, how you relate to the child on a day to day basis is quite another.'

I agreed with her up to a point. Her staff were experienced and their thinking about John was action-oriented, focused on 'what to do next' rather the perennial search for 'explanations'. They were open enough to consider a number of possibilities and welcomed the help and advice of support professionals not because they wanted 'diagnoses' or definite answers but because they valued any ideas which helped them to reflect on their own practice.

In this school there was an ongoing process of reflection, decision-making, implementation and review at all levels. Appreciation of John's 'voice' was an intrinsic part of this. Deborah and her staff were aware they could not predict exactly what he would do. They were always expecting the unexpected. Deborah was confident that there was enough flexibility built into day-to-day operations to counter any fixed views about John as a 'disordered' child period.

The Approach of John's Class Teacher

John's class teacher Jenny Ogden was like all the others, a dedicated, collaborative and creative teacher who thought carefully about her work and had a detailed knowledge of her pupils. Although she might occasionally refer to John as 'possibly autistic', the knowledge-in-action she used on a daily basis derived from a progressive 'open' child development model. She would talk about his strengths and weaknesses in various areas of development e.g. language, cognition, motor, social etc. 'Special' or medical categories did not impinge much on her practical consciousness.

I did not often have the opportunity to discuss children at length with her, but when I did I always found her highly responsive, open to ideas and someone who was willing to experiment and take risks. Like all teachers, she felt under enormous pressure. She worked long hours, staying late after school and often working at home at the weekends. Parents were frequent visitors to her classroom, and she encouraged them to participate in lessons and get to know other children as well as their own. She was very critical of SATs, which she felt had a negative backwash on the education of pupils in her class.

When I spoke to her initially about John, she gave what I thought was a balanced account of his behaviour in class. Clearly, there were matters that concerned her but she felt she was coming to terms with John's 'difficulties', and beginning to understand how to relate to him. She told me about the autism questionnaire and how the report she had written had been based on this.

In the report Jenny said that she felt that he was 'a bright boy' who was making good progress in maths and science, and was beginning to learn to read, but that he was unable to grasp the 'social skills of life'. He found turn taking in a group and speaking and listening to others extremely difficult. There was a tendency for him to treat other children's conversations as 'triggers' for his own experiences, and then he had to 'say his piece, and will not stop until he has said it'. Although he was making progress, he could have achieved much more had he learned to remain on task for longer periods. He would listen and comment on conversations and activities going on near to him or even on the other side of the room, and would interfere with other children's work. He wanted other children to do what he wanted them to do and he got annoyed if they did not do it, 'and that's when he may hurt another child, which is really the biggest problem'. She thought that he talked to children and staff in the same way, as if teachers were not adults! Although he knew the rules and reminded others of them, he did not always obey them himself.

She then went on to list the strategies she had used to address these problems – explaining the rationality behind the rule about sharing and then working with him on sharing in the one-to-one child/adult situation before introducing another child; giving him a time span to complete a task; asking a TA to sit with him to help him focus on the task at hand; talking to parents about how they could reinforce what the teachers were trying to do in school. There had been some small improvements but certain behaviours, like hurting other children, had got worse. He frightened some of the children and targeted certain children for days at a time.

My Observations

I felt that Jenny's report had clearly been influenced by the autism checklist. When I spoke to her, she tended to play down the negative aspects of his behaviour and seemed optimistic that she would eventually, as she put it, 'crack the problem'. But on paper she painted a bleaker picture. When I asked her about this, she made light of it. Reports were for a specific purpose. In this case the purpose was to help the medical professional make a diagnosis. Like Deborah she felt that this would help John in the short and long term by helping to secure a much needed extra resource.

When I observed John in class, it soon became apparent that many of the negative aspects mentioned in Jenny's report varied according to circumstances. For instance, on certain tasks, he was able to take turns. I noted him do this twice in my half-hour period of observation. Also, throughout the period, he was not constantly interfering with others. Like many children in this Y1 class he was often engaged in solitary play. Even when he did 'interfere' with others, they did not always object.

Nevertheless, I did observe him on occasion 'boss' other children and seize their equipment which, as Jenny pointed out, was a lot more frequent in some sessions than others, and depended on a number of factors – his mood that day, how other children reacted, what activities they were engaged in etc. It was a standing joke with teachers in this school that whenever I observed pupils they were 'as good as gold'! There may have been a number of reasons for this. Perhaps the child knew they were being observed and reacted accordingly, or the mere presence of another adult in the class, especially a male in the infant section of a primary school, changed the atmosphere of the class on that day. Or it could have been that behaviours of concern were just not as frequent as the teacher imagined. Good teachers like Jenny knew that there were situational factors at work and that each day was different. But I still felt that her report, which had been forwarded to various health professionals, did not give a rounded picture.

I discussed my observations with Jenny and Deborah and made some suggestions about a 'watching brief'. I asked for a diary of 'incidents' to be kept which would ensure 'positives' were recorded along with 'negatives'. But there was a certain urgency about the situation, which required an immediate response. John's 'violent' outbursts (this word was now used) had caused some of the parents of other children in the class to complain. Head teachers are always understandably edgy about this, and usually want to be seen to be taking swift action. Also, John had been 'picked up' early by the medical services and the process of making a diagnosis was now nearly complete. Deborah felt a further period of observation by me would be perceived by the parents (who had agreed to the referral to our service) as 'starting all over again'. And so I compromised. The 'watching brief' would be for a short period and I would return to the school in a few weeks to assess John.

The Statementing Route

What really exercised Deborah was the lack of flexibility when it came to resource provision. The current situation was fraught with difficulties. As she put it, some of John's behaviours were 'extreme' and Jenny was running out of ideas. She needed support now not several months down the line. Why could not the LEA provide help immediately rather than only when the child had been issued with a statement? Why did the statementing process take so long?

I had discussed these issues with Deborah before. It was possible to provide some emergency support paid for centrally, but statementing was inevitably a lengthy process. It involved a statutory assessment of needs and required reports from all relevant professionals. It had to be transparent and comprehensive. It was concerned with the medium and long term rather than short term. However, I also told her I was unhappy with the system myself for several reasons – it was time consuming, involved formal labelling and often resulted in insufficient or inappropriate support being provided because the decision-making process was not school-based enough.

Deborah agreed but said she would still like to go down the statementing route because 'the system was as it was'. She was confident that the school could take action to prevent John being labelled in a negative sense and as far as decision-making was concerned she thought my input would be important! And so I agreed to see John and give an opinion.

When I returned to the school a few weeks later, I discovered things had moved on and the medical services were now talking about autistic spectrum disorder (ASD) and in particular Asperger's syndrome. There were already a number of other professionals involved – an occupational therapist, a speech therapist, a psychiatrist, a GP from the health side, and the school had called in the Autism Outreach Service from education.

The school was to be offered further advice and support from specialists, which included handouts about the characteristics of a child with Asperger's, accompanied by a list of rudimentary strategies for addressing their needs. At this point, the conversations between teachers and support professionals often revolved around information in these handouts. If they have had no experience of ASD, staff often request more input from the various specialist services. Some teachers are sent on courses aimed at deepening their understanding of the 'disorder'.

I always tried to avoid being directly involved in this kind of input, but occasionally I get drawn in. Deborah clearly wanted to discuss Asperger's with me when I next visited the school. I could have said autism was not my field or words to that effect, but I felt that would have been cop-out.

'An Asperger's Child': Retrospective Interpretations

Deborah was curious to know more about the nature of John's problems. Why was he aggressive at certain times towards other children? How did that tie in with his other behaviours? She said she had been reading up about ASD and Asperger's. If John could not see things from another's point of view, how was this linked to his obsessive behaviour and being a stickler for rules?

I felt this way of describing John's behaviours involved a slightly different but significant shift of emphasis. During our initial conversation, I had not heard much about 'obsessive' behaviours. Deborah insisted that this had always been an issue, but I noted it had not been mentioned on the original referral form. It was a word that she had only begun to use recently, after the diagnosis of Asperger's had been made. Even though, as Deborah insisted, the information from health-based services had only largely confirmed what she and her staff already knew, it seemed to me to derive from a retrospective interpretation in line with the diagnosis. What she would probably have called 'an intense interest in an object or activity' had come to be perceived as an 'obsession'.

There were other examples of this new way of perceiving John, which fitted with his identity as 'an Asperger's child', such as the new emphasis on his literal interpretation of events. Again, retrospectively, Deborah and Jenny could think of examples of this. Apparently, at one point when Jenny had told the class to get down to work, he had got down on the floor under his desk. I did not witness this event but was not altogether convinced by it – he often ended up on the floor for a variety of reasons but usually because he was messing about.

More of his other behaviours were now interpreted as symptoms of Asperger's. On one occasion, when the class was on the carpet, he crawled towards the door as if attempting to sneak out but, of course, could easily be seen by Jenny. Deborah said this could have been because he could not put himself in the position of the teacher – he could not see things from the perspective of 'other'. As with the previous example, I had my doubts. John was a very active pupil and disliked sitting on the carpet. He may have been fully aware that the teacher would spot him, but at that moment just did not care.

I felt that Deborah's and Jenny's previous understanding of John was much richer, more nuanced and more subtle than these simplistic post-diagnostic descriptions based on a simple classification of behaviours. The 'advice' they received seemed to constrain their own powers of observation and channel them in a way which fitted the Asperger's pattern. They did not feel imposed upon, but people whose perceptions are being reconstructed often do not. The process is gradual and involves a seemingly innocuous 'objective' language of observation.

My own feeling was that left to their own devices Deborah and Jenny would have focused more on how John himself perceived things. In all the medical talk about him he was mostly being viewed as a constellation of predispositions and behaviours rather than someone with a consciousness. Rather than talk about John's behaviours as 'symptoms' of a disorder, it would have been more appropriate to talk about the purposes and intentions behind his behaviour, even if we could never have full knowledge of them. Therefore, I felt my intervention should involve putting John's 'voice' back on the agenda. But Deborah insisted on sticking to her 'new' understanding that John was an 'Asperger's child' and so our conversation about him had to start there.

John's 'Voice'

I said that it might be useful to try to understand the 'symptoms of Asperger's' in terms of John's own perspective. For instance, I thought being a stickler for rules and being obsessional might be interpreted as John wanting to gain some control over his social environment. If he was not very good at looking at things from the perspective of another and thus unable to work out what they might be thinking and what they might do next, one way of dealing with this was to make a complex situation less complex by imposing a set of simple rules, which were rigorously adhered to. Enacting a ritual and repeating behaviours over and over again, involved avoiding having to deal with a changing world, particularly when changes were instigated by the unpredictable interventions of others. Why the aggression? John was just asserting himself too forcefully. Why the lack of imagination and the literal interpretation? I suggested that such children can be imaginative but they do not get enough practice at it. And so on.

All this intrigued Deborah and Jenny but I was unhappy with the general drift of the discussion. I realized I may have made a mistake in talking about John in a way which may have merely served to refine their construct of his identity as 'an Asperger's child'. I said as much to Deborah and Jenny, and tried to negate it by deploying the 'discourse of normalization' – an approach often used by EPs to play down sensationalist descriptions of what are often minor deviations from the norm.

After all, this lad was only five. What did we expect of any 5-year old? Surely one of the characteristics of all young children was that they were inexperienced readers of the minds of others? John was less socially amenable than other children of his age but there were probably reasons for this. Whereas other socially immature children may have adopted a passive approach when unable to communicate with or understand others, this was not his way. His strategy was different. He was more assertive than the average 5-year old. He was also being quite rational in wanting to simplify things. In fact, his behaviour could easily be viewed as just a different way of addressing the problems, which most children experienced at school.

Deborah and Jenny agreed but insisted that John's behaviours were still extreme – and one could not get round this. But which behaviours? It was clear what they really had in mind was his 'violent' behaviour not his obsessional behaviour or his literal understanding of language. It is very easy to let meanings 'slide' into each other under an overarching concept of 'deviancy' in a way which closes down discussion and shifts the focus away from an appreciation of the child as a complex individual. In this case, I felt that the process of deviance identification and reinforcement was underpinned by pragmatic considerations, not least those derived from Deborah's interests in managing the situation, reassuring worried parents and securing an additional resource. Like most teachers, her motives were multifaceted and often contradictory.

Deborah even seemed to have accepted a physicalist explanation of John's behaviour as in part genetically determined, even though she did not normally talk about children in this way. She had, she said, read somewhere that 'they' were still investigating ASD but it seemed probable there was a genetic 'cause'. I said that it seemed perverse to use genetic determination as an explanation in John's case when we did not do so with other children who were not such a 'problem' for the teacher. Was this in line with her 'open' approach to children?

These were the kinds of issues I discussed with Deborah – issues that were always alive in her consciousness and mine. They inhered in every decision about the education of a pupil like John. But I was much more wary than she was of 'deviant' labels like ASD or Asperger's, which I felt were not easily reconciled with the child-centred, open-ended, exploratory approach to understanding pupils normally so much in evidence in this school.

My Interview with John

Deborah was still concerned about what she described as the 'practical' issues. 'Practical' for Deborah in this instance meant taking the next step in the process of securing a full, statutory assessment of John's special educational needs with a view to obtaining a statement. I thought this was grounded in a 'theory' of which the foregoing discussion had been critical, but Deborah was either not aware of this or if she was, did not feel constrained by it. Could I see John for an assessment and write a report supporting the school's request for a full assessment? I said I could certainly write a report, although I could not say in advance whether this would be interpreted as supporting her request or not.

I really wanted to do more classroom observation but time was short. I said I would see John in the space just outside his classroom, which was normally used for small group work of one kind or another. It was evident from the start that in the one-to-one child/adult situation involving highly structured tasks there was no evidence of gross communication difficulties. Children with Asperger's are supposed to have a basic grasp of verbal and non-verbal communication, but are said to find more complex verbal interaction confusing. As indicated above they understand language in a literal way but are confused by metaphor and 'figures of speech', and at times can appear 'cheeky' or 'clever' because they understand only a part of what is being said to them.

John's responses did not reflect any of these features to a marked degree but he did wander off the point a great deal and talk to me about anything and everything other than the task that was before him. At one point he kept repeating what I was saying and later in the interview decided that his fingers were more interesting than the puzzle I had asked him to do. But throughout most of the interview he answered my questions and could be encouraged to talk about his interests and activities. In general, John's language did not seem particularly strange to me. His academic attainments were fine for his age. I was more concerned about his alleged aggressive behaviour in class which, according to Jenny, had got worse.

Health and Safety Issues

I saw Deborah directly after this interview and said I would like to see John again in the classroom and discuss him with Jenny. And it was at this point she showed me the report she had written for the LEA with a copy to the medical services. The report made me feel uncomfortable. Everything she had written was true, but she omitted to say the incidents took place over an 18-months period (nursery plus Y1) and said nothing about the time gap – sometimes as long as three months – between each incident. There were also descriptions of other behaviours, which were not included in the original description of his difficulties but which were clearly of great concern to the parents as well as staff at the school. He seemed to have no sense of danger, and had to be watched constantly. He also had a tendency to wander off.

When I told Deborah of my concerns about the report, she said she agreed with me but her overriding aim was to make sure the LEA understood the seriousness of the incidents that had occurred, and the 'health and safety' aspects of the situation. John could at times be a danger to himself and to others. However, I was still unhappy about the tone and content of the report.

A Shoddy Diagnosis Goes Unchallenged

As indicated earlier, the report was sent to the medical services as well as the LEA. John was due to be seen by a psychiatrist in the near future. A few weeks later I rung the CFPS to check on this. A member of the team at the Clinic was willing to discuss John with me over the phone, which was a rare occurrence. She gave me a short spiel about ASD and Asperger's. ASD was recognized as a complex phenomenon and there was apparently more evidence of its association with other disorders such as moderate learning difficulties, severe learning difficulties and ADHD.

In John's case the school reports indicated he was fidgety on the carpet and had difficulty paying attention. The possibility of John being ADHD had been mooted. In fact, she said, the psychiatrist felt that John may have ADHD and dyslexia as well as Asperger's. I asked on what evidence he based these judgments and she referred me to various reports, which had recently been received, including Deborah's. The occupational therapist had observed John and reported that he sat still on the carpet if the teacher was reading a story that interested him but otherwise did not seem to be listening and could not keep still. The psychiatrist felt that a 'percentage' of his difficulties could be due to ADHD, although how much he could not be sure. There was evidence of underachievement because he was three months behind his chronological age on a reading test which might be related to 'possible mild dyslexia'. On the basis of a brief drawing test, John was also identified as having a lack of imagination.

Later, I read in a letter from the occupational therapist to the school that the psychiatrist was considering putting John on medication for his ADHD, which should 'reduce his fidgety behaviour and help him listen to instructions in class'. The psychiatrist acknowledged that this would not help the ASD, which was a 'lifelong condition', but the 'degree of problems associated with it could be reduced'. One or two strategies were then listed for handling John in school – strategies which, I noted, the school had already tried, like making sure at break and lunch times there was always an adult either watching him or at least somewhere nearby.

I was angry about this new diagnosis for several reasons but I was also angry with myself and the staff of the school for not challenging it and therefore by default going along with it. Why was it not challenged? In the 'world of special educational needs' it is in fact rare for a medical diagnosis to be formally challenged. There are disagreements about the contents of reports and plenty of mutterings under breath but this rarely results in a dialogue between education and health professionals where differences of opinion can be genuinely explored. This is partly because of the lack of time which makes regular communication difficult, but there is also a basic structural constraint – professionals have unequal statuses and operate within different accountability systems.

So we end up with a school with a progressive child-centred ethos, whose staff took the ADHD and dyslexia diagnosis with a pinch of salt, but who nevertheless made sure John took his pills (eventually prescribed by the psychiatrist) every lunch time because this was what a medical person via the parents had asked them to do. The teachers also seemed to have accepted the legitimacy of the Asperger's/ASD diagnosis, although the degree to which this construct shaped their day-to-day actions was unclear. Deborah seemed to have gone along with the medical model at least at a formal level mainly because she hoped it would provide further support for her request for a full assessment leading to a statement.

Parental Attitudes

What were the views of John's parents? How did they feel about the diagnosis? It is infra dig. nowadays to associate ASD with 'bad' parenting. The preferred explanations are genetic rather than social. This means there is a tendency for the role of child-rearing practices to go underinvestigated, although a social and medical history is usually obtained.

I had interviewed the parents, Pete and Jill Gregory, just after I had seen John and Deborah. They had told me all about John being a stickler for rules and about his various obsessions. They had clearly expected me to be interested in such matters and seemed to want to give out information which would have helped confirm the ASD/Asperger's diagnosis. I thought they seemed already 'in the know' about this 'disorder', probably because of their involvement with health professionals from an early stage in John's life. But there was another factor. Mr. Gregory, who was not the birth father, had a son who had also been diagnosed as autistic and went to a special school.

Looking through the reports from different professionals it was not evident that anyone had done a thorough investigation of family relationships. However, it was possible that there was more information on the CFPS file. I contacted them again and was told that a history had been taken. I knew from past experience that this involved going through a checklist with the parents. It usually took about half an hour. The member of the team I spoke to said they had noted that stepfather had a son at a special school for autistic children. They had also noted features of John's behaviour at home, which supported the ADHD/ASD diagnosis. What was their opinion about the parents' attitude and family relationships in general? Well, they thought it was possible that John had had his 'nose pushed out' when his mother had taken up with stepfather. Stepfather had talked a great deal about his own son during the interview. John seemed to have a negative attitude towards his stepbrother and there clearly was some jealousy there.

However, although all these aspects had been noted, they did not seem to carry much weight as 'causes'. I had the impression that the ADHD/ASD diagnosis, in all probability made by the psychiatrist after a couple of interviews at most, was assumed to be 'fact' and family relations were possible contributing factors only. I asked if anyone was going to do further work with the family. No, but they would be seen at regular intervals to monitor progress. The parents were thought in general to be 'sensible' and 'caring' and if they wanted more support than had already been offered then this would be considered.

I had heard all this before but it never ceased to amaze me. What might seem obvious to the man or woman in the street did not seem obvious to these particular professionals! Was it not possible that the behaviours which led to the diagnosis of ADHD were a function of emotions which had a social origin? Was not his alleged jealousy and attention seeking understandable? Why were his so called Asperger's 'symptoms' interpreted as a 'disorder', when they were probably a rational if unusual reaction to social and emotional circumstances? Where was the effort in all this to really include John's 'voice'?

The Statement and Review

I did not have the time to pursue this further with the parents or the CFPS. Reports had to be written and submitted in time for the next meeting of the Local Authority Special Needs and Inclusion panel, where in the event it was decided that a statutory assessment should go ahead. Although ASD/Asperger's is a clinical category not a description of an educational need, such a diagnosis, particularly if accompanied by references to ADHD and dyslexia, would be likely to put a pupil on the highest level of need, and generate a resource commensurate with that level. I had previously pointed out a confusion in a document on funding, which referred to the 'severity of autism interfering with learning' at one level and merely to the diagnosis of ASD/Asperger's at a higher level. A diagnosis itself should not generate a resource. In the event, John was assessed, then statemented and allocated 20 hours per week of TA support, which was well over and above what I had anticipated.

At this point, I usually visit the school to discuss the implementation of the statement, but my diary was full for several weeks ahead and by the time I was available, a support plan for John had already been put in place. When I contacted her by phone, Deborah told me that things were going fine and that John was relating well to Claire, a TA who had had a great deal of experience of working with statemented pupils. Deborah had a list of TAs who were 'regulars', and eventually decided upon Claire because she had a good track record with 'behaviour problems'.

I heard nothing of John until the time of the first annual review when I saw Claire for a brief pre-review conversation. She told me that John was making excellent progress and had calmed down a lot since I had seen several months ago. She was not using any special techniques with him, other than providing him with a visual aide-memoire at the beginning of a session so that 'he knew what he had to do next.' She felt that once she had got to know him she had found him an 'interesting and energetic little boy' who had plenty of imagination even if this was often very 'tangential' to the task the teacher had set! She did not think I needed to see him again. At the review, it was clear that John had met all his targets both in terms of learning and behaviour.

One can never be sure if John would have continued to make progress if TA support had been reduced, but one of my tasks was to make a judgement about this. Although most head teachers and SENCOs adopt a professional approach to the quality and quantity of SEN support, the school clearly has a vested interest in retaining the same amount of resource as originally allocated. 'Good practice' in deployment of TAs involves their working in partnership with the class teacher to secure support for all pupils in the class not just those who have been statemented. Twenty hours of TA time in the class could be used to improve the education of all pupils, and so it would always be money well spent. It was not surprising therefore that my suggestion that John no longer needed 20 hours of support and could probably do just as well with 10 did not go down well.

I was a little uncertain about this because I knew that Claire had been doing a great deal of work with the parents over and above the call of duty, and that was probably the main reason why John's behaviour had improved. But I felt ten hours would still have been sufficient even if this contact with the parents had continued. In fact, it would probably have been preferable for her to have spent more time with the parents than with John – a point which Claire appreciated but which could not easily be acknowledged at the review because the parents seemed in denial about the amount of help they had received. From Pete and Jill Gregory's point of view, it was John who had received the support and their expectation was that he would be receiving 20 hours support a week for the rest of his school days, otherwise he would surely need to be in a special school or unit?

I must admit to being ambivalent about my role here. On the one hand, in large classes – and this class had more than 30 pupils – reducing the amount of TA time was likely to impact on the education of all pupils, but on the other the logic of special needs resource allocation suggested that the monies might have been better deployed elsewhere i.e. for a pupil with a higher level of need than John. I also thought that it was important to begin to deconstruct John's 'deviant' identity and halving his support allocation was a step in that direction. In the event, the LEA heeded my recommendation and John's support allocation was reduced.

The Tribunal

Although the parents attended the review, they did not find out about the LEA's decision for several weeks. When they were notified, they immediately requested an urgent review. I was not present at this but I understood that both parents had said they had wanted to 'take the whole thing back to the drawing board'. It appears that John's behaviour at home had become so problematical that stepfather had wanted him sent to a special school for autistic children like his other son. He was blaming the school and the teachers for not having the specialist knowledge to handle John, and this was resulting in John becoming frustrated and taking it out on the family. He thought John was going to receive one-to-one support for at least ten hours but he now understood, after listening to class teacher talking about the support arrangements in the class, that this had not happened. He had rung up various health professionals who had reinforced his view that John was a serious case who needed as much one-to-one specialist help as he could get. The psychiatrist in fact had agreed to write a report to this effect.

I stuck to my guns on this and to be fair the school in the end backed me up. I phoned the parents and pointed out that it would never have been appropriate for John to have received such an intensive level of one-to-one support. He certainly did not need it now; it could well result in his becoming dependent on the TA, just at the point when he needed more opportunities to work autonomously and in a group with other pupils. I agreed that the reduction of support hours was a risk but if it did not work out we could always ask for them to be reinstated.

Jill Gregory seemed to agree with this but Pete was adamant that he wanted to appeal against the decision and if necessary take the matter to a Tribunal. He had been advised to do this by a local group of parents of children with Asperger's. He had already begun to put together a case statement, which included reports from the psychiatrist, the speech therapist and the occupational therapist amongst others.

I had hoped that matters could be sorted out informally but a few weeks later I was informed that the appeal to the Tribunal was to go ahead and I was asked for my comments and an up-to-date report. There is something depressing about quasi-legal processes of this kind. This particular Tribunal is in fact now called SEN and Disability Tribunal. I can appreciate the need for arrangements which make it easier for people to appeal, and can imagine myself supporting appeals in certain circumstances, particularly when disability rights have been violated. But much of my experience of SEN appeals has been negative. The whole business has not been in the child's best interests. Win or lose the process itself has soured relationships between the parents and the school or local authority. The parents no longer regard themselves or are regarded by the school as partners but as adversaries. The resources they have secured as a result of a successful appeal often require the LEA to rob Peter to pay Paul, where Peter is often more needy than Paul.

However, just before the hearing, the LEA received a phone call from Jill Gregory saying that they – the parents – were withdrawing the appeal. There had been developments at home which had prompted this. She and Pete had decided to split up, and Pete was leaving home. The school felt she had never been in favour of the appeal in the first instance, and on leaving home Pete had agreed not to interfere with any decision she might make about John. As indicated above, I felt family relationships were problematical and should have been explored further. The parents splitting up was possibly proof that their attitude was at the root of the 'problem', although it could also be argued that John's misbehaviour and his 'disorder' caused the tensions which eventually led to the breakdown of the marriage.

Coda

I had a long discussion with Deborah about these developments. We both agreed that the ADHD and dyslexia diagnoses were suspect but she was adamant that John was 'an Asperger's child' and that the label had not and would not do him any harm. She and her staff would always treat him as an individual and now the 'dangerous' misbehaviour had stopped, it was becoming a pleasure to teach him. The label and the statement had provided a much needed resource, which had been deployed to good effect, so what was the problem?

I agreed the school was doing a good job but said I would still query the emphasis at an earlier stage on a deficit view of John and the subsequent medical diagnosis. What had it added to our understanding of John's psychological or educational needs? Treating John as an individual, and assessing and providing for his support needs in relation to a broad, child-centred curriculum should have been sufficient. We could not know how the Asperger's label might be regarded in the next phase of the education system or what the long-term implications were. Why should features of John's behaviour be highlighted in this way when we did not go through this process with other children? Why should he be described as having a 'disorder'?

The differences between Deborah and me seemed to relate our different perceptions of the relationship between two discourses. I felt the child-centred pedagogy/ developmental psychology and the special needs discourses were essentially contradictory, whereas Deborah was able to accommodate one to the other without difficulty. I am not sure it is even true to say that Deborah was making 'strategic connections' (Carter and Burgess, 1993) between these two discourses. This would imply she was conscious of possible contradictions and felt the need to 'work' them together for various political purposes, in this instance in order to secure an appropriate level of funding for support. If I had had the chance of a longer 'conversation' (even longer than usual!) with her she might eventually have acknowledged the contradiction. But equally she may have argued for a progressive version of the special needs discourse, one where the notion of 'disorder' or 'deficit' had been expunged. In relation to autism, for example, Hacking (2006) quotes Lorna Wing, a well-known authority in this area, as having developed a questionnaire which does not ask: 'Does this person have autism?' but 'What problems, what advantages and what skills does this person have?'

From my own point of view I would have preferred a discussion about other matters. In terms of the discourses operating in the infant classroom (see Tunstall, 2001), I would liked to have drawn out the differences between a social constructionist/ hermeneutic and a child development/psychological approach. Tunstall identifies various metaphors for learning associated with each of these – the former relies on the metaphor of teaching as 'a collaborative work of art' (Lakoff and Johnson, 1980), and the latter on the metaphor of 'growth, tending, shaping'. In conversations with infant teachers, I have always tried to connect with the moral imperatives of their commitment to a child-centred developmental psychology.

There is a certain 'care for the individual' within this discourse which appeals to me and by and large seems compatible with my own moral position. However, the idea of 'development' is problematical for a social contructionist because it assumes that the curriculum can be grounded in predetermined psycho-biological needs.

Finally, despite what appears, certainly in the short term, to have been a relatively successful outcome, I am still prompted to query the statementing process itself even when it does not involve the deployment of deficit models of the child. Given that this school had experienced staff, a good track record on inclusion, good relations with parents and actively sought advice from various external professionals, it is difficult to see what the point was of going through the rigmarole of statutory assessment and statementing. There was amongst staff a continual process of discussion, reflection, action and evaluation. Deborah made every effort to distribute resources according to need. Of course, more resources were needed but statementing was a clumsy and inefficient way to identify and allocate these. It took up far too much professional time – time that could have been better spent, for example, on developing shared understandings between professionals so that shoddy diagnoses could have been avoided!

Chapter 7
Action Research, Learning and Football Culture: A Successful Intervention?

Introduction

Janet Parke, the SENCO at Dewsberry Primary School, wanted to discuss a number of pupils who had made virtually no progress in reading despite all the support they had received. The head teacher was worried because it looked as though the school's targets in literacy were not going to be achieved. Moreover, this was the third year running that these particular pupils had fallen well short of what the class teacher expected of them.

There were a number of primary schools on my patch in the same position. In any given cohort there were always a number of children – mostly boys – who had difficulty in mastering the basics of reading. Sometimes a change of approach and a little extra support from a TA was all that was required to get them started, but it was often the case that even an extended intervention under the Code had little effect. The problem seemed intractable and left SENCOs like Janet scratching their heads about what to do next.

Janet did not have a class of her own and within the framework of routines which constituted the primary school day was free to create her own timetable. Each year she was able to find time for extended discussions with me about inclusion policies and strategies in general, but this year she said she wanted us to take a closer look at why interventions with a particular group of pupils had failed and what could be done about it. Although there had been periods of steady progress, these were rarely sustained and too often the pupils had slipped back. Now in Year ten (Y10) with secondary school looming, their literacy skills were still very limited.

For the past year Janet herself had done some intensive work on word building using a variety of strategies but with a great deal of emphasis on phonics. She was aware of the dangers of focusing exclusively on the mechanics of reading and understood the importance of encouraging 'reading for meaning', but she felt compelled to 'go over some old ground' because the pupils' mastery of the basics was not secure. They had acquired some rudimentary word-attack skills. They could blend phonically simple words and some more complex words, and recognize a number of common words with irregular spelling. They could even manage to derive meaning from a simple text. But all this was at the same level as last year and there was no evidence of progress.

Identifying the Problem: 'Within Child' Explanations

Like many good teachers, Janet usually identified the 'problem' as hers rather than the pupils' – if they were not learning, then she was not teaching them correctly. She worked pragmatically, dealing with issues as they cropped up, and spent little time thinking about 'causes'. But when she had 'tried everything' and felt she needed a 'complete re-think', she often wanted to 'bounce' ideas off me. Why had these pupils made such little progress? Was it because they could not retain things? Was it a function of poor memory? She knew of research which demonstrated a link between deficits in certain cognitive functions like working memory and 'reading difficulties'.

Janet was a reflective practitioner who was prepared to seek out relevant research and use it to inform her practice. She was a full-time SENCO who, unlike most others on my patch, gave reading research journals and accessing research on the Internet a high priority, particularly when she was 'stuck', as she put it. She usually wanted to talk to me about the research articles she had just been reading.

One of the misconceptions about the role of an EP relates to the nature of their expertise. Despite my protestations to the contrary (!), Janet always assumed I was an expert on clinical 'conditions' like 'dyslexia', and that, because I was always stressing the importance of research, I was up to date on all the research in this area. If she has just read an article on, say, the neurological aspects of reading difficulties, she would assume that I knew all about this and more.

In fact I did not read any of the research on 'dyslexia'. I found it repetitive and largely unhelpful, locked as it usually was within a research paradigm and a perspective on special needs with which I had little sympathy. And so when Janet wanted me to provide her with further references and insights from the research, I always wanted to say to her 'which research do you mean?' But I felt I could not put it like that. If I did, I knew from past experience that I would be accused by Janet of being too 'philosophical'.

A Paradox: Playing Down the Importance of 'Research'

Strangely, one of the strategies I deployed in this situation was to initially play down the importance of 'research' and emphasize the value of 'common sense'. Strangely, because I perceived 'good practice' in education to be research based, and frequently argued for this position at conferences and in professional journals! But I knew that Janet had a particular view of what research was which was not easy to shift and that she enjoyed reading about 'reading difficulties' and 'dyslexia'.

Had she been a student on, say, a Master's course where various research paradigms were identified and discussed then I would have talked to her about the different 'theories' of research. But she was not.

I knew, however, that her 'common sense' was sound, and that she merely used research selectively to legitimate innovative practices, which she had either 'picked up' from other teachers or evolved herself. (Ironically this was a feature of practice of which I was usually critical i.e. practitioners claiming that some minor modification to their practice represented the implementation of radical ideas from research!). And so I tended to play down the 'research' element and concentrate on developing a reflective dialogue around her own ideas and practices.

A typical example of this was the conversations we had about Brain Gym. Even before Brain Gym became fashionable in the Authority as a whole, Janet had developed a workable scheme for her school based on ideas from the research literature on dyslexia. The programme of activities assumed 'learning difficulties' had a neurological base. The activities had descriptors like 'brain buttons', 'cross crawl' and 'hook ups', which were all supposed to exercise the brain and help establish neural pathways. Cross crawl, for example, involved putting the right hand across the body to the left knee as you raised it, and then doing the same thing for the left hand on the right knee, just as if you were marching. Pupils were encouraged to drink plenty of water to 'grease the wheel' i.e. the work of the brain.

Janet had spoken to me about this development with great enthusiasm. I wanted to express doubts and did so obliquely, but when I saw the programme in action it was evident that, suspect neurology or not, the pupils seemed to derive great pleasure from it. They enjoyed all the activities, even those they found difficult. In fact, Brain Gym was so successful that it was incorporated into the curriculum as a regular activity for all pupils. Teachers liked the activities because not only were they supposed to improve the functioning of the brain but they also acted as a benign control mechanism. If the class was becoming too 'lively', instead of telling them to 'settle down', you could achieve the same results by encouraging them to move their bodies in a disciplined way while standing next to their seats. Pupils got to know the routines so well that in one class I observed the teacher only had to shout out 'Brain Gym!' for the whole class to start moving. Sometimes pupils went into the routines spontaneously and incorporated them into their own play. And of course, as I argued, it did not have to be called Brain Gym! Its 'success' presented a golden opportunity for curriculum development in physical education, which Janet felt had been neglected in recent years due mainly to the increasingly sedentary nature of education at the primary stage linked to various 'reforms' like the National Literacy Strategy (NLS).

However, Brain Gym had done nothing to motivate or improve the functioning of the children who now concerned Janet. 'Poor memory' was now in the forefront of her thinking as a possible explanation. She wondered if there was a programme available which 'trained the memory'. She had read in a dyslexia journal about research which suggested that memory could be improved by 'metacognitive' exercises, that is, exercises which encouraged children to reflect on their memory processes and develop strategies, like mnemonics, for example, to aid recall.

I had discussed the question of poor memory with Janet on previous occasions, and could perfectly understand the appeal of this as an explanation. After all, these pupils could not even retain, as Janet put it, an 'infant level sight vocabulary' despite extensive 'overlearning' and revision. But as I had pointed out before, we already knew these children found it difficult to remember words, and so to suggest that the 'cause' was 'poor memory' did not really add anything to our understanding.

An Opportunity for Action Research

Very often the matter would be left there because frankly I did not have the time to follow it up, but on this occasion I did have some space in my diary and would have been able to create a block of time for that particular school. Janet suggested that it would be useful for me to see fewer new referrals, and use the time released to investigate the educational development of these Year 10 'problems'. I felt this was an opportunity not to be missed. As well as addressing the needs of this particular group – who were as much a puzzle to me as they were to Janet – it would also enable me to introduce the intervention as a form of research, albeit research of a different kind to the 'positivist' research with which she was familiar. I therefore told Janet that I was prepared to carry out a small action research project in the school which would focus on the needs of these pupils. It would be a collaborative process that would involve us working as team.

Janet agreed to this and set up a series of planning meetings. It is my experience that many teachers have an intuitive understanding of action research because it involves similar strategies to those they deploy in their day-to-day practice, although they do not call it research. Janet was one such teacher. As indicated above, she was a reflective practitioner who was continually thinking about how she could improve her own teaching.

At the first meeting it was agreed that we should begin by looking at the pupils' experience of the whole curriculum as well as their literacy development. Pupils should be told about the project and asked for their views. We would then explain why we wanted to observe them in the classroom. This would also provide an opportunity to observe children who had responded successfully to previous interventions under the Code, and perhaps match them up in a rough and ready way with those who had not done so well. What were the similarities in the experiences of these groups, and how did they differ?

Gary and Sam

Initially, however, we thought it would be better to focus not on the whole group but on two individuals, just to get an idea of what information we might need and what questions it would be useful to ask. We decided to begin with two pupils from the same class, Gary and Sam. Work with these two turned out to be so engrossing that they were the only pupils ever involved in the project! In the file, on a standardized test administered by Janet, Gary was reported to have a reading age of 8.5 years and Sam 6.5 years. Both pupils were 10 years old and were summer births, and thus relatively young in the age group. At the end of the previous year, Gary had an RA of 6.4 and Sam 6.6.

Janet agreed that since she knew the pupils well (I had seen them briefly the previous year), it would be useful for me to interview them individually myself to get an outsider's initial impression, which may help to stimulate some 'fresh thinking'. In the interviews, it soon became apparent that both pupils were keen to participate in what we told them was 'a project about learning'. Despite the difference in their measured attainment, they appeared to hold similar views on their reading skills. Both thought they were 'good at reading', enjoyed reading in class and were willing to talk at length about their latest reading book. Both thought they had improved since last year. I then went on to broaden the discussion in an attempt to find out about what they thought of school life in general and the degree to which they felt 'included'. Each said he had plenty of friends and could name many activities he did with his friends. Each could identify 'work' he had done recently, which he thought the teacher was pleased with. Gary thought he had done some 'good art work'; Sam that he had done some 'good writing'. They could name several lessons they liked. Both of them liked going out to play at lunchtimes. Neither of them felt bullied. Both could think of something they were good at that was not to do with work. I gave them some options, here. How about being a good friend or helping at home? Both said they were friendly towards other people.

In the classroom Gary and Sam did not have much to do with each other. I had the impression that Sam was not as popular as Gary. Gary seemed to apply himself to tasks for longer periods, and seemed to work more quickly. To get a broader picture, I went through an inclusion checklist with the class teacher. She identified a number of similarities but also a number of differences between them. Sam communicated less effectively with her than Gary, who was always asking questions and making contributions in class. Both pupils played with other pupils at break times and lunchtimes, and there were no noticeable differences in the frequency with which other pupils initiated interactions with either one. Over the course of the term both had had work put up on the wall by the teacher. She was conscious of trying to give positive feedback to both pupils, although she could not be sure she had succeeded in this. Neither was very disruptive in class, but Sam engaged in more low-level disruption than Gary. Sam was 'off task' more of the time than Gary. She knew both sets of parents well. Sam came from a larger family and had more siblings. All the parents worked and the marriages seemed stable. There had been no unusual events in either family in the last year, which may have had an impact on either pupil's functioning, although she did not know this for certain.

I did not think it was appropriate to give Sam and Gary any further cognitive tests. They had both been tested on the Wechsler Intelligence Scale for Children (WISC) by my predecessor and were both said to be 'in the below average range relative to peers'. After years of developing in parallel, Gary was now shooting ahead.

Neither of them qualified as having 'specific learning difficulties'. The Authority deployed a discrepancy model in identifying this group. Pupils had to have IQs well within the average range to qualify! This model has been much criticized in the research literature. Some of the teachers in the school felt it discriminated against certain groups of children who did not fit an arbitrary profile. These two boys had received less support than a child whose scores matched the profile but whose 'difficulties', according to Janet, were 'less severe'.

I discussed these findings with Janet who said that this roughly confirmed what she knew already. This was just another situation when there was no ready explanation for low reading scores. As she had said to me on more than one occasion, there were no 'extreme ends' here; nothing you 'could put your finger on and say with certainty "that's it". It's just your common-or-garden reading problem.'

The Inadequacies of a Cognitive 'Story'

Of course, it would have been quite easy to construct a cognitive 'story' about Sam's literacy development. For instance, his performance on various language and cognitive tests in the past revealed relative weaknesses in verbal comprehension, sequencing, directional skills and word retrieval, and relative strengths in mental arithmetic, spatial awareness and speed of visual search. Tests also suggested that his capacity for immediate auditory recall, as well as his ability to recode information in working memory, were within satisfactory limits. Examination of his visual memory suggested that he was about average for his age in retaining and consolidating visually meaningful information in the short and medium term. It was possible that Sam's difficulties derived from a history of weakness in speech-sound awareness and analysis. But tests revealed no undue problems on a phoneme deletion task or on a test of auditory organization, which involved verbal memory as well as rhyming and alliteration.

I discussed this with Janet who was still interested in explanations in terms of 'cognitive deficits' and knew I had scrutinized all the test information to hand. I said I thought Sam's profile was not markedly different from many other pupils who were not considered to have 'reading difficulties'. Neither was it so very different from Gary's. Of course, one could pursue this further in the hope of finding some direct connections between linguistic, cognitive and perceptual weaknesses and his reading difficulty, but ultimately it was not as if, once you had discovered this, there was much you could do about it. I repeated my view that programmes specifically designed to address cognitive and perceptual weaknesses directly, like exercises to improve sequencing, might be of some help in certain circumstances but had a poor track record. Even when they were successful, it was never clear whether increases in reading scores were due to improvements in the 'enabling process' or in some other factor like teacher enthusiasm or pupil self-confidence. In any case, there were plenty of other pupils who managed to learn to read despite these alleged deficits. If they really were deficits, then they were quite common in the population at large and most pupils seemed to readily compensate for them.

Talking all this through with Janet gave me something of a déjà vu experience. Even when I said to her 'We've had this conversation before haven't we?' and she laughed, this was also something I could remember having said many times before! This time I felt some fresh thinking was required and she agreed. It might be an idea for Gary and Sam to work as a pair on their literacy skills. She had used a paired learning approach before, but on this occasion I felt it was important for us to develop strategies collaboratively. Janet had mentioned 'metacognition'. There might be some ideas here we could work on together.

Metacognition

I was myself interested in metacognition or at least a particular version of this. For me, metacognitive knowledge in an educational context was knowledge about all those factors which constrained or facilitated learning in that context. It was 'meta' because it implied an active agent – the 'I' – who was capable of reflexivity i.e. of reflecting on the self and developing awareness of the self as learner, which included memory awareness, but also an understanding of the social factors involved in learning.

I suggested it would be useful to get Gary and Sam together perhaps once a week for sessions which involved reflection on and discussion of their own learning, supported by Janet or a TA she had trained. Gary in fact was still being seen on a regular basis by Janet because, in the light of his previous record, she was worried he might 'slip back', and she wanted to consolidate the gains made.

These sessions were to be recorded so that the boys would later be able to reflect on what they had said previously. Such reflections on reflections might provide further insights and help them to move forward. In the first session, we felt they should be encouraged to talk about 'things about themselves', which they thought helped them to learn. We came up with questions like: how do I remember things; how do I learn from mistakes; how do I get ready for learning; how do I try things out; how do I find things out; how do I come up with ideas; how do I enjoy learning?

Each of these questions can generate discussion on important aspects of learning. The focus on memory typically leads to reflection on ideas and activities around the notion of practice, rehearsal, repetition, mnemonics etc. 'Learning from mistakes' can lead to reflection on self-correcting strategies; 'getting ready' to self-organization and independent learning, planning, setting targets; 'trying things out' to application and 'rough drafts'; 'finding things out' to experimentation, research, gathering information and accessing libraries, the Internet, etc.; 'coming up with ideas' to ideas-storming, word association, using previous experience; 'enjoying learning' to the range of emotions involved in learning. All these aspects, of course, feed into each other, so that it does not matter which question you start with.

However, Janet and I agreed these kinds of questions only represented half the story. They left out an examination of 'external' factors and the pupils' perception of the role of significant others, like teachers, peers and parents, who shared responsibility for their learning. However, since Janet herself felt more at ease with this more individualistic approach as a first step, she decided to go ahead. I listened to sections of the tapes afterwards.

Janet decided that before pairing Sam up with Gary she would see Sam on his own to model a metacognitive discussion. She provided lots of examples of learning situations and asked Sam how he would have responded in the same situation. For example, the boy in the picture was worried that he could not remember his home telephone number? What should he do? Sam, however, showed little interest in these exercises. Who could blame him? For him 'learning' per se was not an interesting topic. He was not motivated and soon 'switched off'.

I have had similar sorts of experiences myself with pupils in the past. All the rhetoric about teaching pupils to 'learn how to learn' implies that this kind of learning is easier to teach than it actually is. Sam needed to be motivated to become a 'good learner'. And that really was the main point about teaching pupils to 'learn how to learn'. Facilitating learning awareness had to go hand in hand with improving motivation.

A More Social Approach

I suggested that a better way forward would be to stick to the idea of a paired approach but involve the class teacher more and if possible the parents. Reflexivity could still be fostered but as an integral aspect of an enjoyable and worthwhile learning experience. And so the following plan was proposed. In the first phase, Sam and Gary would be given a few teaching sessions on a topic that interested them; this would probably involve football since both lads were keen footballers. They would be asked to carry out an investigation. During this, they would be encouraged to participate in reflexive discussion about the learning process. For example, how did they find things out? Could they have done it any better? They would be encouraged to feel that they were 'in charge'. They would also be encouraged to discuss each other's contribution and how they had worked together and how this could have been improved.

In the second phase, the class teacher would give Gary and Sam an opportunity to transfer whatever they had learned about learning to a classroom context. The idea of learning from peers as a valid classroom activity would be reinforced but so too would be the idea of teaching others. All peer teaching strategies (e.g. paired reading, talking partners) are thus beneficial to both parties. The more 'expert' peer is learning to be altruistic but is also learning more about the process of learning and this is beneficial to his or her own future learning.

The Setting for Paired Work

The paired sessions of the first phase were held in Janet's room. This was a well resourced room with plenty of books on the shelves, a computer with the latest literacy skills software, boxes full of games and activities to help this or that aspect of literacy, and filing cabinets with records, samples of work, pupils folders etc. Janet was aware that the room was called the 'special needs' room by staff but she had always tried to discourage this. She felt that calling it a special needs room rather than, say, a learning support room would 'send out the wrong message' and she tried to make sure the room was used at least some of the time for teaching children other than those on the special needs register. Thus, the room was also used for sessions with a 'gifted and talented' group for what one of the teachers described as 'stretching purposes'. Janet had doubts about this because she thought it was wrong to single out such a group, and I did too. I saw no reason why 'stretching' these children along with the rest of their peers should not be carried out in the regular classroom context.

How did the pupils themselves perceive the room? Janet felt there was no stigma attached to going there for extra work. Pupils left their classrooms for many reasons, to go to the library for instance or to access computers in another classroom or to attend 'positive play' sessions. There were lots of comings and goings, and pupils just accepted them in a matter of fact way as part and parcel of daily life. In fact the room seems to have been popular with most pupils, including Gary and Sam, probably because it gave them a break from the routines of the regular classroom.

It was apparent that Gary and Sam were under the impression they were also coming to the room to be 'stretched', which is a word I supposed they had picked up from the class teacher. Janet made use of this. She told them that that was correct – they were indeed coming to her room to be 'stretched', and she wanted to see how well they could do a project.

The investigation got underway and the two boys worked well together. For the next session they brought material from home in the form of cuttings from newspapers and magazines. Luckily, there was one article about football training, and Janet used this to negotiate a particular direction for the project, which she felt should not just be about collecting pictures of footballers.

The Project

I had had previous experience of secondary school pupils becoming conversant with the various methods of team organization in football, like 4–2–4 and 4–3–3, which resulted in some of them, even those who tested as weak in 'spatial awareness', coming to grips with quite complex scenarios of how and for what purpose space on a football pitch could be controlled. But I felt this would be a bit too much for Gary and Sam. Janet saw other possibilities. It was clear to her that the idea of 'training' could be put to good use. After all, we wanted the pupils to reflect on 'how they helped each other learn' and this was precisely the kind of skills a good football coach would want to encourage.

Sometimes projects like this catch fire, sometimes they do not. What teachers might feel, from past experience, should 'work' does not always. What captures the imagination of one group gets little response in another. The affinity between football coaching methods with metacognition or meta-learning seemed obvious to us and a good 'jumping off' point for the project but would Gary and Sam see the links and be enabled to make use of them? As it turned out, the first step, which was to gain their interest, proved unproblematical. Janet managed to set up a meeting with a member of the Parent Teacher Association (PTA) who ran a local football team. Janet briefed him on the project and suggested it might be useful for him to bring along some of the team to talk about their experiences. Most of the players, who were young men from the local community, neither had the time nor inclination to participate but the one or two who did were enthusiastic and a great hit with Gary and Sam.

One player told them about his failures and as well as successes; how he had lost confidence at one point and nearly given up the game. He also, with the encouragement of Janet, told them about his strengths and weaknesses, about how he learned from his mistakes and how he tried to think of himself as a 'creative ball-playing dynamo'. His imagery was colourful and evocative, and both Sam and Gary latched on to it. He spoke about the 'wheels coming off his train once' when he had had an injury; how 'you shouldn't try to kid yourself you can do something when you can't.' As well as characteristics of the self he also talked about the role of other – how the nickname of his best coach was 'big ears', which seemed to imply that he listened but sometimes listened too much; how his best coach was also 'almost like a father to me' and how some of his teammates were 'selfish' and others 'supportive'.

My Ambivalence

I must confess I was ambivalent about all this (see later in the Coda). Football discourse was prevalent in the peer culture, and although girls joined in, it was essentially male dominated. But there was certainly a great potential for involving parents, particularly fathers. Sam and Gary's fathers both actively supported the local professional club. Footballers have contributed to programmes to get boys interested in reading, and have been involved in various community projects, like disability awareness and 'kick racism out of football'. But not all attitudes and values imported into the school were, to put it mildly, consonant with democratic educational goals. The elitism, the extreme competitiveness and the league table mentality seemed allied to some of the most anti-inclusive educational policies and practices. Football was also a powerful global business, with all the implications this had for the future of local clubs and the survival of minority sports.

Although I enjoy watching football myself, I am appalled by certain aspects of the game. Football cropped up all the time in my conversations with boys in secondary and to some extent in primary schools. Unlike Gary and Sam, who named the local team, most of them when asked which football team they supported would name a Premier League side. For many pupils interested in football, a visit to the local club would always be second best to any activity, like watching a game on television, involving a Premier League club. Of course, there were some boys who said they were not interested in football at all, but they were exceptions and this fact alone would certainly position them as 'odd' in the dominant male-pupil culture.

Although I had my doubts about the direction of the 'investigation', I did not express these to Janet, whose approach I thought was original and interesting. The research questions that emerged were: what would they learn about learning through reflecting on learning in two contexts – the context of football coaching and the context of their own collaboration on the project; and, in the next phase of the project, would this learning about learning make any impact on their learning in the classroom?

The Language of Dialogue

The metacognitive or meta-learning discussions with Janet in the debriefing sessions went quite well. Sam and Gary showed they were capable of articulating concepts about learning. In some sessions, they were encouraged to discuss the 'language of dialogue' in their own collaborative context. I was able to attend one or two of these. At one point, I asked what would happen if they disagreed with each other – what would they do then? Sam said he would say 'tell me more about it' and Gary said that he liked asking people questions because the answers could be 'fun – you might get a surprise'. They were also asked about what they felt would prevent them learning from each other and 'having a good conversation' in class. Sam said that 'those who were your friends would be all right but others would just mess about.' Gary said that 'some people would get annoyed and start an argument.' I then asked if having an argument could be a good thing? They did not think so because it just led to people 'falling out' and 'getting on each others nerves'.

I asked them to compare a football coach with a teacher. Gary said the coach told people 'who to pass to' and did 'team work with you'. Teachers did not do 'team work', they told you to 'write things down on your own'. Sam said the coach had spoken about 'what people were doing right and wrong' and 'watched them when they did it again'. The teacher watched you and then sometimes 'forgot you'. This prompted further questions about what they could do in this situation – how did they let the teacher know about their views and experiences; how did they tell the teacher if things were going wrong; how did they ask for help? They took the opportunity to be quite critical of the teacher. They said she was always shouting at Sam and when they asked for help she told them to 'wait a minute' and then the lesson would end and 'it was too late'. They also thought the teacher did some 'some good things with them' and they had a 'learned a lot'.

What were we to make of this first phase? Janet felt happy about how the sessions had gone and thought Gary and Sam had been well motivated. But would they be able to use this 'knowledge' about learning in specific areas like literacy? Janet kept returning to what she described as 'the bottom line'. Would it help Sam develop his literacy skills? They had at least made a start with learning 'the language of dialogue and learning', but would this transfer to the classroom?

The Second Phase: Transfer to the Classroom

Janet and I now hoped Sam and Gary would be given an opportunity to demonstrate their 'new' knowledge about learning in the classroom context. A lesson was set up where the teacher was asked to include a reflexive discussion about learning. During the course of this, she was to address various questions about learning to Sam and Gary referring back to their experience of 'learning how to learn'. To make sure the two boys would ask and answer questions, their understandings from the football project were reinforced in a pre-tutoring session with Janet where they were encouraged to practise dialogical interchanges.

In the first session I observed, the class teacher made every effort to do as agreed. It was a lesson on the 'simile'. When she had explained the idea of a simile, she set up an exercise, which involved pupils identifying appropriate similes for certain objects, events and experiences; 'like when our skin felt smooth, how could a simile be used to bring out the idea of smoothness?' Just before allowing them to get on with this, she asked if anyone had any questions. Gary and Sam had been primed by Janet to ask a question about being allowed to work in groups, but neither said a word. The class teacher then informed the pupils she would like them to work in groups and asked how they would go about this? One or two pupils including Gary responded. 'We should share things with each other.' 'We should give everyone a chance to speak.' 'We should discuss things.'

Sam still said nothing. Later, in a small group session, the two boys worked quite well, asked questions and made contributions. But in a further whole-class reflexive session on the carpet, Sam made no spontaneous contribution, and when a question was aimed at him directly by the teacher, he just mumbled inaudibly. Gary, however, rose to the occasion, and asked a whole range of questions.

What was going wrong? In a debriefing session in Janet's room she asked both boys for their thoughts on the class sessions, and Gary was clearly more enthusiastic than Sam. Both Gary and Sam felt that Sam's problem was that he did not like to speak in front of the whole class. Sam said he felt 'nervous' and 'forgot what to say'. Janet seemed disappointed but in fact it may have represented progress.

At least Sam was now articulating the difficulties he experienced. It also seemed to explain the difference between Gary and Sam – a difference which was less noticeable in the small group session, although as Janet pointed out, in their reflexive discussions, it was usually Gary who took the lead. Gary was clearly the more confident learner.

Sam Becomes a Teacher

I realized at that point that Sam's orientation throughout the process may have been too passive and dependent. In the 'learning how to learn' project the learner was supposedly in a position of being an active agent, but in fact Sam was only being active in seeking help from others – peers, teachers or parents. Although Sam was asked to think about how he helped others and how others helped him, the former was in fact underemphasized. And so in order to boost Sam's confidence in his own abilities as a learner, Janet and I felt it would be a good idea if he became a teacher! Janet tried this in the next paired session with Gary. Gary had to play the part of a learner, listening and asking questions, while Sam played the teacher, which also included listening and asking questions but from a position of being more of an 'expert' in the knowledge at hand. It was not easy to find a topic where this relationship could be sustained, but football cropped up again, because Sam knew a great deal more than Gary about the local club.

By this time Gary and Sam had become close friends and Janet had no difficulty in encouraging them to collaborate on this new approach. Sam was hesitant at first, and the early interchanges just involved Gary quizzing Sam about the club. Sam often did not know the answers to Gary's questions. Janet then attempted to structure this a little more. Sam was given some teaching goals. He knew a bit about the recent history of the club, and Janet obtained further information from the Internet and had a brief one-to-one with Sam in which she went over this with him. Sam then acted as a teacher would and told Gary what he hoped to teach him. He gave a short spiel about the club – how it used to be in a higher league, how it used to have bigger crowds, how it did things in the community and for charity, how spectators used to stand up but now they were all in seats etc. He also spoke about family history. Both his father and his grandfather supported the club and his dad had told him his grandfather's father was a supporter as well. There was also an opportunity for the conversation to be broadened to include local history, particularly the history of work and how jobs were different now from what they used to be.

Sam did this falteringly at first but his confidence grew. Janet was particularly pleased when he responded to a difficult question from Gary by saying 'I don't know that but I shall look it up'. I did not have a chance to observe all of these sessions or what followed afterwards in the classroom but on a later visit I was told by the class teacher that Sam was now generally much more confident in class, and on one occasion had even managed to speak about his interests in front of the whole class.

A few months later I was asked to see Sam in connection with his end-of-term review. The parents were also invited and said they would like to see me. Everyone felt that Sam had made a great improvement and although he was still well below his peers in literacy achievement as measured by standardized tests, he was approaching reading with more confidence. It was impossible to say for certain how much the intervention had contributed to this. Sam seemed to have become more mature and was now able to make better use of the extra attention he was receiving. I like to think the intervention had made a difference. Sam's father said things at the review which I felt provided some evidence of his progress. He recalled a recent incident when Sam had told him to 'sit down and listen'! Sam had then proceeded to play the teacher with his own father, telling him about 'science' and then quizzing him to see if he had taken it in.

Coda

Like all the stories in this book this one is unfinished. All I can say is that this intervention felt 'successful' on a number of levels. I felt the school's thinking about 'learning difficulties' had been broadened and connections had been made between 'within child' cognitive concepts and more social and, in my view, more productive interpretations of 'learning' and 'learning how to learn'. An attempt was made to encourage the school to think of the latter in interactive (see Quicke, 2003a; Quicke and Winter, 1994; Mercer et al., 1999; Ogden, 2000) rather than individualistic terms. Likewise, ways of looking at 'reading difficulties' which relied on discrepancy definitions (see Solity, 1996) and deficit models were avoided. The football project had demonstrated how psychological intervention could take the form of collaborative action research; and how different research paradigms gave rise to different concerns and approaches. The pupils seem to have enjoyed the experience and derived benefit from it.

However, I could not help feeling rather despondent about the future. I did not know how Sam would fare in the secondary school. On his primary record it still referred to his 'learning difficulties'. The secondary school he would be attending, had a mixed record with pupils so labelled. Sam was a perfectly able boy, but he would need to make rapid progress if he was not to be dubbed, as many were in that school, a 'boy with special needs in literacy skills'. His confidence had been undermined once, maybe it would be again. Would the school be able to sustain his motivation? Would they be able to learn from the successes of the primary school or merely see a low reading age as symptomatic of his not having been taught the basics properly?

As far as football culture was concerned, whilst I accepted that football as a cultural practice was a vehicle for some very unsavoury anti-democratic and anti-educational values, some associated with the 'unacceptable face of capitalism', others with hegemonic masculinity, the fact that one might talk of it being 'corrupted' by such associations implied that one could envisage a more 'pure', uncorrupted practice in MacIntyre's (1981) sense, and that this perhaps could be 'glimpsed' in certain actions in the here and now. Thus, one might say that 'football' was a contested practice. In its 'pure' form it could give rise to relations between participants characterized by moral qualities e.g. courage, solidarity, consonance, honesty; and contribute to the development of social and cognitive 'skills' e.g. planning, team work, rule following. When people refer to 'what's good for football' or 'what's good for the game' and 'love of the game', they are acknowledging that genuine practitioners are motivated by more than just love of money or desire for status.

But is not any form of competitive game exclusive? How does this emphasis on football square with inclusion? All games involve friendly competition, and in so far as this involves virtues such as 'respect for an opponent' and 'appreciation of another's skills' it is morally and educationally positive. Games are exclusive but only in the sense that they are rule following and if one does not follow the rules then one would be excluded from the game. Most culturally valued human activities are exclusive in that sense. This does not mean that one cannot take an interest in the game as a non-player – as a spectator, for example, or as citizen concerned with the various moral and political issues the game gives rise to.

Chapter 8
On the Social Meaning of 'Throwing a Wobbly' and the Question of Survival in a Primary Classroom

Introduction

There was a message on my voicemail from David Grant, the Head teacher of Bawden Primary School. He would like to see me urgently. Several of his pupils were 'getting out of hand'. Other schools had children with 'behavioural difficulties', but Dave had always said he would never call me out just for that! He was making a point, of course, about the severity of 'problems' typically encountered in his school.

I had a gap in my diary due to a cancelled appointment and so I was able to get out to the school that afternoon. The school was in an area of poor housing and high unemployment. The Edwardian terraced houses were in a rotten state and in some streets many of them were uninhabitable and had been boarded up. There was a small industrial estate nearby but even that had seen better days. Many of the units were unoccupied, and those that were employed few people who lived in the area. At one time it was a settled neighbourhood but now it contained many families in transition, often renting accommodation while waiting for a local authority house. All the comings and goings had a disruptive impact on the school. New arrivals could come at any time, and, as Dave put it, pupils were suddenly 'whisked away' when the family 'flitted' to another location. He could not deny that the staff often breathed a sigh of relief when certain pupils were 'transferred out'.

However, there was a well established British Asian community in the area, and approximately a third of the pupils were of Pakistani ethnic origin. Their faith, along with Christianity, was pictorially represented in the entrance area of the school and all signs were in Urdu and English. They had come to Britain originally to work in the steel industry, and had suffered from economic upheavals in the same way as the whites in the area. Although a more stable community than the white population, they were just as poor and were just as likely to be involved in drugs and crime.

Dave felt the geographical location of the school was a problem. The staff were always finding needles discarded by drug users on the school yard and on the small playing field next to the school, which was now not too well guarded by a solid metal security fence. Despite the school having a caretaker and being fitted up with several security devices, burglaries were still averaging one or two a month.

The usual targets were the computers. There were just too many for them to be locked up in cupboards overnight. Vandalism was also a problem – windows were smashed, the school garden wrecked and teachers' cars scratched. There had been three attempts to set fire to the school in the last year, each of them spotted in the nick of time by the caretaker. Dave said the area as a whole was 'deprived' but this particular neighbourhood, where the school was situated, was especially bad. He felt that all the most 'turbulent' families lived nearby and saw the school as a resource in more ways than one! This did have an upside in that it was easier to get parents to keep appointments. If they did not turn up, he would just walk round to the house and knock on the door. But there were plenty of downsides, not least that pupils from other streets had to 'run the gauntlet' to and from school. A number of parents regularly escorted their children, even the older ones, to school but many were not in a position to do so.

A Class at the 'Tipping Point'

When I arrived at the school I signed in and, as usual, was given an identification tag, which I duly attached to the lapel of my jacket. Dave was waiting for me in his office and after a few pleasantries, we got down to the main matter in hand. He wanted to talk to me about a Y5 class. Ideally, the class teacher, Linda Stokes, should also have been here, but he wanted to 'put me in the picture' prior to my meeting with her. Although four pupils in class X were known to me, there were several others who, he said, could be referred if I thought it was appropriate. It was one of those classes which was almost at some kind of 'tipping point' – there were so many 'extreme behaviours' that it was on the verge of becoming unmanageable.

Many things had come together to produce what amounted to a crisis. There had been a rapid turnover of staff in the last year and this class had had three different teachers. Their current teacher, who was newly qualified, was dedicated but inexperienced. There had been several new pupils, including three asylum seekers, who had not integrated well. The existing problems were becoming more severe. Moreover, the school had 'serious weaknesses' in OFSTED jargon, and the staff felt under enormous pressure to improve standards as measured by the average point score on National Curriculum tests, which was well below what was being achieved nationally in allegedly similar schools.

The school was being supported by the local authority in a variety of ways, but Dave felt he could not really 'turn things round' without a more stable staff and ideally two or three extra teachers. Although he adopted the language of managerialism – a language now so dominant that it was difficult for any of us to resist its embrace – this still went hand-in-hand with a language from what seemed like a bygone era. Dave had been in post in this school for nearly 30 years. He had seen enormous changes in the catchment area, which even in the 'old days' had always been a 'priority area'. Now, more than ever, it needed 'positive discrimination' on a large scale, and although he was thankful for all the support he had received from the LEA services he needed a lot more.

Linda's Account

Dave then called Linda in to update me on the current situation. When teachers wanted to impress upon me how difficult a situation was, they often resorted to unprofessional language and to 'shock-horror' stories, which emphasized extreme behaviours. Dave was careful to use appropriate language to describe pupils, but Linda was not.

She said that, although she did not like to use the term, some of the pupils in her class were 'psychos' – not just naughty but 'at the extreme end of the continuum'. There was, for example, Josh, who used to 'throw wobblies' which could involve messing himself and refusing to go to the toilet. He was frequently found on the school roof where he perched precariously and shouted down at staff. He often hid under desks, lying prostrate on the floor, and refused to move.

Then there was Ryan who went in for 'tattooing' himself using razor blades and biros in a way which amounted to self-injury. He had even had a go at tattooing the initials of all his friends on his upper arm. He had tried to erase these when he had fallen out with them but in the process had made an awful mess of his skin.

Another boy, Daniel, had recently been in trouble with the police for pointing an imitation firearm at a police car in the early hours of the morning on a dual carriageway near his home. He had apparently caused panic in the car, which had swerved and nearly hit some traffic lights. The school had found this out from the parents when they were asked to see Dave on account of Daniel's spending a lot of time in school asleep. He often absented himself from the classroom and curled up on a comfy chair in the library-cum-resource area.

Kyle had a reputation as a firebug. Linda suspected his involvement in the various arson attacks on the school, although she felt he did not have a grudge against the school. He was just fascinated by fire. On one occasion he seemed to want to involve her as a co-conspirator, showing her his favourite box of matches and actually striking one to demonstrate how he could do it with his fingernail.

Then there was Imran who was a British Asian boy from a family notorious in the area for theft of one kind or another. He was always stealing mobile phones, which he gave to his brothers who sold them in the local secondary school. Like Josh, he tended to throw 'wobblies' although did not mess himself in the process. She felt that with Imran the 'wobbly' seemed to be more calculated.

Dysfunctional Families?

All these pupils came from families whom Linda described as dysfunctional. They were disliked in the neighbourhood and people tended to avoid them. At least two of the families were feared because of their alleged links with drug gangs. All kinds of stories circulated in school about these families, most of them based on hearsay but some clearly deriving from actual experience. Kyle's brothers and sisters had been involved in the intimidation of their next door neighbours, threatening to beat them up if they did not stop complaining about them. Josh's father was said to be a burglar who was always in and out of jail. Imran's was said to be a Godfather, the boss of the extended family. He did not attend mosque and their community had an antipathetic attitude towards him and the rest of the family.

Linda acknowledged that Dave had tried to avoid putting all these 'problems' into one class but in a relatively small school his options were limited. In any case, in this particular year group, Y5, they were only the 'tip of the iceberg'. There were several other pupils who did not have the same reputation but whose behaviour was just as problematical.

Linda felt that from an inclusion point of view these families seemed to be self excluding. Their children could be quite malicious and tested teachers to the limit. The behaviours were often so bizarre that other pupils called them 'nutters' or 'mental', and many lived in fear of them. Imran in particular was feared by the other British Asians in the class. He was only ten but staff felt he was already an accomplished schemer, manipulator and thief, who bullied other pupils and seemed to have the other British Asian youngsters under his control.

My Reflections on Linda's Account

It is easy to be critical of Linda's account, which clearly involved unprofessional language and a deficit view of her pupils. She was, however, deliberately highlighting the deviant and sensational aspects of their behaviour for a particular purpose. She wanted to make sure I understood how challenging this behaviour was. I had every sympathy for her but I did need to work from a more balanced view of the situation. These pupils presented themselves as problems but it was wrong to lump them together as 'problem pupils' when in fact they were all different as individuals. For reasons of space I cannot give details of my own and other agencies previous involvement with the four pupils who had been referred to the EPS. Suffice it to say, in all cases efforts had been made to highlight the 'positives', few though these were, and to think in terms of how classroom interactions could be made more educationally productive.

Positive Handling

I had observed this class on several occasions, and had seen some of the pupils for individual interviews. The parents had been invited to see me at school but only two had ever turned up, despite the efforts of the Dave and the EWO to secure their attendance. Even I was on tenterhooks in this class. At any point, usually without warning, the class would erupt. If the teacher left the room for a brief period,

I started to get the treatment meted out to any stranger. Imran would gesture to me, often rudely, and when I ignored him would shout across the room perhaps to Josh or Ryan. One of them might then wander over to me and start up what the teachers would describe as a cheeky conversation. He might want to know if I was seeing him today, and could he come along after break and if not why not? Did I like Miss Stokes? Was I a teacher? This would set things off and before long they were all out of their seats and roaming around the classroom interfering with others. The TA, Joan Perry, was respected by individual pupils but her role was not to discipline whole classes and the pupils knew this.

There were days according to Linda when they were all 'hyper'. 'One would start then they all would.' He (it was usually a boy) would get 'wound up' by the others or at least pretend to get 'wound up', and start shouting and even screaming his complaints. A fight would sometimes break out but usually they just bad mouthed each other at the top of their voices. Sometimes they would damage property. On one occasion Ryan threatened to throw a chair through a window. Sometimes Linda had to resort to physically holding a pupil whom she felt was becoming a danger to himself and to others. I discussed with her the advice she had been given about 'positive handling'.

She was aware that under the Education Act 1997 teachers were allowed to use reasonable force to control or restrain pupils, provided the head teacher had authorized this, which in this school he had. She was concerned, however, about the interpretation of 'reasonable force' and how these particular pupils might exploit the situation.

It was quite the thing in this class for pupils to feign anger. They seemed to know that a person in an angry state was threatening to others because they might do things which they would not dream of doing in a calm state, like lashing out wildly without fear of the consequences. They might even take on a pupil much bigger than themselves and even one with a reputation for being a bully because in an angry state when they went 'mental' they just did not care. What might be described as the 'cult of anger' was rife in this class, and may perhaps have been reinforced by the emphasis placed on 'anger management', a control strategy advocated by support professionals and in this school used by the LM and SENCO. It was quite typical for the LM, for example, to run sessions on anger management with individuals or groups of pupils whose misbehaviour was considered to be a reflection of their anger.

Whether a pupil was feigning anger or not, he or she often managed to work themselves into a state which involved Linda having to resort to physical restraint. The idea was to hold the pupils until the anger passed and some form of self-control regained. In this way the physical harm a pupil might have done to themselves or someone else could be avoided, but it also demonstrated to the pupil that they were within safe emotional and physical boundaries. I noticed however that after Linda, with the support and advice of Dave and the Behavioural Support Service, had started to use a holding technique, there were more and more incidents involving angry outbursts. Was this because pupils' behaviour was becoming worse or could the holding technique itself have had something to do with it? Pupils may have been more willing to express their anger now a safety net was available but they may have just behaved in this way in order to be held. Did they actually like being held? It was difficult to say, but it is well known that actions designed to eliminate behaviour can sometimes reinforce it. One could cite many examples of this with which teachers are only too familiar, like pupils' attention-seeking behaviour being reinforced by 'punishment' because it gives them the attention they crave.

But although these pupils might have liked to be held, they could also exploit the situation in other ways. A teacher was allowed to push a pupil in situations where 'reasonable force' was used to contain their movements but not allowed to 'shove' the pupil in a way which might cause them to fall over. The pupils did not know the details of the advice given to schools, but they sensed that it was not right for a teacher to push them too forcefully. On one occasion Josh had an angry outburst and started attacking another pupil, who had called him 'smelly'. Surprisingly enough this did not normally worry Josh who took great delight in other pupils backing off from him holding their nose. But on this occasion he decided to be offended and take it out on the culprit, Jane. Linda told me she held Josh briefly (she also told me that she 'nearly gagged because he reeked') and then as she released him he fell over in an exaggerated way, in common parlance 'took a dive'. He bitterly complained about being 'hit' and said he would tell his dad. Luckily there were two TAs in the class at the time who witnessed the incident.

The Science Lesson

Although Linda felt she was just about on top of the situation, it was a 'hard struggle' and she was not sure whether she would be able to 'survive the year'. She told me she would think about job-related matters 'morning, noon and night – at home, in bed or in the bath (!)' – and found it difficult to 'switch off' even at the weekend. Although she was pleased with the support she received from the support services and the head teacher, she felt that 'people had no idea what it was like to teach this class.' She followed the school's behaviour policy with its hierarchy of intervention (a reprimand in class to begin with leading up to a talking to by Dave in his office and the parents being called in). There was some relief when pupils went to see a LM or were taken out by Joan for small group work. She felt she was 'winning' but at what cost?

I watched an amazing lesson in Science, where Linda was determined to teach the subject creatively by allowing the pupils to work in groups on an investigation. She set up the lesson during break. It involved each group having access to water and observing whether substances dissolved or did not dissolve in water. They were supposed to record their observations, discuss their findings and draw conclusions. Plenty of opportunities here for creating a mess under the perfect cover of doing an experiment! And so Linda had to be more vigilant than usual, and make brief, low key disciplinary interventions continually to 'nip misbehaviour in the bud'. Each communication about science was followed by a communication about discipline. She told them about 'dissolving' and then immediately moved to a nearby table to take something out of Josh's hand, and this was quickly followed by an instruction to Kyle to keep his feet to himself. It worked. She got through what she described as a 'dangerous lesson'. In the staffroom afterwards she collapsed into an easy chair, saying 'I could just go to sleep.' Five minutes later she was marking books.

The Need for Expertise

I could not help thinking that, although Linda was doing a good job, it was not right to put a newly qualified teacher in such a difficult situation. There were several pupils in her class who needed expert handling by an experienced teacher.

Similar points have been made by the special school lobby who have a legitimate interest in the development of expertise with pupils with these particular needs. However, the mere fact that this expertise derives from teaching in the rarified environment of the special school tends, in my experience, to detract from its relevance for the mainstream. The education of such pupils in the mainstream does not require a 'special' teacher; it requires an expert in mainstream education, one who is au fait with teaching strategies, which address the full range of educational needs. Such experienced mainstream teachers are aware of just what can and cannot be done in this context, and what might and might not work.

Someone with Dave's expertise would have been ideal. He had a vast knowledge of how the school system worked, of various tried-and-tested teaching and learning strategies, of the historical, social and cultural background of the pupils, and of what had to be done to make positive and productive relationships with them.

Attempting to 'Manage' Josh's Behaviour and Anger

As it was, Linda had to make do with the support that was available, which included my involvement. We began by negotiating some targets that Josh thought he would be able to attain – to tell the teacher every time he was about to throw a 'wobbly' and leave the room with the TA; to go to the toilet every time he messed himself and clean himself up (eventually we hoped he would stop messing himself but this was not realistic in the short term); to collaborate with others on an investigation. A realistic reward for achieving these targets would be allowing him time on Fridays to play with his cars (he was keen on cars and had a collection at home, which he would be allowed to bring to school).

We discussed the criteria for achieving these targets e.g. what collaboration actually meant and what evidence we were looking for. We both felt that parental involvement was important and this itself should be a target. The LM and the Education Welfare Officer (EWO) agreed to help with obtaining the parents' cooperation. A contract with Josh was drawn up, which would run for a short period and then be reviewed. There were to be plenty of 'incidental reinforcers' with Linda using a lot of praise and 'catching him being good'.

This strategy was successful for a short time but eventually broke down mainly because of peer pressure; in behavioural terms, the rewards from peers were more powerful than the official rewards. In a one-to-one interview with the LM or me, he expressed his intention to be more cooperative, but within seconds of leaving either one of us all promises were forgotten, or seemed to have been. As soon as he was back with his peers it was as if he felt compelled to misbehave.

The parents were not uncooperative but they both worked unsocial hours as cleaners and found it difficult to keep appointments at the school. However, the LM felt that her counselling sessions with Josh had helped him. He was beginning to reflect on his feelings and in particular his anger, and she thought it would be useful to put him on an 'anger management programme'. As indicated above I had misgivings about such programmes on the grounds that they might have served to fuel a 'cult of anger'.

Such programmes typically focused on what the pupils could do to 'manage' their own anger, but a great deal of the anger pupils were supposed to self-manage was generated by the way the school system itself was managed! There was also an ambiguity at the heart of the programme. A part of it seemed to suggest anger was a negative emotion, which should be avoided (in which case it should have been called anger avoidance), whereas the rest assumed that anger was neither positive nor negative in itself but was a form of emotional energy which should be 'channelled'. In all cases, it was generally considered best to avoid acting on impulse, to 'lengthen the fuse', to give yourself time to think and to take action based on evidence. And so pupils addressed such questions as: think about the motivation of the person who made you angry; think about the situation that gave rise to your feelings; think about how to calm yourself down using calming techniques.

However, although some progress was evident initially, Josh still had difficulty in transferring what he appeared to have learned in the one-to-one to the whole class context. This was a familiar story. Josh had a reputation to live up to. The 'pecking order' had to be maintained and social relations were so volatile that actions to maintain 'status hierarchies' were more intense and frequent than in the average class.

Conflicts were breaking out all the time even between pupils who claimed to be 'friends'. Josh, Ryan and Kyle could be good mates one minute and arch enemies the next. As Linda said, each of them wanted to be 'top dog'. There was also, of course, the usual insults thrown at pupils who were perceived as 'teacher's pets' or 'boffs', and two rather timid girls in the class who were on the receiving end of much verbal and sometimes physical abuse. Josh and the others always defended themselves by claiming to be 'only playing' but when they punched they punched hard. I observed a 'play fight' in the playground between the boys which ended in tears and severe bruising on arms and legs. Linda said bloody noses were quite common. But if all this happened in the morning, they could be friends again by lunchtime and for the rest of the day.

Incipient racism was rife but during the period of my involvement it seemed to be mostly directed at the children of asylum seekers, with the whites and the British Asians ganging up against the three in this class. I had no details on these pupils who were from countries in Africa and the Middle East. The school itself knew very little about them. Although Dave was not against the dispersal policy and certainly felt that asylum seekers should be welcomed and viewed as a positive addition to the community, he wondered whether his school, in view of all the difficulties, was really suitable. He did not want to regard them as an 'extra burden' but that in effect was what they were.

'Circle of Friends' and Pupil Culture

It was clear that up until now the support strategies, which I had gone along with, had been too individualistic. Not enough attention had been paid to 'misbehaviours' which I felt derived from conflicts endemic to pupil culture in this classroom. A strategy was required that was group-oriented and took account of features of pupils' cultural practices which were salient for behavioural change in the classroom context. There were several such strategies but the one with which I and some of the staff were most familiar was 'Circle of Friends'. Connections with issues in pupil culture to do with 'solidarity', 'fairness' and 'friendship' could be made via this technique.

C of F involves selecting a small group of pupils, including a target pupil, to work with a facilitator e.g. the EP or other support worker. In the first meeting the facilitator identifies the overall purpose of the group, which is to help each other and in particular to help the target pupil. The pupils introduce themselves and are asked to list some positives about their behaviour in class as well as areas they all need to 'work on'. Since the target pupil usually has more things to 'work on', it is likely the group will spend more time on that pupil's problems. The group then agrees a name for itself – the troubleshooting group, the helpful group, the listening group, the research group etc.

A weekly meeting is set up, which lasts 30 minutes or so. The content of the sessions can vary enormously but usually involves talking about issues to do with behaviour. The most important part involves pupils developing a plan for helping each other, and the target pupil in particular, when dysfunctional behaviour occurs in class.

In this way the facilitator attempts to build up friendships and develop them in directions conducive to learning and positive behaviour. This obviously has to be a 'whole class' process, with other Circles of Friends eventually being set up for the rest of the pupils. Selecting one group and one target pupil is only a start.

Imran

My own role in the process would be to take the first session with a group set up by Linda. Joan Perry, the TA, would then takeover and I would not see them again until the final session when I would help Joan facilitate 'closure'. Linda was doubtful about the procedure. She felt that by the time we had got round to working with the whole class, the first group would have 'forgotten it all'. But she agreed to 'give it a go'.

Who would be chosen as the target pupil in the first group? I suggested Imran for several reasons, not least because I felt that in addition to problematical behaviour it might be possible for some of the underlying racial tensions to be addressed (in fact the latter did not happen, see Coda). I knew Imran and his family quite well having interviewed him recently along with two of his elder sisters who in effect were his main 'carers' in the family. It was a large British Asian family who were not very religious. As indicated earlier, Imran's father was considered to be a kind of Godfather in the neighbourhood because of his links with organized crime. I had no way of independently verifying this, but since it was the reliable Dave who informed me, I had no reason to disbelieve it.

In the one-to-one, I found Imran a delight, extremely easy to talk to and full of 'worldly wisdom' about life outside school. He was refreshingly honest. Yes, he had 'nicked' mobile phones but that was in the past. No, he did not think the teachers or any other member of staff treated him unfairly. He wanted to do well at school. He was a bully but he saw this as a way of helping the weak to get their own back! He only bullied other pupils who deserved it because they themselves were bullies. It is easy to be cynical about such accounts, but the fact of the matter was that, although feared by others, he only tended to get into fights with pupils like Kyle with whom most other pupils dare not tangle.

Imran was not one of the school's successes from an academic viewpoint, unlike his sisters who were high achievers. Linda felt he was probably 'underachieving'. Some of his behaviour in school was no doubt in part a function of his self-perception as a failure in school, and thus his desire to compensate for this by devaluing the official system and seeking an alternative form of status in the 'deviant' unofficial system. On the other hand, Imran was a participant in a subculture outside the school, which reflected the family's immersion in petty criminal activities. His sisters were also participants. They had in fact done quite well in school and college but subsequently had had brushes with law in connection with local scams. Imran already had a reputation in the community which followed him into school which is why he was feared by other British Asians.

Imran's siblings, whose ages ranged from two to 20, all lived at home, and he clearly had plenty of access to young person and adult conversation. He could talk about the nature of work in the area, about international conflicts, like the Iraq war, about food and how to cook curry, about makes of cars. Like Kyle he had been involved in car crime and claimed to be able to drive a car, even though he could hardly reach the pedals. He explained how he could manoeuvre his body to do this. One teacher described him as 'like a ten year old going on sixteen', even though he was not tall for his age.

The Group

Linda felt it should be a balanced group, containing two boys and two girls. We would clearly have to avoid the situation where the girls started to play little mothers, and looked after the boys in a one-way caring relationship! Ideally, we felt the girls should be ones who were themselves dominant and assertive in the class group and relatively mature socially but not overly conformist. Linda felt there was a small group of girls with these credentials, two of whom, Janice and Judith, were willing to participate. The fourth member was Hanif, a boy with whom Imran sometimes worked and seemed to like. Hanif himself was no angel and was frequently in trouble, but not as often as some of the other boys. He was one of the few British Asian pupils not dominated by Imran, although once or twice had been led into trouble by him.

The first meeting of the group was held on a day and at a time when all pupils in the class were allowed to choose from a range of practical activities. I saw the group in the library-cum-special needs area. I explained what the group was about and asked everyone to introduce themselves, but otherwise avoided lengthy explanations and too much talk. To relax them and get them in the right mood, we began with some activities similar to those used in Circle Time (see Coda) e.g. Simon Says, Story Roundabout. I envisaged all future sessions being activity based, and revolving around themes like friendship, working as a team, solving problems, resolving conflicts, expressing feelings. For instance, resolving conflict would focus on modified versions of Circle Time activities, which encouraged the pupils to see things from the point of view of the other e.g. Someone Else's Shoes, Everybody's Different, Arbitration. Sessions should start with a warm-up game and end with a fun game.

All activities should lead to a plan about what to do in concrete situations to help someone. The first step was to get to know each other a bit better by discussing likes and dislikes, how different people have different points of view, and how some pupils might be bored in the classroom whilst others might find lessons interesting. Each member of the group had to explain why they found something interesting or why they were bored. Then they had to suggest reasons why some pupils messed about, and why others did not. This was a difficult example because it seemed to imply that messing about had a certain legitimacy, but the hope was, it would lead to a discussion about everyone being able to express their opinions, and how this was important because we were all different. This was likely to lead to a consideration of limits: what happened if your free expression interfered with the right of others to free expression; was it right for some pupils' learning to be disrupted by others? The next step would be to help pupils find ways of expressing their feelings and frustrations that did not interfere with others. Appeals would be made to pupils' sense of justice, what was 'fair' and what was not 'fair'.

I hoped the group would gel after an exchange of thoughts and feelings about issues and practices which were of genuine concern to all of them. Linda agreed to continue to facilitate the 'growth' of the group in the broader context of the classroom e.g. by altering seating arrangements and changing the way she organized the class in groups. What happened in between the C of F sessions would be the real test. Would there be any evidence in day-to-day behaviour that the group functioned as the benign form of social control in the classroom we hoped for?

Pupils' Reactions

The pupils clearly enjoyed the first session and were keen to come back next week. Joan Perry took all the sessions apart from the first but I managed to observe the session on Someone Else's Shoes. Imran proved to be a willing participant. When the question of throwing 'wobblies' came up, Judith and Janice said they thought he went 'mad' and although he 'couldn't help it', it did have an effect on other people. Imran denied that he was 'mad', and it was explained to him that nobody was saying he was 'mad' all the time; it was just that he had these spells that affected other people. Imran gave the standard reply to this. He felt he was 'wound up' deliberately by other pupils. A lengthy discussion ensued about name-calling and how to deal with it. Various strategies were discussed, like replying with a joke to show you have not been 'got at'. Janice said she would just ignore what people said to her, but Joan pointed out that this might work sometimes, but more often than not 'the way you looked' was a give away! A slight twitch or a nervous glance told the aggressor that their taunts had struck home. Joan noted that in a future session they could perhaps discuss the role of body language – gesture, posture, eye contact etc. – in greater depth.

Negative Gossip

As mentioned above going 'mad' or 'mental' could well have been a strategy for achieving status in a 'deviant' unofficial culture. Assuming that Imran's behavioural extremes did have some such purpose, could the group counter this in any way? Would the friendship of Judith, Janice and Hanif be able to act in a sense as a counter-cultural force, one more in line with democratic educational values? Perhaps a way forward here would have been to talk about those pupils whom Imran was trying to impress. This was not usually considered an appropriate topic for Circle Time, particularly if it involved negative criticism of other pupils, and maybe even racist and sexist language. But gossiping about others was often the stuff of chat amongst friends. It served all kinds of purposes – as a repository for angry feelings towards a friend, which could not be expressed directly, or as a way of marking out the cultural boundaries of the group and of identifying group values.

For this kind of chat to be off limits for this group would have made it a very 'artificial' group indeed. Yet, it seemed inappropriate for an adult to sit in on such conversations.

Joan Perry made this last point to me. But I felt such gossip was so important for group development that I suggested she went along with it, and only intervened if she felt it was going too far, even if this would be very difficult to judge. We agreed it was important to avoid moralizing about the rights and wrongs of such conversations. However, the advantage of being present would be precisely that she could intervene and ask the pupils to reflect on this or that opinion or attitude.

Judith as a 'Crossover' Person

These sessions seemed to go quite well. Judith proved to be a key figure in the group. In cultural terms she was a 'crossover' person. She could use the language that would appeal to teachers. At one point she said that Imran should 'think for himself' and try harder not to be wound up by people like Ryan, Josh and Daniel. It was important to 'step back' and consider 'what might happen' if he acted in a certain way. But she also expressed her views in the style of the unofficial pupil culture e.g. 'Ryan is just stupid. I wouldn't go out with him. He's got girlfriends tattooed on his arm but I think he's gay.' (This homophobic remark went unchallenged. Should we have intervened?)

Imran, of course, grinned when Judith said this. He was quite happy to have a conversation which involved putting Ryan down because although Ryan was his friend he was also a rival. Imran's attitude was distinctly ambivalent. He wanted to impress him as a member of the same macho-cultural grouping, but on the other hand he expected Ryan on occasion to join others in ganging up against him. So was he a good friend, asked Joan Perry? 'Yes'. Why? 'Because he makes me laugh and we have a good laugh.' Is he always on your side? 'Yes and no. Yesterday, it was me and him against Hanif.'

Joan Perry then asked how the group was going to help Imran. Janice suggested that when he thought he was just about to throw a 'wobbly', he should be allowed to leave the class and one or two of the group should go with him to calm him down. Janice had clearly remembered a strategy that Joan had described earlier. It would require Linda to trust all three pupils since an adult would not be involved.

The group discussed this at some length and decided they would all have to remove themselves to the LM's room and if she was not available (she was only part-time) to the head teacher's office. In each case, the 'friends' role would be to talk to Imran on the way and try to calm him down, and then get back to the class as soon as possible. Later Linda said she would try this strategy but she was not sure if Janice, Judith or Hanif could be trusted. There was also the question of whether it was right for the 'friends' to do this. Why should they miss out on their education? What would the parents think?

Imran in fact did not throw any 'wobblies' during weeks the Circle of Friends was in operation. The group worked well in the sessions and there was some evidence of transfer to the classroom context. Linda felt that Judith and Janice were interacting more with Imran and Hanif than they had been previously, and Imran seemed a great deal calmer. She did not see any of the strategies discussed by the pupils in C of F sessions actually deployed in the classroom (!) but it seemed that even talking about what they might do to help each other had had a positive effect.

Coda

In the final session, the group decided that they had enjoyed the experience and that they would like to continue to meet in the future. Imran did most of the talking. He thought that Judith and Janice were 'great' and agreed they were 'good friends'. It was evident that the C of F was becoming part of the social fabric of the classroom, but as Linda pointed out Imran was still associating with the macho group and she felt it was only a matter of time before 'things blew up again'. As it turned out, she was correct. Unfortunately she was not able to pursue the C of F strategy in a 'whole class' way. It would have been just too time consuming, and there were other pressures on her. Imran's behaviour deteriorated but he did not throw any more 'wobblies'. Both she and Dave agreed that the class had 'moved on a little' and, as Dave put it, was now more 'normally naughty' and no longer at 'a tipping point'.

I felt that Linda had begun to see Imran in a different light. Although his behaviour was still problematical, she had seen a positive side to him. She appreciated the role of the C of F strategy in bringing out Imran's 'good points' and saw what needed to be done to improve the 'social climate' in the class as whole using this strategy, even though she was unable to implement a 'whole class' approach at this time.

Interventions like C of F are clearly not cure-alls. They are at best starting points for the development of a deeper understanding of pupils' cultural practices and how these might be engaged with. Most of the professional literature on C of F is not sociologically informed and makes no mention of such cultural practices. The rationale is similar to that underpinning another technique typically used in primary classrooms – Circle Time, which involves the whole class sitting round in a circle and addressing various moral and 'emotional' issues to do with themselves and their relationships with others. In the dominant 'practical' texts in this field, like Mosley's manuals and resources (see e.g. Mosley, 1998), the activities are explained and justified with reference to self-theories (e.g. Rogers, 1961, 1980), humanistic psychology, reality therapy (e.g. Glasser, 1965) and psychoanalysis (Benson, 1987).

This story illustrates how the cultural context can be taken account of in psychological interventions which address issues to do with 'extreme' behaviours in the classroom. I feel that EPs should be able to support teachers whilst at the same conveying a sense of the limitations of psychologistic approaches which ignore the social and cultural realities of the classroom. Not that these realities can be identified unproblematically. The reader will have noticed that although 'race' is alluded to, the question of racism does not really figure in the story. Why? I can give no clear explanation. The school had an explicit anti-racist policy, but, as one of the teachers pointed out to me, the fact that racial groups tended not to mix (although there were many exceptions at an individual level) seemed to suggest the existence of certain underlying tensions. When it came to derogatory language in the peer group, nothing overtly racist was ever stated in the C of F group as far as I was aware, but a racist discourse was clearly evident in attitudes to the children of asylum seekers.

Section C
Parents at the Extremities

In terms of attitudes towards inclusion, the parents of children described as having special educational needs are a diverse group. Some value 'difference' but want their child to be included and educated as a regular pupil in mainstream school. They are suspicious of all labels, particularly psycho-medical ones, not because they are 'in denial' but because they are worried about the psychological and educational consequences of a label of abnormality.

But there are many parents who actively seek a medical explanation and want a 'diagnosis' as soon as possible. What they imagine will follow from this is usually unclear, but most embrace the logic of the medical model. Once the problem is diagnosed then an appropriate treatment can be administered. Many see the 'treatment' as involving placement in a special school or unit, and push for this through their own contribution to the statementing process. The diagnoses often reflect genuine needs, albeit couched in psycho-medical jargon and unhelpful labels, but sometimes they do not. In extreme cases, the parents want a diagnosis which is clearly unwarranted.

The two stories in this section reflect contrasting parental attitudes. The first, 'We might be losing him' (Chapter 9) is about Betty and Ralph whose son Fred had been diagnosed as dyspraxic. At the age of 11, Fred was transferred from a primary to a special school, which catered mainly for pupils with physical disabilities. Betty and Ralph, however, wanted him to go to a mainstream school and Fred himself had said that he would have liked to 'have a go' in an ordinary school. The parents did not deny that the local secondary school would be extremely challenged by Fred, but thought that attendance at this school would be in his best interests in the long term. Unfortunately, he did not settle in the secondary school and decided for himself that he wanted to go back to the special school.

The second story, 'That's our boy down to a "T"' (Chapter 10), is about Ben who was referred to our service by his mother, Felicity, who wanted him seen by a psychologist as soon as possible. Her GP had said he was dyslexic and she wanted to know what I was going to do about it. She said she had found out from browsing the Internet that dyslexia could be associated with ADHD. Later she discovered that there was a condition called Pathological Demand Avoidance (PDA) and thought Ben might have had this as well. Her story is an extreme case of a phenomenon with which support professionals are only too familiar – the parent who seems to want their child to have a disorder. Although Felicity was the one with whom support services had the most contact, in fact, as I suggest, it was family relationships as a whole which probably should have been the main focus.

Chapter 9
'We Might be Losing Him'

Introduction

Fred was a 12-year-old pupil who attended a school for children mainly with physical disabilities but who wanted to 'have a go' in the mainstream secondary school. His parents, Betty and Ralph, had never wanted him to attend a special school in the first instance but claimed to have been 'talked into it' by teaching staff.

Fred had been diagnosed as severely dyspraxic by an occupational therapist on account of his difficulties with motor control and organization. The speech therapist thought that his understanding of spoken language was very good but that he had a 'delay' in expressive language and the social use of language. On tests, all his answers to questions were relevant but he found it difficult to explain or convey information or talk at length about his interests and activities. His speech was intelligible but his tone of voice was indicative of palatal incoordination, which meant that his utterances were produced on a level tone so that his voice appeared monotonous. His intonation patterns were slow and staccato, giving a laboured and pedantic quality to spoken language. The speech therapist commented that these 'prosodic features of communication could be part of a dyspraxic pattern'.

In junior school he was sensitively handled by teaching staff who tried to find alternative ways for him to record work. He was said to have outbursts of temper if anyone put pressure on him to write. He tried to be friendly and cooperative in the one-to-one but was said to have poor eye contact and was clearly uncomfortable in face-to-face situations where he was expected to interact.

The EP in the previous local authority felt that he was a boy with 'above average learning potential' who appeared to have genuine motor difficulties. His reading skills were well above average for his age, but he was weaker in spelling. The EP noted that in class, unless constantly prompted by the teacher, he would drift into self-absorbed behaviour, which often tended to be repetitive. He also tended to become upset over minor matters. Communication with his classmates was sporadic and they tended not to involve him in their activities unless prompted to do so by a teacher or TA.

The EP felt the most worrying feature of his behaviour was his poor social contact with peers. He told the school he felt that some of Fred's ritualistic and repetitive behaviours needed further investigation. Although there may have been some dyspraxia, the diagnosis was not clear cut, and some of his 'symptoms' fitted more with a diagnosis of Asperger's Syndrome.

I was asked to see Fred when he was in attendance at a secondary school although he was still on the register at a school for children mainly with physical disabilities, where he had been placed initially on moving to the area. His parents felt that this was not an appropriate placement for him, since he was not physically disabled in the usual sense of the term, but apparently he himself had decided that he did not want to go to secondary school straightaway.

Betty's Record of Fred's Progress

Before seeing Fred, I interviewed Betty, his mother, who had asked to see me to 'put me in the picture', she said, about his history. She gave the impression of a sensitive and caring parent who wanted the best for her son and was adamant that it was in his long-term interests to attend a mainstream school. She had kept a record of his progress through the school system and of all the interventions that had taken place, and was happy that the schools he had attended had 'bent over backwards' to include him. She had read about dyspraxia, autism and various speech disorders and she felt that Fred showed various 'symptoms' which pointed to all of these.

But although she accepted that Fred needed a statement she had always been reluctant to agree to further assessments by 'specialists'. She was aware that some people might think she was 'in denial'. Indeed, a speech therapist had said as much on her last visit to the clinic. There had been great pressure on her in the past 'to go down the autism route' but she could not see the point of doing this. She had previously gone through the process of diagnosis and intervention in relation to dyspraxia. Although this had all occurred some time ago, she could still remember many of the details, like having to complete a questionnaire etc.

At that time she was not sure what all this would imply for Fred's education but she was told that it would help to secure a 'special' placement or extra support for his inclusion in the mainstream. She had a copy of the questionnaire in her record. It included questions about whether he could use scissors; whether he bumped into chairs regularly or knew his left from his right; whether he could go to the shops on his own. She was also asked about his personality and behaviour – did he get frustrated easily, was he disorganized, did he rush through work, could he cope with direction to tasks by others, did he have difficulty dressing?

She had known for years that he was poorly coordinated and rather awkward, and both she and his teachers had worked out ways to address problems arising from this. He had been encouraged to use alternative means of recording, like a computer or a tape recorder. The school had provided him with a checklist for self-organization on an educational task. She herself liked the checklist idea because it reminded her of her own weakness – she felt she had a poor memory and would draw up a checklist for everything – holidays, walking tours, even what things to take with her when she visited a relative. She had encouraged him to draw up a list of items he needed for school and that he had to make sure were in his rucksack before he set off. He did this 'obsessionally' and never ever forgot anything, although the school reported that he had difficulty in finding things in his rucksack which he knew were there.

As for getting to school, she still had to take him, but over the years she had encouraged him to make journeys on his own, with some limited success, for instance, going to the local shops. She had worked up to this in easy stages. First, she waited outside a shop while he went in to make a simple purchase; next time she moved further away and the time after that a little further, and so on, until eventually she was nearly back at her front door. She never felt she could let him out of her sight, though, apart from when he was actually in the shop. This was all described in a caring way and certainly, when I first spoke to her, in a way which reflected her optimism and avoidance of a maudlin preoccupation with Fred's difficulties.

When the diagnosis of dyspraxia came back, Betty was at first pleased but later wondered if it had been worth it. She knew this was not the whole story. There were also other issues to do with speech and communication. Most of the intervention strategies suggested were 'too general, not fine-tuned enough', and in any case the teachers and herself had been working in this way with Fred for a number of years. He was already receiving support for his speech and she was continually aware of the need to develop his communication skills. Later, when the question of autism came up, she was reluctant to go through such a lengthy diagnostic process again because it would just mean that Fred would have another medical label attached to him. All she wanted to happen was what was already happening in school, but, as she put it, 'even more so'. She would be happy for the speech therapist and occupational therapist to give further advice, but she also wanted them to follow Fred's progress in more detail and consult her and the teachers more regularly.

Interviewing and Observing Fred

Fred was clearly uncomfortable in the one-to-one. To each question, he responded with a short phrase which seemed to imply that he thanked me but thought the interview should now be ended. It was the same phrase each time, although I could not quite make it out. It sounded something like this: 'Yes, that's OK. Thank you. I'm tired now.' He gave the impression of being rather remote and disinterested. As in all one-to-ones when things are not going well, I assume the situation may be distressing for the pupil and terminate the interview. From my discussion with the Jane, the SENCO, it became apparent that Fred exhibited similar behaviours with everyone, adult or pupil, in the one-to-one or in a group. She was not sure at the moment exactly what his needs were but communication – 'how we get through to each other' – was definitely a problem.

I felt I needed to get an impression of how Fred was currently coping in the classroom. A geography lesson was in full flow when I arrived. It was a small class and several pupils were sitting on their own. Three were in places where there was no one in the seat in front or behind. Fred was one of these. There was no TA support in this session but the teacher managed to get round to all the pupils during the course of the lesson and spent several minutes with Fred. He made no contribution in the oral part of the lesson, which involved a discussion about the train system in France. The other pupils were well motivated and most of them made what I thought were interesting contributions. According to Jane this was a 'good class' and that was one of the reasons he had been placed there.

During the class discussion, Fred just sat quietly seemingly not taking much interest in what was going on. He repeatedly flicked through his text book. Several other pupils were behaving in a similar way, constantly fiddling with pens, books, rucksacks – anything that was to hand. The teacher then set the pupils a task which involved drawing a map. They were allowed to work individually or in groups. Several pupils, including Fred, chose to work individually. I thought this task would be too difficult for him but he had a go at it. He spent longer on the task than other pupils and what he produced was not what the teacher had asked the class to do. It was a crude, inaccurate map of France with a railway line drawn out of all proportion. It looked like a piece of work done by a much younger child.

Afterwards I discussed Fred with Jane who felt he would have been quite able to grasp concepts in geography and other lessons but would not have been able to convey his understanding 'because it was not easy for him to express his thoughts either verbally or non-verbally'. Although he gave the impression of not being particularly interested in what the teacher was saying, 'he took in more than you might think'. The lesson I saw was, according to Jane, fairly typical. He participated to a degree, but the task set was not one that brought out his strengths. However, we both agreed this was not the main issue at this stage. It was sufficient at the moment to get him to attend school regularly and into the routine of going to classes. Peer relations were also important. How would other pupils act towards him and how would he react to them? The school had a 'buddy' system which was used mainly to facilitate the induction and integration of asylum seekers.

A 'Buddy' for Fred?

There was some doubt as to whether Fred would respond well to a 'buddy'. He did not seem to like attention from other pupils, even when this was friendly. He had never had any friends per se either in or outside of school. When he first arrived at the school, some pupils went out of their way to befriend him but he did not give them much back. In fact, Jane said that on one occasion she observed him get up and move away when a girl sat next to him and tried to engage him in conversation. She had also seen him turn his back on a speaker in the middle of a conversation. On several occasions pupils had attempted to escort him to class. He was a slow and ungainly walker, tended to lose his way in corridors and was very often late for class, but he indicated that he preferred to walk on his own.

Nevertheless, Jane felt she ought to pursue this. He was not a regular butt of bullies in the school, perhaps because he did not respond to bullying like the average victim. He just did not appear interested in what people said to him. However, he was bullied on occasion and she nominated several pupils in the class to be on 'bully watch'. These pupils knew that Fred did not want much social contact, and so they merely watched him from a distance, and reported back if they actually saw or suspected any bullying was taking place. Fred, of course, would probably not have told anyone even if he had been bullied, not because he was frightened of being thought a 'snitch', but because he would just not have wanted to talk to anyone about it. In the event, there was some bullying witnessed. Two rather immature pupils were seen walking beside him along a corridor imitating his walk. The 'bully watchers' did report this to Jane eventually but not before they had sorted it out themselves with the pupils concerned!

Fred Gets Agitated

The staff felt that Fred usually 'showed little emotion' around the school but had become very agitated recently in an incident that occurred at lunch time in the dining hall. When his dinner was being dished up, he asked the dinner server a question. She did not quite hear what he had said and asked him to repeat it, whereupon he picked up a knife and threw it at her, accompanying this with a stream of abuse, involving the 'f' word together with many other swear words. A teacher who was in the hall at the time said she had never heard him speak so loudly or so clearly!

Fred was not suspended but actually absented himself the next day, and the parents were asked to attend an interview with Jane and me. The head teacher knew of the incident, which was serious enough to warrant his direct involvement, but he thought in this instance the matter would be best dealt with by the SENCO.

Betty, Fred's mother, attended for interview on her own. She said she was very upset about the incident and could not apologize enough. Jane said that up until that point Fred had been making fairly good progress and seemed in his own way to be adapting to school life. The problem in this case seemed connected with his frustration at not being understood by the dinner server. Betty agreed. There must have been many problems of communication occurring daily which were frustrating for him. Perhaps he was 'bottling it all up' and the incident in the dining hall was 'the final straw'? If the build up of frustration was the problem, then what were the early signs? If the school knew these they could nip it in the bud, so to speak. What did Betty feel we should be looking out for?

Parents are usually in the best position to detect subtle changes of mood in their children. But Betty confessed she was increasingly unable to 'read' Fred's behaviour and was in no better position than anyone else in trying to identify signs of frustration. Of course, she realized this was an exaggeration. There were obviously some behaviours she could interpret better than teachers, but she wanted to emphasize that he was becoming more remote even from her, and periods when he withdrew into himself were becoming longer and more frequent.

Betty's Apology

At this point Betty became tearful. She apologized for not having told me at the first interview about her current worries. She said she felt matters were coming to a head. Her main worry was that they, i.e. Ralph and she, felt they were 'losing' Fred: 'He might be slipping away from us.' As the years went by, he was becoming less and less communicative. At one time she could have a conversation with him but now this was almost impossible.

She had discussed this over and over again with her husband. Both had made strenuous efforts in the past to get him interested in something outside 'his own little world'. Sometimes, he would latch on to a television programme or a sporting activity but only, she felt, if this was related to a current obsession, and even then it was not 'a normal sort of interest'. He took in information and talked about it, but could not really hold a proper conversation and never exuded enthusiasm. He showed no emotion until he got into these rages which were a fairly new development. Previously, he became distressed about what appeared relatively minor matters but which were important for him. Now, his outbursts of temper were still sparked off by seemingly trivial incidents but had become even 'wilder' and also more frequent.

She had maintained her optimism throughout his primary school years and had hoped his progress could be sustained in secondary school. It was only now that this optimism was, as she put it, 'fraying at the edges'. She had never been 'in denial', although she admitted she may have underestimated the 'depth' of his communication difficulties. Looking back on it, as the years had gone by, he had become less and less communicative. And she did not think this had anything to do with his having reached 'a bolshie adolescent stage'. It was a function of his wanting to become more self-contained and shun the rest of society.

But she repeated that she had never been 'in denial'. In fact, just the opposite. She was only too aware of his needs and the fact that there had been little sign of improvement at secondary school, was beginning to depress her. She wondered whether she was getting to the end of her tether. Fred was not able to 'give much back'. Sometimes he spoke to her as if she were a stranger. She tearfully repeated that she felt they were 'losing' him.

A Revised Statement?

I was not sure what to do at this point. I felt the only option was to think of further strategies to address Fred's educational needs. Would it be worth trying to secure more support for him via a revised statement? I could certainly advise the school to carry out an interim review (the annual review was several months away). But I felt we already had a clear view of Fred's educational needs, sufficient to know what needed to be done. Betty in any case did not want to pursue a revised statement, and I was not going to persuade her. Was this remiss of me? I did not think so, but there are many who would think otherwise.

I discussed Fred's progress with Jane and we decided on a course of action which involved a revised timetable for Fred with more time in the Special Needs Department, where he could receive one-to-one help from a TA, who would be advised by a speech therapist. The covert (!) buddy system was maintained. Fred's routes through school were identified and he would be supported in between as well as in lessons.

This new regime ran until the end of term. I thought things were going quite well, when to my surprise on the last day of term Fred declared that he wanted to go back to the special school.

Jane and I immediately arranged to see Fred and his parents. Again, only Betty turned up. Ralph, her husband, apparently was away on business, but as Betty pointed out he had not given up on Fred. He just felt he had little to contribute to the discussion. As far as he was concerned, Fred was Fred and that was it! He did not think he would change much in the future. He was not a great problem at home. In fact, apart from the occasional outburst of temper, which was usually to do with school, he got on with his life at home 'quietly', reading books, watching television, playing with his computer and looking after the dog. He did not want to do much with his dad or mum, although they always insisted that he accompany them on family trips. Sometimes, Ralph took him to a football match. Although he never showed much interest in a 'live' game or understood what was going on, he knew a lot of facts about football and was brilliant at football quizzes.

The Parents Look to Their Own Future

Betty said she had also accepted that Fred was not likely to change a great deal. A doctor had once told her that these things sometimes cleared up in adolescence but she knew now this was not going to happen. She repeated again her concern about his becoming more and more distant from her and Ralph: 'In the end there might be hardly any communication at all.' She still spent a great deal of time with him at home and she would see this continuing, but the last 12 years had been 'all about Fred and his needs' and she felt Ralph and she should 'think about ourselves a bit more'.

Although she loved Fred, she longed to have a normal child who could 'give her love back to her'. Recently she had applied to become a part-time TA, a job for which she felt well qualified. It would get her out of the house, give her more of a social life and enable her to relate to children whom she felt she could help. Although she would still love Fred and do everything she could for him, she also had to think about her own life. Her marriage was not under threat but she felt she and Ralph needed to do 'other things'.

As far as the place at the special school was concerned, Betty said she was reluctant to agree to this but if that was what Fred wanted, then 'so be it'. Although his mainstream placement had not been a waste of time and there had been periods when he seemed quite happy, she felt they had now come to 'the end of the road'. In a sense it would be easier for her. He would be picked up and brought home in a taxi, so she would not have any worries about getting him to and from school. There was a greater chance of his receiving one-to-one input from a speech therapist at the special school. He would be in a smaller class and in a simpler environment and so would have less difficulty getting around. But she felt all this did not really compensate for his (self) exclusion from the mainstream.

Coda

So that was that! Since he was still on the register of the special school, there would be no problem about re-admitting him. I was left wondering about my intervention and whether there was anything more I could have done. Communication with Fred was problematical but he had a number of strengths. He was capable of taking in information on any subject. He could read at a good level for his age and answer questions on what he had read; and was achieving at an average level in maths. Would it have been worth considering a placement in another kind of special facility, one that was more of an 'integrated resource' i.e. part of a mainstream school? On balance, I felt that Fred should have been given and given himself more time in the mainstream. I said this to Betty who said she would talk to Fred. I do not know whether she did or did not, but next term he returned to the special school.

Jane felt the parents had given up on inclusion and finally decided special school was the lesser of two evils. She also hinted she thought Betty and Ralph were beginning to give up on Fred himself. I was unsure, but I did not really agree with this view. I am always suspicious of parents who sacrifice everything for their children. There comes a point when the parents have to think about their own futures and their own lives. On the few occasions I saw Fred I got the impression that he did not necessarily want a lot of adult attention. Betty may have had to accept what Ralph may have already accepted – that Fred wanted less contact with them than they did with him. It was not really a question of 'losing him', so much as just allowing him to be himself. They could still cater for his needs whilst at the same time improve the quality of their own lives.

On reflection I felt there were other avenues in the mainstream school that could have been explored. Fred may have been able to benefit from a more intensive speech and language input carried out in a small group and linked with school curriculum support strategies. Betty and Ralph's concerns had to be taken seriously, but what the implications were for addressing Fred's educational needs were unclear. Although Fred chose to go back to the special school, I do not think this should have been taken at face value and just accepted as an inevitable outcome of his 'condition'. The special school told me they anticipated his return to them at some stage but I felt they had based their opinion on a very dated view of what support systems at secondary level might be capable. The idea of Fred withdrawing into himself was a key factor but I felt the school-generated aspects of this were poorly understood. If Betty and Ralph had themselves been encouraged to become more involved collaboratively (e.g. acting as 'listeners', say, in small group discussions in the SEN Department, as some other parents did) they might not have thought the 'end of the road' had been reached as far as inclusion was concerned.

Chapter 10
'That's Our Boy Down to a T'

Introduction

I received a phone call from Felicity Marsh, the parent of a child at Ferndale Primary School. Could I see her 9-year-old son, Ben, as soon as possible? Her doctor, a General Practitioner (GP), had told her he was dyslexic. She wanted to know what I intended to do about, how soon could he get a statement and how much one-to-one specialist help would he receive? I explained about our procedures – how I was happy to accept her referral but my next job was to ask Ben's school about his progress and take it from there. She agreed to this as long as it would not 'hold things up'.

I duly rang Paula Ferris, the SENCO at the school. I was told that Ben was not even on the special needs register! In fact she had considered putting him on last week but this would have been for his behavioural not his learning difficulties. He was slightly below his age level in literacy skills but there were plenty of pupils who were 'a lot worse' than him. I told her what Mrs. Marsh had told me and that it might be a good idea if she asked her to visit the school to discuss his progress. Paula agreed to this and I left a message on Felicity's answer phone saying she would be receiving an appointment from the school in the near future.

Sometimes parents accept this course of action and I never hear from them again. Others are less happy and ring me up to tell me so. If the latter, I know it will take time to sort out – time that I will have to take out of my allotted time for that school. However, I feel I cannot walk away from this situation. If a parent thinks his or her child is dyslexic and the school does not, then that child has a need which has to be addressed – a need to do with having a parent who is going to act on the belief that his or her child has a 'problem'.

Felicity Marsh rang me again a fortnight later. When was I going to see Ben? She reiterated her concern about 'things being held up'. I asked her about her visit to the school. She had had a long talk with the class teacher and Paula but she got the impression they did not believe her, and she wanted me to go into the school and tell them about dyslexia. I asked for more details about what the school had said to her. Apparently they did not think Ben had a 'serious learning problem' but she knew that he did. In comparison with his younger brother Aden – 'well, there's no comparison. Aden is way ahead of him.'

Ben 'Down to a T'

When I contacted the school later, Paula, as I suspected, felt that Felicity had not listened to a word she had said and seemed determined to get Ben statemented. Felicity knew all about this procedure. A friend, who also had a dyslexic child, had told her she should not be 'fobbed off' with all the 'jargon' about special needs registers and stages of the Code of Practice. She needed to cut through all this and demand her child be seen by an EP for an assessment. I told the school that I did not intend to see Ben at that point and if Felicity rang me up I would tell her this. I would, however, monitor his progress by checking the termly reviews.

I had no further contact with the school or Felicity for several weeks. Then I received a phone call from the school asking if I could go in as a matter of urgency because Ben had poked a fellow pupil in the eye with the 'blunt end of a biro'. There was no serious damage, and the parent of the child had accepted it was probably an accident (the pupils had been pretending to conduct an orchestra), but Felicity Marsh, when told of the incident, had withdrawn Ben from school, and demanded he be seen by the EP. The school had now become more concerned about Ben from a behavioural viewpoint and they were going to refer him anyway.

Felicity asked to see me on my own without a teacher present and I agreed to this. She said that she felt Ben's behaviour had taken a turn for the worse because he was frustrated and this was obviously due to the fact he had dyslexia and no one was doing anything about it. She had also looked up dyslexia on the Internet and found out that it was sometimes associated with ADHD or Attention Deficit Disorder (ADD), and that she recognized the symptoms in Ben – he was fidgety, could never sit still and often flew into a temper. She had brought with her printouts of articles by various 'specialists', which she thought I might like to read. I was then handed a checklist of the symptoms of ADHD on which she had ticked nearly all the boxes. She said she had spent hours on the Internet searching for information and had shared this with her husband and her other children who all agreed that some of the descriptions of disorders were Ben 'down to a T'.

An Odd Discrepancy

I said that the school had also become concerned about his behaviour, so I would certainly look into the situation. Would I be seeing Ben? In fact, yes, I probably would now see him. A week or so later I duly did. Felicity asked to be present and I said this was no problem. I have always felt it a desirable practice for parents to be present when I see pupils, although in fact it rarely happens.

Ben presented as a rather immature boy who was quite chatty in the interview. He was now pleased to be back in school. He told me about his friends, his interests and his brothers and sisters. I noted from the school referral form that he had become quite disruptive recently but there was no evidence that he could not sit still or was unable to concentrate on a task for long. Towards the end of our conversation, when asked about his behaviour in class, he said that he could not help it because 'I often go silly in the head'.

I decided to investigate his reading using the Neale Analysis of Reading Ability, which gave scores for Accuracy, Reading Rate and Comprehension. Ben seemed to enjoy doing this test and applied himself well, but I was rather surprised to find that although Reading Rate and Accuracy were commensurate with his age level (9 years), his Comprehension age was well below this, in fact at the 6-year-old level. Maybe Felicity was right after all? Maybe the school had got it wrong? I did not say this to her, but terminated the session saying that I would have further discussions with the teachers. Felicity wanted to know how long the statementing process would take and was clearly put out by my saying that if we went down this route it should not be hurried because we would want to gather as much information as possible.

Paula showed me Ben's academic profile. There was nothing in it which suggested a comprehension problem. He was reading a book at an appropriate level and when Paula had questioned him about the story, his answers had been satisfactory. He answered questions in class and made contributions to discussions. The disruptive behaviour was the main problem and this had got worse recently. She was very surprised by the results of the Neale test. Paula herself often administered this test, and so I asked her to check my results. To my surprise, she found no difference in Ben's scores on all three aspects of the test. His Comprehension was at the same level as Accuracy and Reading Rate. His spelling too was on a level with reading, and so there was no specific problem in that area.

What was going on here? I decided to make some suggestions about how the school might deal with Ben's disruptive behaviour, which was still at quite a low level despite the biro-in-the-eye incident, and to keep the situation under review. But I was uncertain about the best way forward. I had never previously experienced such a disparity between the school's assessment of reading and my own, and I felt I needed to see Ben again, perhaps on his own this time, which would be difficult because Felicity would now expect to be present.

Referral to the Cherry Tree Centre

I expected a phone call from Felicity but it never came. I was then off sick for a week and on my return managed to re-arrange my schedule to fit Ben in towards the end of the week. Felicity in fact was unable to keep this appointment and I rescheduled again for three weeks after that. This is often what happens in my kind of work. Diaries get so full that one cancelled appointment means a person cannot be seen again for several weeks by which time the situation has changed.

And the situation did change. Felicity was obviously frustrated that things were not moving fast enough from her point of view. She had probably thought that I was prevaricating, and had decided to take matters into her own hands and get Ben referred by her GP to a health-based clinical facility, the Cherry Tree Centre, for an assessment. This process did not take as long as it usually did and reports from the Centre had been sent to the LEA by the time I was due to see Ben again in school.

The reports were passed on to me, and I was astounded by the content. Not only did they confirm that Ben had 'severe attention and behavioural difficulties, possibly a reflection of ADHD', but they also suggested that he was 'a low functioning dyslexic', as indicated by his poor scores on reading tests and pattern of scores (most of which were in the low ability range) on an individual intelligence test, the Wechsler Intelligence Scale for Children (WISC 111). The LEA, on receipt of these reports, thought that the case should be referred to the Special Needs and Inclusion panel for a decision about whether a full statutory assessment should be carried out.

I was very unhappy about this decision but there was not much I could do about. I saw Ben again in school, on his own this time because Felicity failed to arrive on time for the appointment. He must have been fed up with the Neale test but I was curious as to how he would perform. I used a parallel form of the test, and this time Ben performed as well as on Comprehension as he did on Accuracy and Reading Rate. I told him he had done better than last time. Why was that? He said that it was 'easy' this time but would say nothing more. I was left wondering whether the previous form of the test had been genuinely more difficult for him. Or was it to do with lack of concentration? Or had he deliberately done badly?

The Full Picture

Felicity eventually turned up at the school accompanied by, Brian, her husband (Ben's stepfather), and her oldest daughter, Karen, who was at a college of further education. She explained that she had asked her husband and daughter to attend so that I would obtain a 'full picture' of what Ben was like at home. Felicity had the reports from the Cherry Tree Centre to hand and she asked if I had read them. I said I had and had been a little surprised because there appeared to be no evidence of many of these behaviours and learning difficulties in school. Also, I was now able to say that I could find no serious problems with his reading. Whereupon, all three accused me of siding with the school and only listening to what the school had to say. They knew that the school was wrong.

Brian, in fact, became quite angry, spoke about Ben's rights and said he would 'take matters further' if he did not get satisfaction. Karen, the daughter, was also vehement in her condemnation of the school and me. Her account, though, posed further questions about life in this family. During the course of her detailed description of what Ben was like at home, she gave as an example of his 'weird' behaviour that he sometimes wanted to sleep with mum. On these occasions, dad would end up in Ben's empty bed. It was usually in mum's bed in the morning that he counted his collections of finger nail clippings and other 'strange' things in matchboxes. I asked her if she had told anyone else about this and she said they knew all about it at the Cherry Tree Centre. What did she herself think? Well, Ben needed comforting because he was 'a very sick boy'.

The rest of her account contained descriptions of difficulties which had not been mentioned in any of the reports I had read. She talked about his speech – how he could not speak properly and kept mixing up his words. If anything was changed in the house or routines were disrupted, he used to panic and become fearful. This was an angle on Ben's behaviour I had not heard before. I thought, maybe unfairly, that it sounded as if she had memorized information from the Internet, but under the heading of autism rather than ADHD! I found out later that Karen wanted to follow in her mother's footsteps and work in some form of health care. She used to sit with her at the computer for hours looking up information about 'child disorders' on the Internet.

I told the family that as far as I and the school were concerned Ben's educational progress was satisfactory, and my report to the LEA would be along these lines. I appreciated that they saw things differently, and that they were concerned about his behaviour at home. The best course of action would be for them to return to their GP and ask for a referral to the Child and Family Psychiatric service where they, as a family, might be helped. They were not pleased by this suggestion. Felicity accused me of ignoring the mounting evidence that it was Ben who had the 'disorders', not her or any one else in the family.

The Question of Abuse

At this point I was worried that the situation at home was more serious than the school or anyone else had realized. I kept turning Karen's comments over in my mind. The family's determination to get support for their view that Ben was 'disordered' was a real concern. I was wondering about 'abuse'– was the family covering something up? How should I pursue this? The school was a little suspicious because of the parents' attitude towards it but other than that there was no evidence to go on. Ben was not the happiest of boys and his behaviour at times was a cause for concern but on most days he was on an even keel and got on with life in much the same way as most other children in the school. Social Services had never been involved with the family. The clinical professionals who had seen Ben for assessments had interviewed the parents. In one report it referred to Felicity being 'overanxious', but no other questions were raised.

I explained all this to the LEA who were inclined to support the school's view and mine, but said the reports from other professionals that mother had obtained could not be ignored. I had no option but to go back to the school and repeat some of the psychological tests carried out by psychologists in the Cherry Tree Centre. I was reluctant to do this for three reasons. First, it would mean putting Ben through yet more tests, and although he might have enjoyed this, why should he have to miss yet more schooling for no good reason? Second, a technical point, repeating tests such a short time after a previous administration could affect the validity of the results. Third, my time allocation for that school was almost used up, and there were plenty of other children the SENCO wanted me to see whose needs, she felt, were greater than Ben's. On the last point, of course, it could be argued that in view of the attitude of the family, Ben's situation was more dire.

When Felicity was informed that I was to see Ben for a further assessment she demanded to be present but I said that, although I would see her afterwards, it would be too distracting for Ben if she were there. She queried my decision because she had always been present when Ben had been tested previously. She said she had been upset about my seeing him the last time without her being there. I had to give in on this. Insisting she not be present may have been construed as my trying to hide behind a professional smokescreen. Also, although it was unlikely that Ben would have become upset, he just might have, and that would have made a difficult situation worse.

Was Ben Faking it?

I had no option but re-test Ben on the WISC test with Felicity present. Ben began quite well on the general knowledge and psychomotor subtests but on the comprehension test he started to say 'don't know' to questions which I felt he should have been able to answer. On a test of spatial reasoning involved manipulation of blocks he gave up quickly on the easiest items. He performed slightly better on two other performance tests before again giving up quickly on a verbal reasoning and a vocabulary test. Overall, his scores were similar to those obtained by the other psychologist. In terms of age-related measurements on this norm referenced test he came out in the bottom 1% on several subtests.

I was puzzled by these results. Ben had probably faked the reading test, but deliberately getting low scores on an IQ test and not giving the game away was a much more difficult business. But I could not accept these scores at face value. Either Ben had faked it or the test was just not valid in his case. I noted how his personality seemed to change in Felicity's presence. He seemed less mature and more dependent.

I had had previous experience of 'sick' families who selected one of their own as a repository for their own anxieties and insecurities. Indeed, I had once seen a girl who obtained similar scores to Ben and whose mother thought she would never have been able to cope in mainstream secondary but who had in fact thrived in that environment. As in that case, my own position was difficult. I had to defend a view which my own evidence seemed to contradict! My report on Ben was a bit of a mishmash. I did not include the actual test scores but said they concurred with those obtained previously. However, I stressed the results were probably not a reliable indication of Ben's 'functional capabilities' in class. His literacy skills were up to speed and his numeracy was only just below what one might expect for a boy of his age. His behaviour had been a cause for concern recently but socially there were no obvious problems – he had several friends and was not the isolate his parents insisted he was.

Felicity received a copy of this report and rang the LEA saying that it confirmed that Ben needed to go to a special school both for his learning and his ADHD. The LEA was in a difficult position here and could see an appeal looming but insisted that the main evidence was equivocal and they could not at that point issue a statement.

Ben Continues to Make Progress

Things went quiet after this. I expected the parents to taken action and appeal against the LEA decision, but they did not. I was relieved in one sense in that it would mean I could get on with other work in that school. But I was still concerned about what might be happening in that family, and how it might be affecting Ben. This exemplifies one of the great frustrations of the job. I suspected the family itself had deep-seated needs which should have been addressed, but unless there was an issue which directly impinged on Ben's adjustment to school, I could not devote more time to the case. All I could do was to ask the school to keep a watching brief and inform me or Social Services if they felt the situation was deteriorating.

Several weeks later the school informed me that the parents wanted another meeting to discuss Ben. I asked the school for an update on Ben and they informed me that things had not changed. He continued to make progress. His behaviour was still problematical but not seriously so. They were providing him with no extra help. There had been one development, however. Ben's school attendance had dropped off recently, not seriously, but just enough for enquiries to be made. They were not sure why the parents wanted to see me. I thought maybe they had obtained some more 'evidence' from another agency and wanted to submit this to the LEA.

Felicity arrived for interview accompanied by Karen. She said she had been back the Cherry Tree Centre and they had agreed Ben should be statemented, even though the psychologist had thought the school report had suggested he was making some progress. Reading between the lines I suspected that the Centre had begun to realize there were certain anomalies and the 'case' was more complex than they had at first thought. Perhaps that was the reason the parents had not taken further action regarding an appeal against the LEA's decision.

Another Disorder: Pathological Demand Avoidance (PDA)

I was anticipating yet more complaints from Felicity, and this was what happened, but her description of what she saw as the problem had a new twist to it. Apparently she now felt that the Centre had got 'some of it right' but had missed some crucial aspects of Ben's disorders. Felicity had by this time reached the stage of regarding me as someone who was not an expert on 'disorders'. Had I heard of PDA? I had but I wanted to know what she meant by it, and how she had come across it. She said she thought Ben had autism as well as dyslexia and ADHD but no one agreed with this. Karen, however, had looked autism up on the net and had come across this 'condition' – PDA – which was like autism in some ways but very different in others. It was another disorder the symptoms of which again fitted Ben 'down to a T'. From an early age, he had been very 'obstinate', and this was not just 'normal naughty behaviour', it was 'obsessional'. What did she mean by that? 'He couldn't stop doing it; it seemed to be his main goal in life.' She appreciated it was not a disorder many people knew much about and that was why they had missed it at the Centre. But there was another Centre she had read about which specialized in this particular disorder, and she was hoping to get Ben assessed there.

The previous diagnoses seemed to have come under closer scrutiny at the CT Centre and I felt Felicity may have been searching for another 'coat-hanger' for her and the family's beliefs about Ben. She clearly wanted this on the agenda of our meeting and I said I would be happy to talk about it but I stressed that I also wanted to discuss Ben's behaviour at home and at school, and why there appeared to be such a difference. The family still did not think there were any discrepancies. As far as they were concerned the school had just got it wrong.

I listened to what they had to say and then tried to give a more balanced account of Ben's behaviour, some of which I hoped they might have felt able to acknowledge. He could be quite assertive and could stick up for himself, and although this was 'normal' he could on occasion 'overdo it' mainly because he lacked experience. His truculent behaviour might have reflected a phase of his development. It was better to be like this than too passive and to 'bottle everything up'. Felicity agreed but said that it was far worse than I could ever have imagined. He had been like it for a very long time and, of course, there were lots of other things I did not know. The rest of the conversation continued in this vein and superficially we seemed to be getting nowhere, with Felicity and Karen continuing to counter my views with 'evidence' from home.

However, there were some hopeful signs. At least, at an emotional level, I felt they were more willing to engage with alternative views, which previously they had not even been prepared to listen to. Also, there was some indication that Felicity was beginning to acknowledge it was not just Ben who had 'problems'. When I mentioned the attendance issue, she said she was aware of this but had been a 'bit depressed' recently, slept in herself and forgotten to wake Ben. Yes, Ben did sometimes end up in her bed when he had had a 'nightmare or something'. I quickly mentioned that it might be possible for the EWO to visit her at home to discuss this, fully expecting her to refuse, but to my surprise she agreed.

I heard nothing more from the head teacher of the school or Felicity after that. It was the end of the year and the school was just about to break up. The SENCO had not mentioned Ben on my final visit. Next term, this school would not be on my patch.

Coda

I was very dissatisfied with my involvement with this family. When I contacted the Cherry Tree Centre I was unable to get hold of the psychologist who had seen Ben. I had worked with the Centre before but two-way effective communication had always been difficult to establish. Philipsen (1995) has suggested that the actions of different professionals can be coordinated even when there is disagreement on 'meanings', but I have always found this problematical. A way forward would be for everyone to accept a shared view of practice as reflective, open, enquiry-oriented and collaborative. But there have historically been many constraints on the development of this model stemming from a variety of factors – the different epistemological orientations both within and between professional groups, the lack of time, and the differences between groups in terms of power and status. Genuine challenges to each others' views, so necessary for the accomplishment of negotiated meanings (see Mehan, 1983; Salmon and Faris, 2006), have been few and far between in my experience.

Negotiating with the Centre would in any case have been a frustrating business. A great deal of time would have been taken up with a discussion of conflicting assessments and different views of the family's, particularly mother's, attitudes. I felt the Centre had obviously given too much credibility – initially, at any rate – to Felicity's interpretation of events. Later, there was some evidence that they had begun to see the situation in a different light, but by then things had moved on.

What could have been done to help this family? They could have undoubtedly benefited from intensive family therapy of a kind beyond the brief of an EPS. Perhaps Ben was a scapegoat, perhaps the family were projecting on to him their own anxieties and insecurities? It would have been easy to identify Felicity as the main protagonist in all this. Her views seemed to count for more in the family group and she did most of the talking in the interviews. Much of the research in this area seems to focus on mothers. For example in their study of Munchhausen's syndrome by proxy, Adshead and Bluglass (2005) describe attachment representations in a cohort of mothers with this syndrome, finding evidence of insecure attachment relationships in their own childhoods. But this approach shifts the emphasis on to mother's psychology as a major factor and away from any detailed consideration of interactive processes in the family.

I felt the school should have reviewed the way they worked with the parents. Their approach was overly influenced by their view that rather than being helpful partners, Felicity and the rest of the family were undermining what they – the school – were doing to help Ben. I could have played a greater role here in establishing a dialogue between the school and the parents. The school should have seized every opportunity to 'keep the conversation going' with the parents. They could clearly not be 'neutral', but should have tried to deploy a language of 'neutrality' in relation to certain content (see Stancombe and White, 2005). The aim would have been to pick out the positives in family talk, few though these were, and just listen in an apparently non-judgmental way to the rest. I felt my final interview with Felicity and Karen suggested a possible way forward along these lines, but I never managed to get this across to the school.

Chapter 11
Conclusion: Promoting Inclusion via the Creation of Democratic Learning Communities

In the LEA in which I worked, there were clearly many barriers to the successful implementation of an inclusion policy. However, what constituted a barrier, why it existed and the best way to overcome it were all open to interpretation. In Chapter 1, I attempted to identify the genesis of my interpretations – the values on which they were based and the 'traditions of enquiry' in which they were located, traditions which were critical and radical in the sense that they involved analyses which problematized much that would have been taken for granted by more conventional and 'conservative' advocates of inclusion. For instance, they involved questions about the discourse of special educational needs itself – including the contribution of support professionals like EPs – and how it could be construed as inherently anti-inclusionary; and questions about the education system which was regarded as dominated by priorities which worked against inclusion. For many critics like me these defects were rooted in factors beyond the school context and were linked to the pervasive social inequalities and injustices endemic to the kind of society in which we lived.

Inclusion and Reconstruction

For the critical EP, inclusion is not just about the integration of pupils identified as having special educational needs. It involves working for changes in a school's values, priorities and curricula so that the education of all children will be improved. The special/normal distinction (and other distinctions like that between the pastoral and the academic) are seen as barriers to the realization of this goal in that ultimately they are based on the assumption that it is not the system itself which is the problem. For the radical critic, it is the educational needs of most children that are not being met in schools where a competitive and meritocratic ideology is dominant. Children who disrupt the smooth running of this system are defined as having problems which they 'bring with them' to school rather than as problems that have been partly constructed by the school in the first instance. To put this another way, schools have failure built into them and then identify the 'cause' of failure in the deficiencies of individual children. Integration implies that certain pupils are deviant, dysfunctional for the system and need to be incorporated, whereas inclusion implies that it is the system which is dysfunctional for the education of most children and needs to be reconstructed.

Such reconstruction in my view involves a vision of schools as democratic, inclusive learning communities, an ideal which I hope guided my interventions and which I shall flesh out later in this chapter. In the stories I have described how I tried to engage with various 'discourses of remediation', like the SEN and the pastoral discourses, in ways which were deconstructive and pointed to alternatives. All the schools had SEN policies but I tended to be more involved with these in the primary than the secondary school where interventions had as much to do with pastoral as SEN policies and structures. What all these 'remedial' policies had in common was an emphasis on individual or small-scale structural rather than 'whole school' and 'whole curriculum' solutions.

The Role of the Educational Psychologist

The reader will have to judge whether the interventions described in the stories were consonant with the wider aim of reconstructing schools as democratic learning communities. From my own point of view, given the schools' expectations of my role and function as an EP, the constraints were evident from the very first day of my appointment when I had to 'pick up' ongoing 'cases'. I learned of decisions taken in schools with reference to my role without my being aware of this at the time. I found out a school had not referred a child with a putative 'behavioural difficulty' because they had decided not to go down the statementing 'route', implying that my role was solely to expedite this formal process. When obtaining parental agreement to a referral, a head teacher or SENCO often interpreted my role in a way of which I did not approve. Schools often assumed that I was an expert in ADHD or autism or that I wanted to see a child for individual assessment using tests. These communication problems were ameliorated after good working relationships were established but they were never completely resolved.

The problem for the critical EP working from the 'inside' is how to pursue his or her own practice in a way which contributes to the construction of an alternative discourse whilst not inadvertently reinforcing the 'discourses of remediation', like the SEN and pastoral discourses. Will so-called alternatives be accommodated within these discourses in ways which leave the latter's central concepts and principles intact; will radical action turn out to be about limited 'reform' rather than 'radical change' or will it even be 'regressive'? Discourses work in mysterious ways. Their rules are more likely to be implicit than explicit.

The 'Baggage of History'

As a critical EP in a reforming local authority, I had doubts about whether the 'baggage of history' could be as easily offloaded as some of my colleagues imagined. In relation to the SEN discourse, for example, the very existence of special structures – a Code of Practice, a statementing process, special schools and various special administrative arrangements and services – were dependent on the assumption that special educational needs were 'attached' to individual pupils and could be identified uncontroversially and 'neutrally' by positivist experts. The EP was one of these experts, arguably the most important in that he or she was often regarded as the most 'scientific' and objective. In pushing for an alternative discourse (which at the very least would require that the 'problem' was located in the 'situation' rather than 'within the child'), the critical EP had to argue against the validity of the very tools e.g. IQ tests which historically reflected some of the core concepts of his or her professional expertise.

However, despite the obvious constraints, it seems to me that working as an EP was not inherently more compromising for a radical than say working as a teacher or, for that matter, an academic educationalist. (What could be more constraining than SATs or the Research Assessment Exercise (RAE)?). The EP was expected to identify appropriate teaching/learning strategies and to support teachers in the implementation of these, in addition to assessing children and producing reports for official purposes. Input around these strategies was subject to constant evaluation and negotiation as these stories indicate, and there was plenty of opportunity to challenge the language, concepts and principles of the 'discourses of remediation'.

Critically Engaging with the Sen Discourse

In relation to SEN policies, I saw my task as trying to work in a way which did not eschew the language of need but perceived needs as always relative to the interactional context in which they were expressed. Critically engaging with the special needs discourse 'from the inside out' meant identifying educational needs but without resorting to the special terminology of that discourse; it meant retaining my power as a player within the SEN framework but only in order that my critical input would carry more weight; it meant following the rules of the discourse at the same time as trying to undermine them. My starting point was always to be critical of the assumption that pupils with special educational needs could be distinguished from pupils who had 'normal' educational needs (see Priestley, 1999) and that this discursive construction often involved a 'label to do with abnormality' (see Armstrong, 2003, p. 132) or 'disorder' which had implications for how the former's needs were spoken about, how and by whom they were treated, how they were perceived by others, and how they perceived themselves.

I asked similar questions to those posed by other radical inclusionists, like those, for example, who drew up the influential Index for Inclusion (Booth et al., 2000); for example, was there an attempt in this school to minimize the categorization of students as 'having special educational needs'; were students who were categorized as 'having special educational needs' seen as individuals with differing interests, knowledge and skills rather than as part of an homogeneous group (see p. 70); and did statements of 'special educational needs' build on the strengths of students and possibilities for their development, rather than concentrate on identifying deficiencies? (see p. 71).

Radicals, of course, may be self-critical and may disagree amongst themselves about various actions taken and compromises made. For instance, it is perhaps clearer why the first two questions from the Index quoted above may lead to a radical change of thinking than the third which seems merely to identify relatively uncontroversial criteria for improving statements. But the context is all. One can imagine situations where pointing to a 'deficit bias' in a particular statement could well be perceived as a serious challenge to the preconceptions of powerful experts whose reports were an important part of the evidence taken into account by a local authority.

Experiencing the Challenge

The stories demonstrate how the challenge of critically engaging with the 'discourses of remediation' was experienced – what aspects were of particular concern, what actions were taken and why, and what problems were encountered. All my decisions and actions involved making judgements in the light of circumstances – some taken in haste, some after a lengthy period of deliberation; some based on hunches, others on ideas from the research literature; some involving acceptable compromises, others compromises that were more problematical – in short a whole panoply of actions, reactions and interactions in a dynamic and ever changing context.

There was never an easy way forward. What would be the medium or long-term consequences of actions that appeared beneficial in the short term? Would actions taken in the interests of an individual also be in the interests of the group, and vice versa? What would be the wider implications of a particular recommendation? Obviously a great deal depended on the context. For example, advising a school to identify narrow behavioural targets (of the kind criticized in some of these stories, see e.g. Chapter 7) may have been acceptable in exceptional circumstances and when no general theory of learning was being invoked. However, in a situation, where a behaviouristic, skills-oriented target culture was dominant, such suggestions might have merely served to reinforce the highly reductive view of learning pervasive in the school as a whole.

Although I was critical of the target-driven culture, even in relation to Individual Education Plans (IEPs), I regularly became involved in discussing targets with teachers partly in the hope that I could eventually raise questions about the way teaching and learning were organized in classrooms. Sometimes this did work out (Chapter 7), sometimes (see Chapter 5) it did not. Or take the example of a strategy like 'circle of friends' (see Chapter 8). This could be regarded as a form of behavioural control that 'worked' for a particular pupil at a certain 'moment' in a certain context. But if this strategy was never envisaged in broader terms as part of a curriculum process, there would have been a danger of it merely being a 'tool' for controlling pupils in the interests of the status quo.

Since compromises were inevitable, it was often a question of judging which was the lesser of two evils. Some compromises were judged to be 'better' than others because they kept more possibilities open for change in the future and seemed less 'harmful' for pupils in the present. For example, I felt that, although I was (and still am) opposed to the idea of LSUs, in the circumstances it was better to get involved in their development than to opt out (as I could with difficulty have done). I thought it was possible to develop them in a way which could have led to changes in pedagogy, curriculum and structures in the mainstream. Chapter 2 demonstrates how this goal was not achieved, Chapter 3 how progressive links were made between pastoral and academic structures via LSUs. In Chapter 6, I describe how I 'gave in' to the school's demands that a child be assessed by me and a report written for the LEA because I thought it would be in the child's interests for me, in this instance, to be fully involved in the statementing process.

Sustaining the 'Vision'

My 'vision' of a democratic, inclusive learning community kept me critically alert and motivated. It enabled me to judge what might have been an appropriate way forward in a particular situation and to tentatively evaluate my actions and those of others in the light of certain principles and understandings. It helped me to see where the current system was failing and what needed to be done about it (see later). However, it is important to emphasize that for me what sustained this 'vision' from day-to-day was not some abstract theory of education, democracy or inclusion. Were this the case it would have been difficult to avoid feelings of pessimism, since my interventions nearly always fell short of what I had hoped for, and even when they were 'successful', in most cases, made only a small difference in terms of achieving overall goals. There were numerous constraints stemming from factors both within and outside school. I met teachers whose stress-related illnesses seemed obviously linked to policies which they felt undermined their professional identity. I also met parents living in dire circumstances for whom there was little help available; and pupils who were alienated, bored and frustrated by a test-driven, ill thought-out curriculum.

What sustained the 'vision' and gave me hope was the embrace of a humanist discourse, which enabled a deepening appreciation of the humanity of individual teachers and pupils as I worked with them over a period of time. There was something about the way certain teachers, particularly in primary schools, spoke about children that reflected a deep care and concern for the latter's well-being. Such teachers knew how to relate to children to get the best out of them, but they also knew that this was not all there was to a teaching relationship. Children needed to be enjoyed, appreciated and 'loved' for who they were in the here and now not just for what they might become in the future. Such teachers wanted to talk to you about their charges and wanted you to know everything about them not just about their educational achievements or lack of them. They took delight in what children said and did.

They often knew their brothers and sisters whom they may have taught in the past or would be teaching in the future. They spoke to parents regularly, not just when there was a problem.

There were many such teachers in the schools on my patch and they were always very welcoming of professionals like me. I got to know them as people as well as teachers. They would talk to me about anything and everything – about their own children, about their own anxieties and illnesses, about education and the 'world' generally, about sport, films on television, cooking and holidays! I looked forward to going into their schools. When I was down, they kept my spirits up and my hope alive. In a sense they supported me as much as I did them.

We often had disagreements over 'inclusion'. Many of them claimed to support policies to which I was opposed but I always had a strong feeling that, in the final analysis, they would know what was and was not in children's best interests and act accordingly. They did not always use words like 'inclusion', 'democracy', 'diversity', 'difference', 'labelling' but their understanding of children and their relationships with them were imbued with a sense of the value of the individual and the importance of mutual respect.

Then, of course, there were the pupils – always full of surprises, always expressing their idiosyncrasies in ways one did not anticipate, and yet on occasion determined to be predictable! Each, like all of us, was a mixture of the undesirable and the desirable – naïve and ungracious one minute, socially astute and good-natured the next. Imran's 'wordly wisdom' (Chapter 8) was as insightful as it was shocking and Peter's (Chapter 2) use of argument as clever as it was 'deviant'. Was David's (Chapter 5) offer to clean up the staffroom table connected with his later request for a biscuit? If so, what a display of initiative! When Kirsty (Chapter 3) handed me a tissue from a box of tissues supposedly meant for 'clients', neither of us could suppress a smile – she was as much aware of the irony as I was. When Sam (Chapter 7), faced with an awkward question, came out with 'I don't know but I shall look it up', both the teacher and I were so pleased to be so surprised.

Towards a Broader Conversation on Inclusion

As I have suggested above, the 'vision' of a democratic learning community helped me to evaluate my interventions and identify how they might contribute to the development of such communities. The stories describe interventions made at the individual level triggered by school concerns about the behaviour and/or learning of particular pupils. But most of them involved conversations with teachers which went beyond immediate issues relating to these pupils and had wider implications for policy and practice in the school. Over a period of time, I could see how my input did or did not make an impact on a teacher's classroom practice, on SEN policy in the school or on broader policy developments.

However, like most critical professionals, I feel I could have done better. It was not that some of these interventions did not make a difference, but with hindsight

I feel I could have made more of them. In particular, I could have made a greater effort to talk to head teachers and staff about how exactly I saw my input contributing to the version of 'inclusion' which guided my actions. These broader conversations would have been difficult to arrange. The teachers were busy people who worked under pressure in a complex, dynamic environment. They were happy to talk about support for individual pupils, but if they felt that my input involved 'just another meeting' they were less keen.

Linking Up With the Curriculum

A way forward would have been to link intervention more explicitly to curriculum development in the school and class context. This would have been an unusual move because the EP is not typically associated with the curriculum. He or she may make recommendations about how a particular child should be handled or what targets within an established curriculum might be appropriate or even about how teaching and learning might be organized in the classroom as a whole to address the needs of pupils described as having 'learning or behavioural difficulties'. But none of this is seen as a contribution to curriculum development per se, which is still generally thought of as involving the development of 'content' in the National Curriculum.

And so a starting point might have been to show how everything a child learns and experiences in school is part of the curriculum. Rearranging maths groups to facilitate the inclusion of a pupil is as much about the citizenship curriculum as it is about the maths curriculum. Raising a child's self-esteem by teaching science in a way that plays to her strengths is as much about the PSHE as it is about science. Identifying IEP targets in collaborative group work in English is as much about the moral curriculum as it is about English.

The Learning Curriculum

The EP is quite well placed to make these kinds of links. Many of their discussions with teachers involve what might be described as 'the learning curriculum' i.e. 'messages' conveyed to pupils about themselves as learners by teaching them in certain ways. These processes can vary according to the perceived needs of the child and the aims of teaching in a specific context. The development of 'the learning curriculum' involves identifying the 'messages' and helping the child and the teacher reflect upon them.

There has been much discussion in the past about an appropriate pedagogy for pupils perceived as having SEN and a continuing debate about whether or not there is a distinctive SEN pedagogy. In one of the most exhaustive reviews of effective pedagogy for such pupils, Norwich and Lewis (2001) conclude that although there is no evidence to support a distinctive SEN pedagogy, there is some justification in talking about 'adaptations to common teaching approaches, which have been called specialized adaptations, or "high density" teaching.' (p. 314). They propose the notion of a 'continua of teaching' which implies a difference of degree rather than kind. The various 'strands of teaching' that can be considered along a continuum might be to do with the amount of practice, overlearning, structure, visual examples, success experience, breaking down into small steps, 'bottom-up' approaches, experience of transfer, and careful checking of preparedness for the next stage of learning. A particular programme may include all or just some of these. They are approaches which could, with a lesser intensity, be used with all pupils. Pupils perceived as SEN might need common teaching approaches at some times and special adaptations at others.

There are, indeed, many 'strands' to the teaching/learning process. It seems to me it is not just a question of adapting some strands and not others, but also making sure that the strands selected are not just confined to those required for skill training. We have to be careful to avoid 'adaptation' which in effect involves an exclusive learning curriculum conveying 'messages' about fundamental differences between SEN pupils and others in the way they learn and what they should therefore learn about learning. The danger is that SEN pupils will receive teaching in a 'high density' way which may teach them 'skills' but do nothing to enhance their autonomy. What pupils learn about themselves as learners may not be conducive to their development as independent learners. Teaching using high levels of practice to mastery will not lead to mastery of the learning curriculum, unless it also involves encouraging the pupil to reflect on processes. In teaching pupils to see themselves as 'better' learners the following, for example, might be added to the list of 'strands': each learner to be given the opportunity to acquire responsibility for his or her own learning, and to learn how to seek help from and actively help other learners.

Treating pedagogy as a learning curriculum would also require helping pupils and teachers understand what did and what did not help learning in the school context. The story in Chapter 7 gives some idea of how this might be achieved in practice but I should have spent more time exploring how these ideas could have been more widely applied in the school.

The Emotional Curriculum: A Way Forward?

The general thrust of these broader conversations with teachers will not be unfamiliar to EPs. They relate not just to a 'learning curriculum' but also to the 'emotional curriculum' and 'emotional literacy'. Versions of the latter vary, but they usually include collaborative approaches to learning for individuals and organizations – working together for a common purpose, trusting each other, sharing experiences and feelings, learning from each other, deepening people's understanding of each other and what is happening in the organization, facilitating communication characterized by mutual listening and response, and developing organizations that value members as persons (see Antidote, 2003). Many EPs regard 'emotional literacy' as an important goal of their work with teachers as well as pupils and parents, and many would feel their professional knowledge would include sufficient expertise in this area to provide a useful input to schools. I certainly think this is a move in the right direction. It potentially involves radical changes to the whole curriculum and the development of relationships throughout the school which are consonant with a democratic, inclusive philosophy.

Many approaches based on some notion of 'emotional literacy' however, suffer from three main weaknesses. First, because of the emphasis 'emotion' and 'feeling' the impression is often given that how people feel about 'policy' is more important than working to change it. I have heard head teachers, for example, encourage their staff to 'get things off their chest' about SATs, share their problems and support each other, but without any prospect of SATs themselves being significantly altered. In short, the only change involved is in the degree to which people feel more comfortable about accepting the new status quo. This is 'emotional literacy' used as a management tool. Second, 'emotional literacy' can easily go hand in hand with the development of a therapeutic ethos which, as Ecclestone (2004, p. 112) argues, can produce a 'diminished view of people and low expectations about people's capacity for resilience and autonomy'. As with certain versions of the psycho-medical model, there is a tendency to overemphasize pupils' vulnerability at the expense of their potential for agency and thus to medicalize their problems. Third, and in the context of the present discussion, the most important weakness is that the 'whole school strategies' promoted by the concept do not include an analysis of what is wrong with the current curriculum – other than that it is too cognitively oriented – or of the sociological and political factors that would facilitate or constrain the development of an alternative.

The Curriculum and Democratic 'Communities of Practice'

However, I am suggesting that the 'emotional curriculum' would be a useful starting point for the development of inclusive policies provided it was socially constructed as 'a community of practice'(see Lave and Wenger, (1991) and involved an interpretation of community as democratic as opposed to, say, hierarchical. The curriculum for such a community would be critical and self-reflexive, valuing a certain form of learning and facilitative of an understanding of this amongst pupils and teachers. It would be an inherently inclusive community in the sense of catering for diversity and difference, and giving expression to the 'voices' of all individuals and groups, within the parameters suggested in Chapter 1. In line with the more progressive definitions of the 'emotional curriculum' (as expressed, for example, in the Antidote literature referred to earlier), learning in such communities would be dialogical and require the establishment of a 'bond' between teachers and learners.

Learning would be viewed as 'situated', thus as an intrinsically social and context-dependent activity. Whereas traditional psychological theories focus on the solitary individual, the universal principles of cognitive development and thought detached from action, the situated approach assumes that learning arises from social interaction in specific social settings and can only be understood in terms of the local and particular rather than the universal. For proponents of situated learning, like Lave and Wenger (1991), learning is about developing an identity via participation in a 'community of practice'.

A dialogical approach to teaching models for the pupil a particular stance towards knowledge, one that involves probing assumptions, asking questions, communicating with others etc. But dialogue in a 'community of practice' is something more than a pattern of cognitive interchange. As Burbules (1993) acknowledges, productive dialogue involves intellectual factors but it also thrives on 'emotions' or moral qualities such as hope, affection, trust and respect which are crucial to the 'bond' that sustains a dialogical relation and the relations of 'belonging' in an inclusive community context. Without such a bond, it is doubtful if the pupil's interest could be held over a period of time, since, as experienced teachers know, pupils often lose interest in the 'argument' of a topic, and appeals have to be made to other commitments e.g. to affection for and trust of the teacher.

The value of such relations is explicitly acknowledged in a 'learning and emotional curriculum' which would clearly have to be a spiral curriculum where content and method were appropriate for the age, level of understanding and experience of the pupil. The aim would be to develop pupils' awareness of dialogical learning – how they perceived themselves as learners, how they interacted with parents, peers and teachers in ways that promoted learning, what barriers there were to dialogical learning in school and outside school, and what action should be taken to make their school a genuine democratic 'community of practice'.

Barriers to Learning

The 'learning and emotional curriculum' would be critical in the sense that it would involve the identification of barriers to the development of democratic learning 'communities of practice' at macro, meso or micro levels. Explanations at a macro level relate to society-wide and indeed worldwide structures and it is important to think in terms of these broader influences in order to understand why change at local level in one institution or one community is so problematical. Bottery (2004) refers to dysfunctionalities stemming from the wider context of market and state, from class, gender, race and other forms of discrimination, and in general from the imperatives of the global economy. However, in practical terms, it is important to act locally and this means engaging with issues at the meso (i.e. school) and micro (i.e. class group and individual) level.

It is sometimes claimed that 'communities of practice' themselves are consonant with the needs of the global market in that they are based on the kind of collaborative and pragmatic learning required to make organizations more effective and profitable (see Lesser and Storck, 2001). But much of the thinking about schools as learning communities has been driven by those who (see Bottery, 2004) see the need for an alternative to the instrumentalist imperatives of the market in education which have become entrenched in recent years. From league tables to individualistic teaching approaches to the governance of schools the thrust of state policy has been in the direction of opening up the school system to competition and embedding market values in the curriculum itself. The suggestion that all this is being done in a way which is aligned with democratic educational values must be treated with scepticism in the light of growing evidence of increasingly unfair and unequal outcomes (Jackson and Segal, 2004).

The National Curriculum

How does the current National Curriculum in England measure up as a curriculum for democracy, inclusion and community? I am concerned here with the 'bigger picture' of curriculum reform rather than with the specifics of the contributions of EPs and other support workers. But I assume that support strategies can help to realize inclusion if they go hand in hand with changes on a broader front.

The National Curriculum, despite all the changes that have taken place in recent years, has always been a barrier to inclusion. There has been never been a serious attempt to relate the subject disciplines and the way they are taught to general principles, like those identified in the first section of the Education Reform Act (1988), which established the National Curriculum and referred to a balanced and broadly-based curriculum which promoted 'the spiritual, moral, cultural, mental and physical development of pupils at the school and of society' (see DES, 1989). As I have pointed out elsewhere (see Quicke, 1995), it has just been taken for granted that a National Curriculum composed of subject disciplines would realize these broader educational goals. But subject knowledge can be and often is structured and taught in ways which undermine rather than promote pupils' moral, cultural, emotional and cognitive engagement in forms of learning which would enhance the collaborative and community ideals associated with inclusion.

Although the NC programmes of study have suggested a view of learning as 'situated' in Lave and Wenger's sense, this is not how things have worked out in practice, where a different view seems to have been dominant – one which is more individualistic and instrumentalist, resulting in a focus on competition and performance in public examinations. Genuinely collaborative group work is still rare and even when practised never the dominant mode of learning. The organization of the curriculum into subjects, with new subjects or new content merely 'bolted on' has meant the curriculum has become increasingly overcrowded and fragmented. In the secondary school, for example, up to the age of 14, pupils study 12 subjects – English, mathematics, science, design and technology, ICT (information and communications technology), history, geography, a modern foreign language, art and design, music, physical education and citizenship. In most schools the curriculum has been organized in terms of weekly 'slots' for subjects rather than cross-curricular themes. For a subject teacher, teaching a large class of students between one to four periods a week, bonding with pupils dialogically, in the sense described earlier, has been impossible.

The Secondary Curriculum Review

At the time of writing the Qualifications and Curriculum Authority (QCA) has begun a review of the 11–14 curriculum which looks as though many of these criticisms of the National Curriculum have been taken on board. The final draft will be submitted to the Department for Education and Skills (DfES) in June 2008. It is proposed that the curriculum needs to focus on how pupils experience learning as well as what they learn. There will be opportunities for a move away from 'subject boxes' to a more integrated approach to learning where learners are encouraged to see and experience the connections between subject areas. A number of curriculum dimensions – global dimension, enterprise, creativity, cultural understanding and diversity – will provide a context and focus for work in and between subjects and across the whole curriculum. The curriculum aims, which should inform all aspects of curriculum planning, include many of the skills and qualities one would expect pupils to develop in democratic learning communities, including the 'emotional' goals of a sense of self-worth and self-confidence; goals to do with the capacity to communicate and work with others; and responsible citizenship goals such as respect for others, appreciation of the benefits of diversity and understanding one's own and others' cultural traditions. Moreover, the curriculum should be seen as the entire planned learning experience, including lessons, routines, events and out-of-hours learning.

These are hopeful signs but it remains to be seen if such proposals will be accepted by Government and, if so, whether the resources for their successful implementation will be forthcoming. As countless studies in the school improvement tradition have shown (see Stoll and Fink, 1996), radical curriculum change requires radical measures which take account of all the barriers to its realization. Although schools will welcome the prospect of greater flexibility and a slimmed down curriculum, these kinds of reform have been advocated many times before, and have always tended to be constrained by certain enduring features of the system. Such features include the continuing subdivision of knowledge into subjects, which, despite all the talk about integration, will remain the main 'vehicles' for curriculum organization; the insistence on the retention of the spurious division of the NC into levels; the tendency for cross-curricular themes like 'cultural understanding' to be ill-defined, misunderstood and a 'bolt-on' rather than an intrinsic element; the underestimation of the amount of time, collaboration and resources required to plan and implement a new curriculum; the erroneous assumption that 'dialogical' teaching can be realized via technology and without making classes smaller; the anti-inclusive hierarchies and divisions constructed through a bureaucratic notion of 'personalized' learning; the regressive 'backwash' of high stakes, summative, formal, quantitative testing; and the use of the latter for the construction of league tables which discourage collaboration between schools.

Schools as Democratic Learning 'Communities of Practice'

It is my contention that if whole school reform is to be accomplished, then schools themselves as well as the subjects they 'house' should be conceived as 'communities of practice', and that as such 'school' should have a learning/ emotional curriculum which fostered and reflected its own development as a democratic community of practice. All participants would seriously consider the impact of school on their learning, how it helped them learn or how in the present circumstances it hindered learning. This would involve a discussion of curriculum content but also of how that was organized and taught. Learning, language and communication would be taught in a way that was not abstracted from the ongoing experience of school as an emergent community of practice, and would be continuous with attempts to develop such a community through the formal and informal curriculum. Thus, pupils would be encouraged to examine their relationships with teachers and between themselves, and teachers would do likewise. The informal cultures of school, including pupil as well as teacher cultures, would be acknowledged and engaged with.

Close dialogical relationships require programmes of study which are more open ended than at present. A fluid, flexible, enquiry-oriented approach suggests a project method, where pupils would spend much of their time pursuing lines of enquiry in areas of interest. The idea of a core curriculum would be retained but this would in fact be a learning/emotional curriculum. The dialogical bonds established in the core would act as a catalyst, generating expectations across the curriculum.

The curriculum for the development of a democratic learning community would avoid being parochial (see Hinchcliffe, 2003) since intrinsic to it would be the development of social relations which encouraged an interest in issues and practices 'beyond school'. A 'good' teacher–pupil relationship would be one which was mutually respectful and facilitated reflection on the learning experience in school but which also encouraged learning beyond immediate experience.

It might be argued that this sort of curriculum is beyond the reach of many so-called SEN pupils. Such a view is basically pessimistic about inclusion because it assumes a fundamental difference between the learning approaches of those so described and the rest of the pupils. Such pupils may well present challenges but it would be wrong to make judgements about their potentialities on the basis of existing academic track records or scores on cognitive and/or attainment tests. At present we just do not know what they might be capable of in terms of the learning/ emotional curriculum. It is evident from their sensitivity to derogatory labelling and other forms of negative labelling that vulnerable pupils are often only too aware of barriers to learning in the school context. It is certainly possible to design a curriculum for low achieving pupils, which encourages a critical understanding of learning (see Quicke, 2003a).

In sum, the curriculum for a democratic learning community would encourage a sense of belonging to the school community by focusing on the communicative context of social relations in the school itself. It would encourage pupils and teachers to be critically aware of aspects of this context (e.g. class, gender, race and disability discrimination; a non-dialogical pedagogy; a formalized, inflexible, overloaded curriculum; a test-based, summative assessment system) which were dysfunctional for the realization of collaboration and autonomy in learning. It would provide ideas and analyses which would enrich the pupils' appreciation of and critical perspective on the school's putative common culture of learning as a democratic learning community. It would be a broad curriculum which included cognitive and affective aspects of learning, and also a spiral curriculum which could be taught to pupils at any stage, age or level of skill/ knowledge.

Final Comment

It remains to be seen how schools seeking to become democratic learning 'communities of practice' would interpret this idea and how they would develop it in the future. There are clearly, in Dewey's (1933) terms, many 'dangers and opportunities' in the current context. Whilst there is plenty of rhetoric amongst educationalists, employers, Government officials and others about the need for schools to become 'learning organizations' and 'learning communities', there is little consistency when it comes to policy recommendations and this usually stems from different interpretations of key terms like 'learning' and 'community' deriving from different ideologies.

It is my contention that making schools genuinely inclusive would require this kind of radical curriculum reform. Democratic learning communities are an appropriate 'vision' for EPs, one that is consonant with much that is aspired to in 'good practice' in support. The challenges for them are defined in terms of the interventions required to facilitate the achievement of such communities. The immediate question should be: will this intervention foster the development of this class group and this school as a community of learners? In pursuit of this we might ask how 'learning' in this school as a whole is understood? Is the ethos one which encourages all pupils to contribute to community life? Is there a concern to ensure that all pupils feel they 'belong' and are equally valued?

Most teachers will be familiar with various strategies for incorporating challenging pupils socially in the class group, but I am suggesting that developing democratic communities of learners is likely to require more than that. Such pupils may feel they belong, but belong to what and belong as what? We want them to belong as critical learners, that is, to be recognized and to recognize themselves if not actually then potentially as autonomous, and collaborative; and to be aware of what impedes their progress towards these goals. Everyone should feel that it is important to devote time and energy to constructing a 'we as learners' group identity where each individual is empowered as a participant. If this does not happen, then it is up to the group – teachers and pupils – to reflect on what has gone wrong and how things might be changed.

I am aware that the psychological interventions described in the various stories are not always consistent with these proposals. Some of them do, however, identify strategies which point in the right direction. I hope they show there is no quick fix as far as creating inclusive schools is concerned, and that inclusion has to be seen as 'a never-ending search to find better ways of responding to diversity' (Ainscow and Tweddle, 2003, p. 173) and a long-term strategy for democratic educational reform.

Glossary

Annual review. The review of a statement of special educational needs which an **LEA** must make within 12 months of issuing the statement or, as the case may be, of the previous review.

Department for Education and Skills (DfES). The government department responsible for education and training in England. Formerly known as the Department for Education and Employment (**DfEE**).

Education Action Zone (EAZ). A group of schools (15–25) which aim to create partnerships to improve education in challenging areas. Smaller **EAZ**s based on a single school and its associated primaries are only being set up in **Excellence in Cities** areas. Additional government funds are allocated for 3–5 years.

Education Welfare Officer (EWO). Person employed by a Local Education Authority (**LEA**) to help parents and **LEA**s meet their respective statutory obligations in relation to school attendance. In some **LEA**s, **EWO**s are known as Education Social Workers.

Excellence in Cities (EiC). A programme launched in March 1999 by the Prime Minister and the Secretary of State, the aim of which was to raise standards in specific city areas through targeted intervention and investment.

General Certificate of Secondary Education (GCSE). The name of a set of qualifications taken by secondary school pupils at age 14–16, or by some older students or adults, in England, Wales and Northern Ireland.

Key Stage. A child's progress through school is measured in **Key Stages**. Each KS covers a number of school years, starting at KS 1 and finishing at KS 4. KS 1 is the infants (3–7 years), KS 2 (7–11 years) the juniors, KS 3 the lower secondary (12–13 years) and KS 4 the upper secondary (14–16 years).

Individual Education Plans (IEP). An individual learning programme devised by a school for a child who has been identified as having special educational needs. It sets out key individual short-term targets for the pupil, the teaching strategies to be used and extra support that may be needed. Plans are usually revised at least twice a year.

League Tables (also called Performance Tables). The **DfES** publishes comparative secondary and 16–18 performance tables each year reporting achievements in public examinations and vocational qualifications in secondary schools and Further Education Sector colleges. Primary school tables are published by local education authorities (**LEAs**) and report the achievements of pupils at the end of **Key Stage** 2.

Learning Support Units. In-school centres in secondary schools set up under the **EiC** providing short-term teaching and support programmes for pupils who are disaffected, at risk of exclusion or vulnerable because of social or family issues.

Local Education Authority (LEA). The authority that has responsibility for providing education to pupils of school age in its area.

National Curriculum. A curriculum prescribed by government covering what children should be taught in state-maintained schools. The **NC** purports to provide a broad and balanced education covering 11 subjects overall and is divided into four **Key Stages** according to age.

National Literacy Strategy (NLS). The **NLS** was introduced to all primary schools in England in September 1998. The strategy was planned for teachers to teach a daily Literacy Hour, which followed a pattern of 30 minutes whole class teaching, followed by group work and concluding with a plenary session.

National Numeracy Strategy (NNS). The **NNS** was launched in 1998 and has been formally implemented in classrooms since September 1999. The aim is to provide primary (infant and junior) school pupils with a firm foundation in maths.

Office for Standards in Education (OFSTED). An official body established under the Education (Schools) Act 1992 to take responsibility for the inspection of all schools in England and Wales, which are mainly or wholly state funded.

School Action. School Action is additional or different support provided by a school when a pupil is identified as having special educational needs. It is part of the graduated response as set out in the Special Educational Needs (**SEN**) Code of Practice. To help plan the support the class teacher and **SENCO** will collect information about the child, undertake further assessments and involve parents or carers in discussions.

School Action Plus. School Action Plus is part of the graduated response to meeting a child's special educational needs as set out in the Special Educational Needs (**SEN**) Code of Practice. It is triggered when a pupil continues to make little of no progress despite having received support from the school through **School Action**. **School Action Plus** involves seeking advice or support from specialists outside the school.

Special Educational Needs (SEN) and Disability Tribunal. An independent tribunal set up by Act of Parliament for determining appeals by parents against the Local Education Authority (**LEA**) about a child's special educational needs, where parents cannot reach agreement with the **LEA**.

Special Educational Needs (SEN) Code of Practice. The **SEN** Code of Practice provides local authorities, maintained schools, early education settings and other agencies with comprehensive advice on how to carry out their statutory duties to identify, assess and provide for children's special educational needs. The Code sets out detailed guidance for a graduated response to supporting children. (See also **School Action, School Action Plus, Statement of special educational needs, Statutory assessment**).

Special Educational Needs Coordinator (SENCO). A member of the staff of a school who has responsibility for coordinating **SEN** provision within that school. In a small school the head teacher or the deputy may take on this role. In larger schools there may be a **SEN** coordinating team.

Standard Assessment Tests (SATs). National tests which together with teacher assessments are undergone by pupils at ages 7, 11 and 14. Test and assessment results are reported to parents as levels rather raw scores. The levels define whether the pupil is working at the expected standard for their age, above or below it.

Statement of special educational needs. A statement of special educational needs (**SEN**) sets out in detail a pupil's special educational needs, the provision required to meet those needs, and the type and name of school the pupil should attend. A statement can only be made by a local authority and only after a **statutory assessment** of the child's needs.

Statutory assessment. This is a formal and detailed multi-agency assessment of a child's special educational needs (**SEN**) carried out (under section 323 of the Education Act 1996) by the local authority.

Teaching Assistants. TAs provide teaching and non-teaching support for classroom teachers. Their qualifications vary, but many only have basic education qualifications. There is now a national framework of qualifications, with the core being National Vocational Qualifications (NVQs). There has been considerable variation across schools and **LEA**s regarding the title, job descriptions etc. Categories include education assistants, classroom assistants, learning support assistants and non-teaching assistants.

References

Adshead, G. and Bluglass, K. (2005) Attachment representations in mothers with abnormal illness behaviour by proxy, The British Journal of Psychiatry, 187 pp 328–333.

Ainscow, M. and Tweddle, D. (2003) Understanding the changing role of English local education authorities in promoting inclusion, in Allan, J. (ed), Inclusion, Participation and Democracy: What is the Purpose? (pp 165–178). Dordrecht/Boston/London: Kluwer Academic Publishers.

Annan, M. (2005) Observations on a service review: A time to move on, Educational Psychology in Practice, 21(4) pp 261–272.

Antidote (2003) The Emotional Literacy Handbook, London: David Fulton Publishers in association with Antidote.

Armstrong, F. (2003) Spaced Out: Policy, Difference and the Challenge of Inclusive Education, Dordrecht/Boston/London: Kluwer Academic Publishers.

Armstrong, F., Armstrong, D. and Barton, L. (eds) (2000) Inclusive Education: Policy, Contexts and Comparative Perspectives, London: David Fulton.

Baldwin, S. and Cooper, P. (2000) How should ADHD be treated? Head to head, The Psychologist, 13(12) pp 598–602.

Ball, S.J. (1995) Intellectuals or technicians? The urgent role of theory in educational studies, British Journal of Educational Studies, 43(3) pp 255–271.

Barton, L. (2003) Inclusive Education and Teacher Education. A Basis for Hope or a Discourse of Delusion? London: Institute of Education.

Baxter, J. and Frederickson, N. (2005) Every child matters: Can educational psychology contribute to radical reform? Educational Psychology in Practice, 21(2) pp 87–102.

Benjamin, S. (2002) The Micropolitics of Inclusive Education, Buckingham: Open University Press.

Bennathan, M. and Boxall, M. (1996) Effective Intervention in Primary Schools: Nurture Groups, London: David Fulton.

Benson, Jarlath F. (1987) Working More Creatively with Groups, London: Tavistock Publications.

Booth, T. (2005) Keeping the future alive: putting inclusive values into action, Forum, 47(2/3) pp 151–158.

Booth, T., Ainscow, M., Black-Hawkins, K., Vaughan, M. and Shaw, L. (2000) Index for Inclusion: developing learning and participation in schools, Bristol: Centre for Studies on Inclusive Education.

Bottery, M. (2004) The Challenges of Educational Leadership, London: Paul Chapman.

Broadfoot, P. (2001) Empowerment or performativity? Assessment policy in the late twentieth century, in R. Phillips and J. Furlong (eds), Education, Reform and the State, London: Routledge Falmer.

Burbules, N.C. (1993) Dialogue in Teaching: theory and practice, New York: Teachers College Press.

Carr, W. and Hartnett, A. (1996) Education and the Struggle for Democracy, Buckingham: Open University Press.

Carter, B. and Burgess, H. (1993) Testing, regulation and control: shifting education narratives, Curriculum Studies, 1(2) pp 233–244.

Charmaz, K. and Mitchell, R. (1997) The myth of silent authorship: Self, substance and style in autoethnographic writing, in R. Hertz (ed), Reflexivity and Voice (pp 193–215). London: Sage.

Colwell, J. and O'Connor, T. (2003) Understanding nurturing practices – a comparison of the use of strategies likely to enhance self esteem in nurture groups and normal classrooms, British Journal of Special Education, 30(3) pp 119–124.

Davies, B. and Harre, R. (1990) Positioning: the discursive construction of selves, Journal for the Theory of Social Behaviour, 20(1) pp 43–63.

Department for Education and Employment (DfEE) (1999) Excellence in Cities, London: DfEE.

Department of Education and Science (DES) (1989) National Curriculum: from policy to practice, London: DES.

De Nobile, J.J. and McCormick, J. (2005) Job Satisfaction and Occupational Stress in Catholic Primary Schools, paper presented at the Annual Conference of the Australian Association for Research in Education, Sydney, November 27th–December 1st, 2005.

Dewey, J. (1933) Democracy and Education, New York: Macmillan. First published in 1916.

Dolby, N. and Dimitriadis, G. (eds), with Paul Willis (2004) Learning to labor in new times, New York: Routledge Falmer.

Ecclestone, K. (2004) Learning or therapy? The demoralisation of education, British Journal of Educational Studies, 52(2) pp 112–137.

Ellis, C. (1995) Final Negotiations, Philadelphia, PA: Temple University Press.

Glasser, W. (1965) Reality Therapy, New York: Harper & Row.

Greene, M. (1995) Releasing the Imagination: Essays on Education, the Arts and Social Change, San Francisco, CA: Jossey-Bass.

Griffiths, M. (1998) Educational Research for Social Justice, Buckingham/Philadelphia: Open University Press.

Griffiths, M., Berry, J., Holt, A., Naylor, J. and Weekes, P. (2006) Learning to be in public spaces: in the margins with dancers, sculptors, painters and musicians, British Journal of Educational Studies, 54(3) pp 352–370.

Hacking, I. (2006) Making up people, London Review of Books, August 17, pp 23–26.

Hill, J. (1994) The paradox of gender. Sex stereotyping within statementing procedures, British Educational Research Journal, 20(3) pp 345–355.

Hinchcliffe, G. (2003) Rethinking Lifelong Learning, paper presented at the Annual Conference of the Philosophy of Education Society of Great Britain, New College, Oxford, April 2004.

Holt, N.L. (2003) Representation, legitimation and autoethnography: An autoethnographic writing story, International Journal of Qualitative Methods, 2(1) pp 1–21.

Iszatt, J. and Wasilewska, T. (1997) Nurture Groups: an early intervention model enabling vulnerable children with emotional and behavioural difficulties to integrate successfully into school, Educational and Child Psychology, 14(3) pp 63–69.

Jackson, B. and Segal P. (2004) Why inequality matters, London: Catalyst.

Lakoff, G. and Johnson, M. (1980) Metaphors we live by, Chicago: University of Chicago Press.

Lave, J. and Wenger, E. (1991) Situated Learning. Legitimate peripheral participation, Cambridge: Cambridge University Press.

Lesser, E.L. and Storck, J. (2001) Communities of practice and organizational performance, IBM Systems Journal, 40(4) pp 32–43.

Lloyd, G. (2003) Inclusion and problem groups: the story of ADHD, in Allan, J. (ed), Inclusion, Participation and Democracy: What is the Purpose? (pp 105–116). Dordrecht/Boston/London: Kluwer Academic Publishers.

Lunt, I. and Majors, K. (2000) The professionalism of educational psychology, Educational Psychology in Practice, 15(4) pp 237–246.

Lukes, S. (1973) Individualism, Oxford: Basil Blackwell.

MacIntyre, A. (1981) After Virtue, London: Duckworth.
Macmurray, J. (1961) Persons in Relation, London: Faber & Faber.
Mehan, H. (1983) The role of language and the language of role in decision-making, Language and Society, 12 pp 187–211.
Mercer, N., Wegerif, R. and Dawes, L. (1999) Chidren's talk and the development of reasoning in the classroom, British Educational Research Journal, 25(1) pp 95–111.
Miller, A. (1996) Pupil Behaviour and Teacher Culture, London: Cassell.
Minnow, M. (1997) Not Only for Myself: Identity, Politics and the Law, New York: The New Press.
Mittler, P. (2000) Working Towards Inclusive Education, London: David Fulton.
Mosley, J. (1998) Quality Circle Time in the Primary Classroom, Wisbech, Cambs: LDA.
Mouffe, C. (1993) Liberal socialism and pluralism, in J. Squires (ed), Principled Positions, (pp 69–78), London: Lawrence & Wishart.
Munt, V. (2004) The awful truth; a microhistory of teacher stress at Westwood High, British Journal of Sociology of Education, 25(5) pp 577–591.
Neufeld, P. and Foy, M (2006) Historical Reflections on the Ascendancy of ADHD in North America, C. 1980–C. 2005, British Journal of Educational Studies, 54(4) pp 449–470.
Norwich, B. (1993) Has 'Special Educational Needs' outlived its usefulness? in J.Visser and G. Upton (eds), Special Education in Britain After Warnock, London: David Fulton.
Norwich, B. and Lewis, A. (2001) Mapping a pedagogy for special educational needs, British Educational Research Journal, 27(3) pp 313–329.
Nussbaum, M. (1997) Cultivating Humanity: A Classical Defense of Reform in Liberal Education, Cambridge, MA: Harvard University Press.
Ogden, L. (2000) Collaborative Tasks, Collaborative Children: an analysis of reciprocity during peer interaction at Key Stage 1, British Educational Research Journal, 26(2) pp 211–226.
Oliver, M. (1996) Understanding Disability: From Theory to Practice, Basingstoke: Palgrave.
Peim, N. (1993) Critical Theory and the English Teacher, London: Routledge.
Philipsen, G. (1995) The coordinated management of meaning theory of Pearce, Cronen and associates, in D.P. Cushman and B. Kovacic (eds), Watershed Research Traditions in Human Communication Theory, Albany, NY: State University of New York Press.
Priestley, M. (1999) Discourse and identity: disabled children in mainstream high schools, in Corker, M. and French, S. (eds), Disability Discourse, Buckingham: Open University Press.
Pring, R. (2001) The virtues and vices of an educational researcher, Journal of Philosophy of Education, 35(3) pp 410–421.
Quicke, J. (1981) Special educational needs and the comprehensive principle: some implications of ideological critique, Remedial Education, 16(2) pp 61–66.
Quicke, J. (1982) The Cautious Expert, Milton Keynes: The Open University Press.
Quicke, J. and Winter, C. (1994) Teaching the language of learning: towards a metacognitive approach to pupil empowerment, British Educational Research Journal, 20(4) pp 429–449.
Quicke, J. (1995) Differentiation: a contested concept, Cambridge Journal of Education, 25(2) pp 213–224.
Quicke, J. (2003a) Educating the pupil voice, Support for Learning, 18(2) pp 51–58.
Quicke, J. (2003b) Teaching Assistants: students or servants? Forum, 45(2) pp 71–75.
Reed-Danahay, D. (1997) Auto/Ethnography, New York: Berg.
Richardson, L. (1995) Writing-stories: Co-authoring 'The Sea Monster', a writing story, Qualitative Inquiry, 1 pp 189–203.
Rogers, C.R. (1961) On Becoming a Person, Boston, MA: Houghton-Mifflin.
Rogers, C.R. (1980) A Way of Being, Boston, MA: Houghton-Mifflin.
Rose, R. (2000) Using classroom support in a primary school, British Journal of Special Education, 27 pp 191–196.
Salmon, G. and Faris, J. (2006) Multi-agency collaboration, multiple levels of meaning: social constructionism and the CMM model as tools to further our understanding, Journal of Family Therapy, 28(3) pp 272–292.

Schon, D. (1983) The Reflective Practitioner, London: Temple Smith.

Schutz, A. (1971) The stranger, in B.R. Cosin, I.R. Dale, G.M. Esland, D. Mackinnon, D.F. Swift (1971), School and Society (pp 27–33). London: Routledge & Kegan Paul.

Selfe, L. (2002) Discussion paper-concerns about the identification and diagnosis of autistic spectrum disorders, Educational Psychology in Practice, 18(4) pp 335–341.

Solity, J. (1996) Discrepancy definitions of dyslexia, Educational Psychology in Practice, 12(3) pp 141–151.

Stancombe, J. and White, S. (2005) Cause and responsibility: towards an interactional understanding of blaming and 'neutrality' in family therapy, Journal of Family Therapy, 27(4) pp 330–351.

Stoll, L. and Fink, D. (1996) Changing Our Schools, Buckingham: Open University Press.

Terkel, S. (2003) Hope Dies Last, London: Granta Books.

Tomlinson, S. (1982) A Sociology of Special Education, London: Routledge & Kegan Paul.

Tunstall, P. (2001) Assessment discourse and constructions of social reality in infant classrooms, Journal of Education Policy, 16(3) pp 215–231.

Vardill, R. and Calvert, S. (2000) Gender imbalances in referrals to an educational psychology service, Educational Psychology in Practice, 16(2) pp 213–223.

Webb, R. and Vulliamy, G. (2006) The impact of New Labour's Policy on teachers and teaching at Key Stage 2, Forum, 48(2) pp 145–158.

Weis, L. (1990) Working Class Without Work: High School Students in a De-industrialising Economy, New York: Routledge.

Williams, H. and Daniels, A. (2000) Framework for intervention, Part 2, Educational Psychology in Practice, 15(4) pp 228–236.

Willis, P. (1977) Learning to Labour, Farnborough: Saxon House.

Woods, P. (1983) Sociology and the School, London: Routledge & Kegan Paul.

Index

A

Ability, 13, 14, 23, 25, 26, 48, 54, 69, 73, 76–79, 81, 83, 110, 151, 152
Action research, 2, 3, 70, 108, 118
Adolescence, 19, 145
Adshead, G., 157
Agency, 1, 15, 27, 44, 52, 155, 167, 177
Agent, 9, 10, 15, 20, 27, 111, 115
Ainscow, M., 173
Alienation, 59
Alternative discourse, 160, 161
Anger, 71, 122–125
Anger-management, 29, 41, 71, 125, 128
Annan, M., 4
Annual reviews, 69, 75, 80
Anonymity, 5–7
Antidote, 167
Anti-racist policy, 28, 135
Anti-social behaviour, 56
Argument, 11, 14, 25, 26, 33, 73, 115, 164, 168
Armstrong, D., 9, 12, 161
Armstrong, F., 9, 12, 161
Arts education, 52
ASDAN, 44, 48
Asperger's, 93–99
Asperger's child, 93, 94, 101, 102
Asperger's syndrome, 13, 70, 92, 140
Attention, 2, 3, 12, 13, 16, 23, 28, 32, 61, 62, 75, 80, 97, 99, 118, 126, 129, 142, 146, 150, 152
Attention Deficit Hyperactivity Disorder (ADHD), 13, 23–27, 32, 33, 36, 37, 97–99, 102, 137, 150, 152–155, 160
Attention-seeking behaviour, 61, 126
Autism, 1, 3, 89, 90, 91, 93, 99, 102, 140, 141, 153, 155, 160
Autism checklist, 89, 91
Autistic Spectrum Disorder (ASD), 13, 92, 93, 95, 97–99

Autoethnographic, 2, 3, 5
Autonomy, 4, 8, 10, 87, 166, 167, 172

B

Baldwin, S., 36
Ball, S.J., 4
Barton, L., 9, 10, 12
Baxter, J., 4
Behavioural difficulties, 11, 12, 19, 60, 63, 67, 121, 152, 165
Behavioural support service, 125
Behavioural targets, 162
Behaviouristic, 44, 82, 162
Benjamin, S., 14
Bennathan, M., 67
Benson, J.F., 134
Bluglass, K., 157
Booth, T., 13, 161
Bottery, M., 168, 169
Bowlby, 67
Boxall, M., 67
Brain gym, 107
British Educational Research Association (BERA), 7
British Psychological Society, 36
Broadfoot, P., 85
Buddy system, 142, 145
Buddy, 142
Bullies, 29, 61, 66, 130, 143
Bully watch, 143
Bullying, 11, 26, 60, 64, 143
Burbules, N.C., 168
Burgess, H., 102

C

Calvert, S., 17
Carr, W., 8
Carter, B., 102

Charmaz, K., 4
Child and Family Psychiatric Service (CFPS), 23, 32, 34, 35, 44, 45, 51, 97–99, 153
Child-centred, 70, 86, 95, 102
Child centred ethos, 70, 89, 97
Circle of friends, 17, 28, 71, 129, 134, 162
Circle time, 131, 132, 134
Citizens, 8, 81
Citizenship, 3, 165, 170
Class, 10, 13, 23, 26, 27, 28, 34, 35, 42, 48, 49, 56, 58, 59, 65, 68, 70, 74
Clinical psychologist, 32
Co-counselling, 33
Code of Practice, 12, 14, 23, 69, 74, 149, 161
Collaboration, 14, 20, 43, 58, 82, 83, 86, 87, 115, 127, 160–172
Collaborative action research, 118
Collaborative approaches, 166
Collaborative group work, 165, 169
Collaborative learning 'skills', 81
Collaborative partnerships, 83
Colwell, J., 67
Communication difficulties, 96, 97, 144
Communication skills, 29, 141
Communication, 13, 96, 127, 139, 141, 143, 145, 147, 156, 160, 167, 169, 171
Communities of Practice, 167, 168, 171, 172
Compromises, 30, 162, 163
Consultancy model, 76
Conversations, 1, 10, 25, 29, 57, 66, 90, 91, 93, 102, 107, 115, 133, 164–166
Cooper, P., 36, 50
Core curriculum, 171
Counter-cultural, 132
Critical autoethnography, 2, 3
Critical EP, 159–161
Critical professionals, 164
Critical reflection, 2, 86
Critical, 3, 9, 10, 21, 44, 67, 79, 90, 95, 107, 116, 124, 159, 161, 162, 167, 168, 172
Cross-curricular themes, 170
'Crossover' person, 133, 134
Cult of anger, 125, 128
Cultural practices, 10, 71, 129, 134
Culture of derision, 4
Curriculum development, 107, 164
Curriculum dimensions, 170

D
Daniels, A., 15
Davies, B., 15
De nobile, J.J., 37
Deficit bias, 162

Deficit model, 12, 103, 118
Democracy, 5, 8–10, 163, 164, 169
Democratic community of practice, 171
Democratic educational reform, 173
Democratic learning communities, 8, 160, 170, 172
Democratic learning society, 8
Department for Education and Employment, 1999 (DfEE), 19, 175
Department for Education and Skills (DfES), 170, 175
Deviance, 41, 95
Deviant identities, 66
Deviant, 19, 66, 67, 95, 100, 124, 130, 132, 159, 164
Dewey, J., 172
DfES guidance (2005), 29, 80
Dialogical approach, 168
Dialogical engagement, 49
Dialogical learning, 168
Dialogue, 4, 97, 107, 115, 116, 157, 168
Difference, 2, 9–12, 32, 52, 56, 57, 79, 81–84, 87, 97, 102, 109, 117, 118, 137, 151, 156, 157, 163, 164, 166, 167, 171
Differentiation, 69, 70, 73, 77
Dimitriadis, G., 68
Disability, 9, 62, 101, 114, 172, 176
Discourse of normalization, 94
Discourse of special educational needs, 159
Discourses, 15, 102
Discourses of remediation, 160–162
Discrepancy definitions, 118
Discrepancy model, 110
Disorder, 9, 13, 23, 27, 36, 37, 64, 70, 92–94, 98, 99, 101, 102, 138, 155, 156, 161
Diversity, 9, 10, 52, 81, 164, 167, 170, 173
Dolby, N., 68
Drama work, 44
Drama, 20, 45, 46, 49, 51, 52, 54
Drugs, 42–49, 56, 57, 121
Drugs culture, 46, 49, 57
Dysfunctional, 123, 159, 160, 168, 172
Dysfunctional behaviour, 31, 129
Dyslexia, 70, 97, 99, 102, 106, 107, 137, 149, 150, 155
Dyspraxia, 140, 141

E
Ecclestone, K., 167
Economic, 56, 68, 121
Economy, 56, 168
Education Act 1997, 125
Education Action Zones (EAZ), 19

Education for citizenship, 3
Education Reform Act (1988), 169
Education Welfare Officer (EWO), 35, 128, 175
Educational Psychology Service (EPS), 1
Ellis, C., 5
Emotional curriculum, 166–168, 171
Emotional literacy, 166, 167
Equality, 8, 79
Ethical issues, 5–7
Ethnographic, 2, 3, 5, 10
Ethnography, 2
Excellence in Cities (EiC), 19, 175, 176
Exclusions, 20, 28, 29
Expressive difficulties, 75
Extreme behaviours, 122, 123, 134

F
Faction, 7
Faris, J., 157
Fink, D., 170
Foy, M., 36
Frederickson, N., 4

G
GCSEs, 20, 49
Gender discrimination, 17
Gender oppression, 42
Gender, 21, 27, 42, 168, 172
General Certificate of Secondary Education (GCSE), 20, 49, 175
Glasser, W., 134
Global economy, 168
Gossip, 71, 132, 133
Greene, M., 52
Griffiths, M., 3, 15, 16

H
Hacking, I., 102
Harre, R., 15
Hartnett, A., 8
Hegemonic masculinity, 118
Hierarchy of intervention, 126
High density teaching, 166
Hill, J., 17
Hinchcliffe, G., 171
Holt, N.L., 5
Homophobic, 133
Hot seating techniques, 48
Humanist discourse, 163
Humanistic psychology, 134

I
Identity, 20, 41, 70, 87, 93, 94, 100, 163, 168, 173
Inclusion checklist, 109
Inclusion services, 1, 4, 5, 12, 17, 54
Inclusion strategies, 1, 74, 78
Inclusive philosophy, 15, 29, 167
Index for inclusion, 161
Individual Education Plans (IEPs), 80, 162, 175
Individualism, 8, 9
Individualistic, 14, 69, 112, 118, 129, 169
Inequality, 83
Informal cultures, 171
Informed consent, 6
Integration, 142, 159, 170
Interactional context, 161
Interactionist, 14, 15
Interactions, 10, 15, 17, 81, 109, 124, 162
Interpretative frameworks, 15
Isolation rooms, 29
Iszatt, J., 67

J
Jackson, B., 169
Johnson, M., 102

K
Key stage, 80, 85, 175, 176
Key worker, 33, 34, 45

L
Label, 25, 37, 70, 102, 137, 141, 161
Labelling, 9, 20, 25, 69, 82, 92, 164, 171
Lakoff, G., 102
Language of dialogue, 115, 116
Lave, J., 167–169
League tables (performance tables), 37, 169, 171, 176
Learning communities, 8, 160, 169, 170, 172
Learning curriculum, 165, 166
Learning difficulties, 14, 67, 69, 74, 78, 97, 107, 110, 118, 149, 152
Learning how to learn, 17, 70, 116–118
Learning Mentors (LMs), 19, 20, 29, 49
Learning organizations, 172
Learning Support Service, 74
Learning Support Units (LSUs), 19, 20, 31, 163, 176
Lesser, E.L., 169
Lewis, A., 165
Literacy, 17, 63, 74, 77–82, 84, 89, 105, 107, 108, 110, 113, 116, 118, 166, 167, 176

Literacy skills, 23, 25, 52, 105, 111, 113, 116, 118, 149, 154
Lloyd, G., 36
Local Education Authority (LEA), 19, 20, 23, 36, 43, 73, 74, 76, 85, 92, 96, 97, 100, 101, 122, 152–155, 159, 163, 175, 176
Low ability, 54, 73, 78, 152
Lukes, S., 8
Lunt, I., 15

M

Macintyre, A., 119
Macmurray, J., 9
Majors, K., 15
Male-pupil culture, 115
Management speak, 58, 59
Managerialism, 4, 122
Managerialist, 4, 20, 37
Market values, 169
Mccormick, J., 37
Medical models, 9
Mehan, H., 157
Mental health, 51
Mercer, N., 118
Meritocracy, 79
Meritocratic ideology, 14, 159
Metacognition, 111, 112, 114
Meta-learning, 114–115
Miller, A., 15
Minnow, M., 10, 52
Mitchell, R., 4
Mittler, P., 37
Moderate learning difficulties, 69, 74, 78, 97
Moral perspective, 1
Mosley, J., 134
Mouffe, C., 10
Munchhausen's syndrome, 157
Munt, V., 37
Mutual respect, 164

N

Name-calling, 25, 132
NASUWT (National Association of Schoolmasters and Union of Women Teachers), 56
National Curriculum, 37, 44, 52, 54, 122, 165, 169, 170, 176
National Literacy Strategy (NLS), 107, 176
National Numeracy Strategy (NNS), 176
Neale, 151, 152
Neale Analysis of Reading Ability, 151

Negotiated meanings, 157
Neufeld, P., 36
Norwich, B., 9, 165
Nurture group, 21, 54, 55, 57, 64, 67
Nussbaum, M., 52

O

O'connor, T., 67
Occupational therapist, 93, 97, 101, 139, 141
Office for Standards in Education (OFSTED), 21, 53, 57, 89, 122, 176
Ogden, L., 118
Oliver, M., 9
Overlearning, 108, 166

P

Paired learning, 17, 111
Paired reading, 112
Parent Teacher Association (PTA), 114
Parents, 6, 13, 17, 19, 23, 24, 33, 34, 43–45, 48, 56
Pastoral, 20, 29, 31, 34, 39, 43, 49, 159, 160, 163
Pastoral facilities, 29
Pastoral strategy, 49
Pastoral structures, 20, 34
Pastoral Support Plan (PSP), 20, 43, 44
Pastoral system, 31
Pathological Demand Avoidance (PDA), 137, 155, 156
Peer culture, 114
Peer group, 40, 135
Peer pressure, 128
Peer relationships, 27, 28
Peim, N., 15
Performance assessment, 37, 57
Performativity culture, 86
Performativity discourse of assessment, 85
Personal narratives, 4, 5
Personalized learning, 78, 171
Philipsen, G., 156
Political issues, 37, 49, 119
Political perspective, 1, 8, 9
Politics, 31, 78
Positive handling, 71, 124–126
Positivist, 4, 5, 16, 108, 161
Pre-tutoring session, 116
Priestley, M., 161
Pring, R., 7
Psychiatrist, 23, 24, 40, 51, 93, 97, 98, 101
Psychoanalysis, 134
Psychotherapy, 51

Pupil culture, 83, 115, 129, 133
Pupils cultural practices, 129, 134

Q

Qualifications and Curriculum Authority (QCA), 170
Quicke, J., 11, 14, 86, 118, 169, 172

R

Racism, 10, 28, 71, 114, 129, 135
Radical, 37, 84, 107, 159–162, 167, 170, 172
Radical action, 160
Radical curriculum change, 37, 170
Radicals, 162
Reading age, 73, 74, 77, 109, 118
Reading difficulties, 49, 106, 110, 118
Reality therapy, 134
Reconstruction, 46, 87, 159, 160
Reed-danahay, D., 4
Reflection, 2, 3, 5, 15–17, 23, 27, 41, 42, 64, 79, 86, 90, 103, 111, 124, 125, 146, 152, 171
Reflective, 1, 2, 5, 15, 33, 43, 61, 79, 106–108, 157
Reflective dialogue, 107
Reflective practitioner, 1, 2, 5, 15, 33, 79, 106, 108
Reflexive, 5, 10, 15, 24, 32, 112, 116, 117
Reflexivity, 111, 112
Regressive, 13, 14, 160, 171
Reintegration, 29, 31, 43, 45, 63
Retrospective interpretation, 93, 94
Rose, R., 86
Richardson, L., 5
Rogers, C.R., 134

S

Salmon, G., 157
Scapegoats, 56, 57
Schon, D., 15, 17
School action, 1, 12, 14, 23, 176, 177
School action plus, 1, 12, 23, 176, 177
Schutz, A., 15, 16
Segal, P., 169
Self reflection, 16, 23
Self worth, 27, 29, 170
Self-confidence, 110, 170
Self-critical, 4, 10, 162
Selfe, L., 13
Self-esteem, 53, 78, 165
Self-reflexive, 2, 3
Self-worth, 170
SEN pedagogy, 165, 166
Sexist, 132
Shutz, A., 15
Significant others, 112
Situated approach, 168
Situated learning, 168
Situational factors, 92
Skills, 23, 25, 26, 28, 29, 31, 34, 37, 44, 47
Social contructionist, 103
Social inequalities, 159
Social justice, 3, 15
Social psychology, 14
Social services, 35, 41, 44, 153, 155
Socially constructed, 2, 9, 10, 167
Sociological factors, 167
Sociology, 14
Sociometric questionnaire, 27, 28
Solity, J., 118
Speaking and listening, 80, 90
Special education, 1, 3, 6, 11, 12, 14, 58, 60, 63, 69, 74
Special Educational Needs (SEN) and Disability Tribunal, 176
Special Educational Needs (SEN) Code of Practice, 1, 176, 177
Special Educational Needs Coordinator (SENCO), 6, 19, 21, 24, 44, 53, 55, 58, 70, 74, 100, 105, 106, 125, 141, 143, 149, 153, 156, 160, 176, 177
Special educational needs, 1, 3, 6, 11, 12, 14, 58, 60, 63, 69, 74
Special Needs and Inclusion Panel, 69, 99, 152
Special Needs Department, 19, 21, 26, 53, 54, 145
Special needs discourse, 73, 102, 161
Special school, 12, 13, 53–55, 69, 70, 73–75, 77, 84
Speech therapist, 75, 93, 101, 139–141, 145, 146
Spiral curriculum, 168, 172
Stancombe, J., 157
Standard Assessment Tests (SATS), 14, 20, 78, 79, 84, 86, 89, 90, 161, 167, 177
Standards agenda, 13, 69, 85
Statement, 1, 23, 69, 70, 73, 74, 76, 84, 92, 95, 98, 99, 101, 102, 140, 144, 145, 149, 154, 162, 175, 177
Statemented pupils, 12, 69, 82, 99
Status hierarchies, 83, 128
Statutory assessments, 12

Stereotypes, 42, 48
Stigma, 25, 113
Stoll, L., 170
Storck, J., 169
Stress, 2, 19, 32, 37, 40, 50, 56, 57, 67, 85
Stress-related illnesses, 163
Subculture, 10, 130
Support package, 42
Support services, 74, 126, 138
Support structures, 33, 79

T
Target setting, 43, 69
TAs, 24, 54, 86, 87, 99, 100, 126, 177
Teacher culture, 15, 171
Terkel, S., 68
Tomlinson, S., 9
Tribunal, 100, 101, 176
Tunstall, P., 102
Tweddle, D., 173
Traditions of enquiry, 8, 9, 159
Targets, 4, 14, 20, 43–45, 58, 70, 80, 81, 84, 87, 89, 100, 105, 111, 122, 127, 162, 165, 175
Transfer, 20, 29, 73, 75, 82, 85, 112, 116, 134, 166

U
Underachieving, 20, 130

V
Vandalism, 122
Vardill, R., 17
Voices, 86, 125, 167
Vulliamy, G., 85
Vulnerability, 27, 32, 167
Vulnerable, 11, 20, 27, 32, 40, 46, 54, 68, 171, 176

W
Warnock committee, 11
Wasilewska, T., 67
Webb, R., 85
Wechsler Intelligence Scale for Children (WISC), 76, 77, 109, 152, 154
Weis, L., 68
Wenger, E., 167–169
White, S., 157
Whole curriculum, 59, 79, 108, 160, 167, 170
Whole school, 1, 59, 81, 160, 167, 171
Williams, H., 15
Willis, P., 10
Wing, L., 102
Winter, C., 118
Within-child, 9, 13
Within child explanations, 106
Woods, P., 15
Work experience, 41, 42, 44

Y
Youth Offending Team (YOT), 43–45, 47, 49

INCLUSIVE EDUCATION: CROSS CULTURAL PERSPECTIVES

1. F. Armstrong: *Spaced Out: Policy, Difference and the Challenge of Inclusive Education.* 2003   ISBN 1-4020-1261-6

2. J. Allan (ed.): *Inclusion, Participation and Democracy: What is the Purpose?* 2003   ISBN 1-4020-1264-0

3. D. Youdell: *Impossible Bodies, Impossible Selves: Exclusion and Student Subjectivities.* 2006   ISBN 1-4020-4548-4

4. L. Barton and F. Armstrong (eds.): *Policy, Experience and Change: Cross-Cultural Reflections on Inclusive Education.* 2007   ISBN 1-4020-5118-2

5. J. Allan: *Rethinking Inclusive Education: The Philosophers of Difference in Practice.* 2007   ISBN 978-1-4020-6093-9

6. J. Quicke: *Inclusion and Psychological Intervention in Schools: A Critical Autoethnography.* 2008   ISBN 978-1-4020-6367-1

Printed in the United Kingdom
by Lightning Source UK Ltd.
124344UK00002BB/1-18/A